First World War

and Army of Occupation

War Diary

France, Belgium and Germany

7 INDIAN (MEERUT) DIVISION
Headquarters, Branches and Services
Commander Royal Artillery
1 May 1915 - 31 May 1915

WO95/3933/5

The Naval & Military Press Ltd
www.nmarchive.com
Published in association with The National Archives

Published by

The Naval & Military Press Ltd

Unit 10 Ridgewood Industrial Park,

Uckfield, East Sussex,

TN22 5QE England

Tel: +44 (0) 1825 749494

www.naval-military-press.com

www.nmarchive.com

This diary has been reprinted in facsimile from the original. Any imperfections are inevitably reproduced and the quality may fall short of modern type and cartographic standards.

Contents

Document type	Place/Title	Date From	Date To
Heading	Meerut Division H.Q Div Artillery 1st to 31st May		
Heading	War Diary With Appendices Head Quarters Divisional Artillery Meerut Division From 1st May To 31st May 1915		
War Diary	Fosse	01/05/1915	07/05/1915
War Diary	Rue Du Puits M 27 a	08/05/1915	11/05/1915
War Diary	Fosse	12/05/1915	15/05/1915
War Diary	Rue Du Puits M 27 a	15/05/1915	16/05/1915
War Diary	Rue Du Puits	16/05/1915	23/05/1915
War Diary	Fosse	24/05/1915	31/05/1915
Miscellaneous	Appendix 155		
Miscellaneous	Tactical Progress Report	02/05/1915	02/05/1915
Miscellaneous	Tactical Progress Report	03/05/1915	03/05/1915
Operation(al) Order(s)	Operation Order No.29 By Lieutenant-General Sir C.A. Anderson K.C.B. Commanding Meerut Division.	04/05/1915	04/05/1915
Miscellaneous	Tactical Progress Report	04/05/1915	04/05/1915
Miscellaneous	Tactical Progress Report	05/05/1915	05/05/1915
Miscellaneous	Headquarters Meerut Division	06/05/1915	06/05/1915
Operation(al) Order(s)	Operation Order No.30 By Lieut-General Sir Charles Anderson K.C.B. Commanding Meerut Division.	06/05/1915	06/05/1915
Diagram etc	Flags For Marking Position Of Advanced Troops		
Miscellaneous	Headquarters Meerut Division	07/05/1915	07/05/1915
Miscellaneous	Headquarters Meerut Divn	07/05/1915	07/05/1915
Map	Map		
Miscellaneous	Tactical Progress Report	06/05/1915	06/05/1915
Operation(al) Order(s)	Operation Order No.18 By Brigadier General R. St. C. Lecky R.A. C.R.A. Meerut Division.	07/05/1915	07/05/1915
Diagram etc	Flags For Marking Position Of Advanced Troops		
Miscellaneous	Meerut Divisional Artillery	08/05/1915	08/05/1915
Miscellaneous	No.405/45-G Headquarters Meerut Division	07/05/1915	07/05/1915
Miscellaneous	Tactical Progress Report	07/05/1915	07/05/1915
Miscellaneous	Time Table-Indian Corps		
Miscellaneous	No.G.405/38 Headquarters Meerut Division	07/05/1915	07/05/1915
Miscellaneous	The Following Position Marking Flags Will Be Used By Divisions As Under	06/05/1915	06/05/1915
Operation(al) Order(s)	Operation Order No.44 By Brig. Genl. F.E. Johnson, C.M.G. D.S.O. R.A. Commanding Lahore Div. Artillery	07/05/1915	07/05/1915
Miscellaneous	Lahore Divisional Artillery Time Table		
Miscellaneous	Tactical Progress Report	08/05/1915	08/05/1915
Miscellaneous	A Form Messages And Signals		
Miscellaneous	Headquarters Divisional Artillery Meerut Division	09/05/1915	09/05/1915
Miscellaneous	A Form Messages And Signals		
Miscellaneous	Instructions for Meerut Divisional Artillery 10th May 1915	10/05/1915	10/05/1915
Miscellaneous	Headquarters Divisional Artillery Meerut Division	10/05/1915	10/05/1915
Miscellaneous	Tactical Progress Report	10/05/1915	10/05/1915
Miscellaneous	Tactical Progress Report	11/05/1915	11/05/1915
Miscellaneous	Tactical Progress Report	12/05/1915	12/05/1915
Miscellaneous	1st Army G.S. G.S. 32 (a)	13/05/1915	13/05/1915

Miscellaneous	Tactical Progress Report	13/05/1915	13/05/1915
Miscellaneous	1st Army General Staff No.G.S 82 (a)	13/05/1915	13/05/1915
Operation(al) Order(s)	Operation Order No.31 By Lieutenant-General Sir Charles Anderson K.C.B. Commanding Meerut Division	14/05/1915	14/05/1915
Miscellaneous	No.G.439/21 Headquarters Meerut Div 14th May 1915	14/05/1915	14/05/1915
Miscellaneous	No.G.439/32 No G 9 Headquarters Meerut Div 15th May 1915	15/05/1915	15/05/1915
Operation(al) Order(s)	Operation Order No.19 By Brigadier General R.St.C. Lecky R.A. C.R.A. Meerut Division.	14/05/1915	14/05/1915
Miscellaneous	Revised Instruction For Meerut Divisional Artillery		
Miscellaneous	Headquarters Divisional Artillery Meerut Division	14/05/1915	14/05/1915
Miscellaneous	Tactical Progress Report	14/05/1915	14/05/1915
Operation(al) Order(s)	Operation Order No.45 by Brig. General N.E. Johnson C.M.G. D.S.O., Commanding Lahore Divisional Artillery	15/05/1915	15/05/1915
Miscellaneous	Time Table And Barrages		
Miscellaneous	Barrage		
Miscellaneous	Points Registered		
Miscellaneous	Tactical Progress Report	15/05/1915	15/05/1915
Miscellaneous	Rocket Signals	14/05/1915	14/05/1915
Miscellaneous	Tactical Progress Report	16/05/1915	16/05/1915
Miscellaneous	A Form Messages And Signals		
Miscellaneous	Tactical Progress Report	17/05/1915	17/05/1915
Miscellaneous	A Form Messages And Signals		
Operation(al) Order(s)	Operation Order No.32 By Lieutenant General Sir Charles Anderson, K.C.B. Commanding Meerut Division	18/05/1915	18/05/1915
Miscellaneous	A Form Messages And Signals		
Miscellaneous	Tactical Progress Report	18/05/1915	18/05/1915
Miscellaneous	Appendix 204		
Miscellaneous	Tactical Progress Report	19/05/1915	19/05/1915
Miscellaneous	A Form Messages And Signals		
Miscellaneous	O.C. R.A. Southern Group	20/05/1915	20/05/1915
Miscellaneous	A Form Messages And Signals		
Miscellaneous	Tactical Progress Report	20/05/1915	20/05/1915
Operation(al) Order(s)	Operation Order No.34 By Lieutenant-General Sir Charles Anderson, K.C.B. Commanding Meerut Division.	21/05/1915	21/05/1915
Miscellaneous	A Form Messages And Signals		
Miscellaneous	Appendix 213	21/05/1915	21/05/1915
Miscellaneous	X Sec BM 273		
Miscellaneous	C.R.A 53 O.C R.A. Southern Group	21/05/1915	21/05/1915
Miscellaneous	X Q 20 to Q 12		
Miscellaneous	C.R.A 54 O.C R.A. Southern Group	21/05/1915	21/05/1915
Miscellaneous	O.C. 4th Bde RFA	21/05/1915	21/05/1915
Miscellaneous	A Form Messages And Signals		
Miscellaneous	Tactical Progress Report	21/05/1915	21/05/1915
Miscellaneous	No.G-126 Headquarters Meerut Division	21/05/1915	21/05/1915
Miscellaneous	Tactical Progress Report	22/05/1915	22/05/1915
Miscellaneous	Tactical Progress Report	23/05/1915	23/05/1915
Miscellaneous	Tactical Progress Report	24/05/1915	24/05/1915
Miscellaneous	No.G.768 Headquarters Meerut Division	24/05/1915	24/05/1915
Miscellaneous	M 20 M 23		
Miscellaneous	Tactical Progress Report	25/05/1915	25/05/1915
Miscellaneous	Tactical Progress Report	26/05/1915	26/05/1915

Miscellaneous	Tactical Progress Report	27/05/1915	27/05/1915
Miscellaneous	Tactical Progress Report	28/05/1915	28/05/1915
Miscellaneous	Tactical Progress Report	29/05/1915	29/05/1915
Operation(al) Order(s)	Operation Order No.37 By Lieutenant-General Sir Charles Anderson, K.C.B. Commanding Meerut Division.	30/05/1915	30/05/1915
Miscellaneous	Tactical Progress Report	30/05/1915	30/05/1915
Operation(al) Order(s)	Operation Order No.20 By Brigadier General R.St.C Lecky R.A. C.R.A. Meerut Division.	31/05/1915	31/05/1915
Miscellaneous	Tactical Progress Report	31/05/1915	31/05/1915

Meerut Division,

H. Q. Div. Artillery.

1st To 31st May

65.

121/5799

With appendices.

Head Quarters Divisional Artillery, Meerut Division.

1st May 31st May

HEADQUARTERS DIVISIONAL ARTILLERY
MEERUT DIVISION

Instructions regarding War Diaries and Intelligence Summaries are contained in F. S. Regs., Part II. and the Staff Manual respectively. Title pages will be prepared in manuscript.

WAR DIARY
or
INTELLIGENCE SUMMARY.
(Erase heading not required.)

VOLUME X.

Army Form C. 2118.

Hour, Date, Place		Summary of Events and Information	Remarks and references to Appendices
4.20.a.m.	1st May 1915....... FOSSE.	4th Brigade Batteries replied to Heavy Hostile bombardment by shelling enemy trenches and O.P's for about 1¼ hours. 8th Battery opened fire on enemy's trenches owing to report of heavy shelling of PORT ARTHUR and RUE du BOIS and report by Infantry that enemy were using poison gasses. Rate of fire was reduced as enemy's fire slackened.	
4.30 to 5.a.m.	do.......	2nd Battery fired on enemy trenches opposite Southern Section, ~~xxx~~report as above being received.	
4.30 to 5.45.a.m.	do.......	Enemy kept up a screen of fire continually over our support trenches along ~~xx~~ the RUE du BOIS(extending from NEUVE CHAPELLE to about point S 9 d 5'7) and on the open ground in S 3 c and d and S 4 c and S 9 b. A continuous and well directed fire swept the road from PONT LOGY to about ROUGE CROIX, and the road from WINDY CORNER(S 9 a 6'10) to point M 32 d(St VAAST). There was a strong smell of Sulphur at REVOLVER House(S 3 c 4'4) apparently caused by the bursting shell, which in some cases had a thick yellow smoke. At the commencement of the bombardment the German Machine Guns registered all their points on our trenches and then stopped.	
4.45.a.m.	do.......	5th Siege Battery engaged the following objectives:- (i) Houses 400 yards N.W. LA TOURELLE cross roads to Distillery. (ii) Breastwork S 11 a 8'4. (iii) Point where German first line trenches cut LA BASSEE Road.	
5.50.a.m.	do.......	Firing ceased. During the whole of the above time there wasno machine gun fire and very little rifle fire.	
6.2.a.m.	do.......	Hostile aeroplane AVIATIK sighted flying high, bearing 105°,engaged with 34 rounds then turned S.S.E.	appendix x 154
7.5.a.m.	do.......	Hostile aeroplane AVIATIK sighted flying low, bearing 150°,engaged with 13 rounds then turned E.S.E.	
7.45.a.m.	do.......	Hostile aeroplane FOKKER sighted flying high, bearing 45°,engaged with 61 rounds then turned E. 8th Battery fired on machine gun at point 59 which was firing on a British aeroplane.	
8.a.m.	do.......	Hostile aeroplane AVIATIK sighted flying high, bearing 90°,engaged with 33 rounds and turned E.	

(9 29 6) W 4141—463 100,000 9/14 H W V Forms/C. 2118/10

Army Form C. 2118.

Instructions regarding War Diaries and Intelligence Summaries are contained in F. S. Regs., Part II. and the Staff Manual respectively. Title pages will be prepared in manuscript.

WAR DIARY
or
INTELLIGENCE SUMMARY.
(Erase heading not required.)

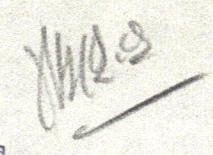

Hour, Date, Place	Summary of Events and Information	Remarks and references to Appendices
8.45.a.m. 1st May 1915...... FOSSE.	Hostile aeroplane AVIATIK sighted flying high at bearing 130°, engaged with 62 rounds and turned E.	
10.30.a.m. do........	66th Battery O.P. shelled by field howitzer.	
10.50.a.m. do........	66th Battery fired on "L" shaped house near point 125.×	×appendix 154
11.a.m. do........	7th Batery O.P. was shelled by heavy howitzer or gun, five hits on house.	
11 to 11.30.a.m. do........	44th Battery position shelled by 10'5 c.m.-one man hit very slightly. five rounds were fired at about 5 minutes interval-apparently from ILLIES.	
11.15.a.m. do........	Enemy shelled DEHRA DUN Brigade Headquarters with five 5'9" shell.	
11.20.a.m. do........	7th Battery fired a few shots into German O.P. at point 63.×	
3.30 to 5.15.p.m. do........	German "Sausage" seen low at bearing 213°.	
	Further information is contained in the Tactical Progress Report attached. Appendix 155.	
4.20.a.m. do........	The G.O.C., No.1 Group Heavy Artillery Reserve was communicated with regarding the expected attack. During the hostile bombardment this morning it was quite impossible to get telephonic communication with the G.O.C., R.A. of the 1st Division(our right) and the 8th Division(our left), the wires being conjested with messages of the General Staff of the Divisions concerned. It is very necessary that Divisional Artillery Commanders should be in through communication with each other and this opportunity is taken of bringing this important matter to notice.	[initials]

Army Form C. 2118.

Instructions regarding War Diaries and Intelligence Summaries are contained in F. S. Regs., Part II. and the Staff Manual respectively. Title pages will be prepared in manuscript.

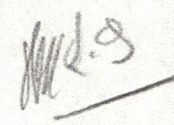

WAR DIARY
or
INTELLIGENCE SUMMARY.
(Erase heading not required.)

Hour, Date, Place	Summary of Events and Information	Remarks and references to Appendices
7.45.a.m. 2nd May 1915. FOSSE.	Light Howitzer shelled ground in front of 14th Battery.	
7.55.a.m. do.	German battery, thought to be at VIOLAINES, shelled just in rear of 28th Battery position(M 27 c 8'9).	
9.a.m. do.	14th Battery registered Salient between 137 and 14±.×	
11.20.a.m. do.	66th Battery fired on enemy's working party in Redoubt N. of 63.×	×appendix 154
11.30.a.m. do.	66th Battery fired on enemy's trench between 51× and 63.×	
11.55.a.m. do.	14th Battery fired on house 124×-man seen leaving house-probably an O.P. This was also fired on at 6.30.p.m.	
12 noon. do.	Enemy shelled NEUVE CHAPELLE and our Infantry in front- 7th and 66th Batteries replied by shelling enemy's trenches and point 65. 2 hits obtained on the house.	
	44th Battery registered the trenches near point 57.×	
2.20.p.m. do.	66th Battery fired on working party S. of point 63.×	
4.30.p.m. do.	20th Battery registered, with aeroplane, the following points:- Cross roads at T 12 c 6'6, N 32 a 6'3, N 31 d 9'1.	
	Further information is contained in Tactical Progress Report attached.*	* Appendix 156.

[signature]

(9 29 6) W 4141—463 100,000 9/14 H W V Forms/C. 2118/10

Instructions regarding War Diaries and Intelligence Summaries are contained in F. S. Regs., Part II. and the Staff Manual respectively. Title pages will be prepared in manuscript.

Army Form C. 2118.

WAR DIARY
or
INTELLIGENCE SUMMARY.
(Erase heading not required.)

Hour, Date, Place		Summary of Events and Information	Remarks and references to Appendices
4.45.a.m.	3rd May 1915...... FOSSE.	2nd Siege Battery registered on advanced post on Salient(56)-unsatisfactory result.	
5.5.a.m.	do.........	PIPSQUEAK fired about 5 rounds between PORT ARTHUR and GOOD LUCK House.	
7.50.a.m.	do.........	Hostile aeroplane "ALBATROSS" sighted, bearing 96°, engaged with 10 rounds, turned E., reappeared at 8.a.m., re-engaged with 11 rounds.	
8.10.a.m.	do.........	20th Battery registered trenches between points 128 and 138.	
11.15.a.m. to) 12.30.p.m.)	do.........	German 4'2" Howitzer shelled the RUE DU BOIS from S 10 a 4'3 to S 9 d 6'6 firing about 20 rounds altogether.	* Appendix 154
1,p.m.	do.........	Trenches of 6th Jats heavily bombed by the enemy. 2nd and 8th Batteries fired a few rounds to stop bombing near point V.6.	
1 to 2.p.m.	do.........	Hose pipes were registered by the Batteries of 4th Brigade R.F.A.	
1.20.p.m.	do.........	German trench mortar at S 10 d 3'8 fired on our trenches.	
1.30.p.m.	do.........	PIPSQUEAK fired 8 rounds over GOOD LUCK House.	
2.54.p.m.	do.........	66th Battery fired on trenches near point 133 where movement was seen.	
3.15.p.m.	do.........	8th Battery registered hose pipe in German trench W. of point 59.	
5.15.p.m.	do.........	20th Battery registered N 31 d 9'1 with aeroplane.	
5.45.p.m.	do.........	5th Siege Battery registered V.6.-5th round into trench.	
5.55.p.m.	do.........	Hostile aeroplane AVIATIK sighted bearing 100°,engaged with 34 rounds and turned S.E. Let off white lights in two or three groups.	
6.30p.m.	do.........	2nd Siege Battery bombarded hose pipe site at S 5 b 7'9 with 12 rounds H.E. and got some good hits into trench. 30th How Battery reported hose pipe removed after they shot at it earlier in the day.	
6.15.p.m.	do.........	Germans fired 5'9" How: at RITZ and along RUE du BOIS. 2nd Siege Battery registered on hose pipe site at S 5b7'9.	
6.27.p.m.	do.........	A few rounds were fired by batteries of 4th Brigade R.F.A. at enemy trenches to check hostile rifle fire on our aeroplanes.	
6.30.p.m.	do.........	5th Siege Battery bombarded with 12 rounds per gun the following:- Point 130-2 hits within 10 yards of hose pipe, pipe looked damaged but remained there. Point 66-trench nearchose pipe was hit, but pipe was not actually hit. V.6. shell hit parapet and threw up sandbags.	
6.40.p.m.	do.........	28th Battery registered "Forkroads" T 7 d 3'6	
		For furtherinformation see Tactical Progress Report attached.	* Appendix 157.

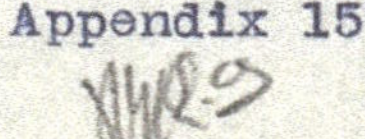

Army Form C. 2118.

Instructions regarding War Diaries and Intelligence Summaries are contained in F. S. Regs., Part II. and the Staff Manual respectively. Title pages will be prepared in manuscript.

WAR DIARY
or
INTELLIGENCE SUMMARY.
(Erase heading not required.)

Hour, Date, Place	Summary of Events and Information	Remarks and references to Appendices
11.5.a.m. 4th May 1915...... FOSSE.	Hostile aeroplane AVIATIK, high, bearing 150°, travelling S.E. and became obscured by clouds.	
11.20.a.m. do.........	66th Battery fired at house at 51 V. ×	
12 noon. do.........	4'2" Howitzer shelled vicinity S 9 d 1'5 firing single shots at 3 minute intervals.	×appendix 157
1.20.p.m. do.........	Enemy bombed ORCHARD S 10 b.	
1.40.p.m. do.........	German field guns shelled cross roads S 9 d 1'5 firing single shots.	
2.50.p.m. do.........	German 5'9"How:(from direction LIGNY le PETIT)shelled S 9 d 1'5.	
3.25.p.m. do.........	German shell fell in RITZ S 9 d.	
4.p.m. do.........	20th Battery registered cross roads S 12 a 6'2, S 12 c 6'6, S 12 c 3'3 and FERME du BIEZ.	
4.10.p.m. do.........	19th Battery registered/fork roads N 32 a 5'3. ×	
4.45.p.m. do.........	14th Battery fired at working party carrying planks-138-support trench. The party were kept busy for some time trying to retrieve planks.	
10.30.p.m. do.........	MEERUT Division Operation Order* No.29 received.	* Appendix 158.
	Further information will be found in the Tactical Progress Report≠ attached.	≠ Appendix 159.

(9 29 6) W4141—463 100,000 9/14 H W V Forms/C. 2118/10

Army Form C. 2118.

Instructions regarding War Diaries and Intelligence Summaries are contained in F. S. Regs., Part II. and the Staff Manual respectively. Title pages will be prepared in manuscript.

WAR DIARY
or
INTELLIGENCE SUMMARY.
(Erase heading not required.)

Hour, Date, Place		Summary of Events and Information	Remarks and references to Appendices
5.a.m.	5th May 1915......... FOSSE.	2nd Battery fired a few rounds on enemy's trenches.	
6.50.a.m.	do...........	PIPSQUEAK fired 6 rounds at 7th Battery's O.P._2 direct hits.	
10.20.a.m.	do...........	14th Battery fired at point 191x	
10.45.a.m.	do...........	A few heavy howitzer shell fell near Hd Qrs Garhwal Rifles.	
11.a.m.	do...........	Enemy bombed area between fire trench and support trench S 10 d 1'1. German Heavy Howitzer shelled NEUVE CHAPELLE. 8" Howitzer put several rounds into PORT ARTHUR.	
12.5.p.m.	do...........	7th Battery fired on working party near 131.x	
2.7.p.m.	do...........	14th Battery shelled party of Germans near point 151x-they took cover.	x appendix 154
3.30.p.m.	do...........	5'9" Howitzer fired few rounds into PORT ARTHUR.	
4.p.m.	do...........	7th Battery fired at activity near point 131x	
4.3.p.m.	do...........	Heavy Howitzer fired 4 rounds at PORT ARTHUR, 2 of which were blind.	
4.5.p.m.	do...........	5'9"s and 4'2"s fired on the area PORT ARTHUR, LA BASSEE Road to RUE des BERCEAUX.	
5.20.p.m.	do...........	German field guns shelled RUE du BOIS at S 9 d.	
5.40.p.m.	do...........	7th Battery fired a few rounds at 125x where snipers reported a nuisance.	
6.30.p.m.	do...........	The 28th Battery registered their zone 46x, 48x, 49x to 66x	
4.3.p.m.	do...........	O,C's Northern and Southern Groups R.A., 9th Brigade R.F.A. and 6th Siege Brigade R.G.A. were informed that the LAHORE Division would take over the Northern Section of the Indian Corps front tonight see 9±6-R.A.(L)*.	* Appendix 160.
		For further information see Tactica Progress Report.≠	≠ Appendix 161.

(9 29 6) W4141—463 100,000 9/14 H W V Forms/C. 2118/10

Instructions regarding War Diaries and Intelligence Summaries are contained in F. S. Regs., Part II. and the Staff Manual respectively. Title pages will be prepared in manuscript.

WAR DIARY
or
INTELLIGENCE SUMMARY.
(Erase heading not required.)

Army Form C. 2118.

Hour, Date, Place		Summary of Events and Information	Remarks and references to Appendices
12.30.p.m.) 1.30.p.m.) 1.p.m.)	6th May 1915... FOSSE.	PIPSQUEAK fired as usual on houses in RUE du BOIS(East end).	
1.p.m.	do......	German Howitzer shelled communicating trench in S 4 c.	
3.p.m.	do......	8th Battery fired on trenches at 54× and V 9× GOOD LUCK House was shelled.	×appendix 152
3.15.p.m.	do......	German 4'2" Howitzer shelled RUE du BOIS from S 10 a 7'7 to S 4 d 2'2.	
3.30.p.m.	do......	PIPSQUEAK shelled vicinity of road in M 33 b, caused by Indian Troops wandering up and down this road and by too much traffic and working parties.	
3.38.p.m.	do......	5'9" Howitzer shelled PORT ARTHUR with H.E.	
4.5.p.m.	do......	5'9" or 8" shelled PORT ARTHUR.	
5.p.m.	do......	~~Exxxxx~~ Neighbourhood of LA COUTURE shelled by 5'9" Howitzers.	≠ Appendix 161(a).
6.p.m.	do......	MEERUT Division Operation Order≠ No.30 received.(*)	(*) Appendix 162.
		For further information see Tactical Progress Report attached.	

[illegible initials]

(9 29 6) W 4141—463 100,000 9/14 H W V Forms/C. 2118/10

Army Form C. 2118.

Instructions regarding War Diaries and Intelligence Summaries are contained in F. S. Regs., Part II. and the Staff Manual respectively. Title pages will be prepared in manuscript.

WAR DIARY
or
INTELLIGENCE SUMMARY.
(Erase heading not required.)

Hour, Date, Place		Summary of Events and Information	Remarks and references to Appendices
7.a.m.	7th May 1915...... FOSSE.	Operation Order No.18 by G.O.C., R.A., MEERUT Division issued. *	* Appendix 163.
10.30.a.m.) 12.15.p.m.)	do........	21 c.m. How: fired on ruined house just behind CRESCENT Trench.	
12 noon) 1.15.p.m.)	do........	PIPSQUEAK shelled, as usual, houses, barricade and trenches at PORT ARTHUR end of RUE du BOIS, also at intervals between 3.p.m. and 5.p.m.	
12 noon.	do........	8th Battery fired on trenches V 9 e× to V.6.×	× appendix 154
12 noon to 2.p.m.	do........	28th Battery O.P. S 10 b 1'7 heavily shelled by PIPSQUEAK.	
1.10 and 3.10.p.m.	do........	14th Battery fired on working party in enemy's communication trenchz	
1.20.p.m.	do........	PIPSQUEAK shelled 7th Battery O.P.,2 hits were obtained on the house.	
3.p.m.	do........	Two batteries of 4th Brigade R.F.A. fired on enemy's trenches to keep down hostile fire on our aeroplanes.	
4.p.m.	do........	66th Battery Observing Officer assisted 28th Battery to register. 8" Howitzer shelled PORT ARTHUR.	
4 to 5.p.m.	do........	8" Howitzer fired on CRESCENT Trench switching till rounds fell between PICQUET House and RUE du BOIS.	
4.45.p.m.	do........	8" and PIPSQUEAK shell dropped close to 44th Battery O.P.	≠ Appendix 163(a)
6.p.m.	do........	≠Orders received for the postponement of operations* for 24 hours. For further information see Tactical Progress Report attached.	* Appendix =164
		ø Time Table, INDIAN Corps, for pending operations attached.	ø appendix 165.
4.p.m.	do.	LAHORE Divisional Artillery Operation Order* No 44 received.	* appendix 165(a)

[illegible signature]

Army Form C. 2118.

Instructions regarding War Diaries and Intelligence Summaries are contained in F. S. Regs., Part II. and the Staff Manual respectively. Title pages will be prepared in manuscript.

WAR DIARY
or
INTELLIGENCE SUMMARY.
(Erase heading not required.)

Hour, Date, Place	Summary of Events and Information	Remarks and references to Appendices
8.5.a.m. 8th May 1915........ RUE du PUITS M 27 a.	Hostile aeroplane AVIATIK flying low, bearing 160°, engaged 15 rounds then turned E.	
8.35.a.m. do.........	Hostile aeroplane AVIATIK flying low, bearing 160°, engaged 24 rounds turned E. and re-appeared at same baering engaged 7 rounds turned S. out of sight.	
9.30.a.m. do.........	14th Battery fired on houses 123 and 124 where sniping was coming from.	
10.10.a.m. do.........	66th Battery had one direct hit ion FERME du BIEZ.	
10.30.a.m. do.........	Hostile aeroplane flying high(AVIATIK), bearing 160°, engaged 7 rounds turned S. out of sight.	
	Hostile aeroplane flying high(AVIATIK), bearing 160°, out of range travelled S.	× appendix 154
11.a.m. do.........	A few rounds of PIPSQUEAK over CRESCENT Trench.	
4.30.p.m. do.........	14th Battery fired on house 140× where Infantry had reported machine guns concealed in house. Machine gun located in large hole in lower half of wall of house apparently at N.E. corner. During registration smoke of discharge of M.G. observed. 6 rounds H.E. 3 detonated properly- 2 on German wire- this was cut but iron posts supporting it were not knocked down.	
	PIPSQUEAKS fell near ORCHARD and PORT ARTHUR.	
5.p.m. do.........	PIPSQUEAK shelled round about East end of RUE du BOIS.	
5.20.p.m. do.........	5'9" Howitzer shell fell near RUE du BOIS.	
5.45.p.m. do.........	German 4'2" Howitzer shelled PORT ARTHUR.	
6.45.p.m. do.........	66th Battery fired 3 rounds at working party at S 11 b 2'2.	
9.p.m. do.........	Headquarters Divisional Artillery established at RUE du PUITS(M 27 a) in farm 100 yards N. of MEERUT Division Report centre. Headquarters LAHORE Divisional Artillery established at the same farm.	
	For further information see Tactical Progress Report* attached.	* Appendix 166.
		[illegible signature]

(9 29 6) W4141—463 100,000 9/14 H W V Forms/C. 2118/10

Army Form C. 2118.

Instructions regarding War Diaries and Intelligence Summaries are contained in F. S. Regs., Part II. and the Staff Manual respectively. Title pages will be prepared in manuscript.

WAR DIARY
or
INTELLIGENCE SUMMARY.
(Erase heading not required.)

Hour, Date, Place	Summary of Events and Information	Remarks and references to Appendices
RUE du PUITS (M 27 a)		
4.45.a.m. 9th May 1915......	4th Brigade batteries fired a few registering rounds.	
5.a.m. do........	All batteries of the MEERUT Divisional Artillery opened fire in accordance with Phase I of schedule of tasks attached to Operation Order By G.O.C., R.A., MEERUT Division No.18.	
5.40.a.m. do........	O.C, 4th Brigade R.F.A. reported no movement of enemy to be seen on front of JULLUNDUR Brigade.	
5.47.a.m. do........	O.C. 4th Brigade R.F.A. reported heavy rifle fire from trenches between 130 and 128.	
5.56.a.m. do........	O.C. 9th Brigade R.F.A. reported we held German first trench, enemy tried to advance but were driven back.	
5.57.a.m. do........	O.C. 4th Brigade R.F.A. reported our Howitzer fire on 63x very effective, and that 7th Battery O.P. being shelled at 5.55.a.m.	x appendix 15x
6.8.a.m. do........	O.C. 9th Brigade R.F.A. reported Gurkhas had taken their trench;but Seaforth's could not get on.	
6.25.a.m. do........	O.C. 9th Brigade R.F.A. reported that Seaforth's still unable to advance-This from O.C. 19th Battery R.F.A.	
6.30.a.m. do........	~~MEERUT Division~~ [illegible] informed that as it was understood we were unable to advance Howitzers ordered to fire on enemy front trenches for 15 minutes,especially near point 59.x	
6.35.a.m. do........	O.C. 9th Brigade R.F.A. wired that Infantry reported machine guns along front trench. The leading half company of the 4th Seaforth's having been wiped out attack stopped.	
6.43.a.m. do........	O.C. 9th Brigade R.F.A. wired that it was reported that 1st Seaforth's had taken half first trench with very heavily casaulties and requiring reinforcements.	
6.48.a.m. do........	Seaforth's reported they were not holding any portion of enemy's trench.	
6.52.p.m. do........	9th Brigade R.F.A. reported M.G. located at point 56x 13th Brigade R.F.A. were asked to knock it out with H.E.	
7.13.a.m. do........	Information received from Advanced MEERUT Division that enemy's front line had been broken by 4th Corps at 6.a.m. in front of ROUGE BANCS, and that Infantry had reached points 827x, 829x and 375x. The 3 R.F.A. Brigades of the MEERUT Divisional Artillery were informed.	

Army Form C. 2118.

Instructions regarding War Diaries and Intelligence Summaries are contained in F. S. Regs., Part II. and the Staff Manual respectively. Title pages will be prepared in manuscript.

WAR DIARY
or
INTELLIGENCE SUMMARY.
(Erase heading not required.)

Hour, Date, Place		Summary of Events and Information	Remarks and references to Appendices
7.32.a.m. 9th May 1915...... RUE du PUITS M 27 a		Observing Officer 19th Battery reported through O.C. 9th Brigade that some of the Gurkhas got into the German front ~~trench~~ line of trenches and Gurkha Reserves held up owing to Seaforth's being held up. It is thought that Gurkhas who got into German trenches were taken prisoners.	
7.55.a.m.	do.........	Phase I of the tasks was repeated.	
8.a.m.	do.........	14th Battery was shelled with 5'9" Howitzers-no damage done-shorts and overs.	
8.10.a.m.	do.........	Phase 3 of tasks was repeated.	
8.40.a.m.	do.........	4th Brigade R.F.A. reported very little shell or rifle fire on JULLUNDUR Brigade front and no movement. Orders to re-organise and prepare for fresh bombardment in a few hours.	
8.42.a.m.	do.........	Forward Observing Officer 13th Brigade R.F.A. reported German reinforcements coming up.	
8.48.a.m.	do.........	9th Brigade R.F.A. reported that Black Watch of BAREILLY Brigade now moving up in support.	
9.2.a.m.	do.........	O.C. ~~XXX~~4th Brigade R.F.A. reported AUBERS on fire S. of Church at 8.55.a.m.	
9.5.a.m.	do.........	~~Xxxxxxx~~.No.1 Group informed us that they were putting two 9'2" on DISTILLERY and one on FERME du BIEZ.	×appendix 1??
9,10.a.m.	do.........	PIPSQUEAK shelled NEUVE CHAPELLE.	
9.14.a.m.	do.........	O.C. 9th Brigade R.F.A. reported he was engaging enemy's reinforcements moving by LA BASSEE Road with two batteries.	
10.a.m.	do.........	9th Brigade R.F.A. reported that 20th Battery O.P. said Infantry report German front line very badly damaged. No man can go out of trenches without being shot by maxim guns- these guns are evidently dug in right down to the ground level.	
10.19.a.m.	do.........	Report from 19th Observation Post that enemy had reinforced front about 56× strongly- 3 F.A. Brigades of MEERUT Divisional Artillery were informed.	
10.25.a.m.	do.........	Heavy Howitzer shelled PONT LOGY.	
10.33.a.m.	do.........	28th Battery F.O.O. reported that enemy strongly reinforced about 55× and 56× may counter-attack. Guns of 28th Battery laid ready to meet this. MEERUT Division, G.O.C. R.A. LAHORE Division and 13th Brigade R.F.A. were informed of this.	
10.[illegible].a.m.	do.........	MEERUT Division message* regarding repetition of bombardment and assault to commence- 2.p.m. the former and 2.40.p.m. the latter. 3 F.A. Bdes and Divisional Ammunition Column were informed≠ accordingly.	* Appendix 167 ≠ Appendix 168

Instructions regarding War Diaries and Intelligence Summaries are contained in F. S. Regs., Part II. and the Staff Manual respectively. Title pages will be prepared in manuscript.

WAR DIARY
or
INTELLIGENCE SUMMARY.
(Erase heading not required.)

Army Form C. 2118.

Hour, Date, Place	Summary of Events and Information	Remarks and references to Appendices
11.13.a.m. 9th May 1915..... RUE du PUITS (M 27 a)	F.O.O. 13th Brigade R.F.A. reported wire in front of German trenches appeared to be well cut and that their machine guns must be level with ground- 1st Division was held up in same way by machine gun fire.	
12.45.p.m. do.........	Two companies enemy seen at MARQUILLIES about 12 noon which may indicate perhaps that reinforcements may arrive from this direction.	
1.p.m. do.........	3 Brigade R.F.A. MEERUT Divisional Artillery were informed that time of commencement of second bombardment altered see Appendix 169.	Appendix 169.
2.15.p.m. do.........	Phases of second bombardment were altered vide Appendices 170 to 173.	Appendices 170,171, 172, 173.
3.20.p.m. do.........	Second bombardment commenced with Phase I and new phases.	
4.p.m. do.........	Infantry should have assaulted.	
4.24.p.m. do.........	Black Watch reported that general effect of bombardment very slight.	
4.32.p.m. do.........	13th Brigade R.F.A. reported no signs of advance and machine guns just as active.	
4.53.p.m. do.........	F.O.O. of 28th Battery reported Infantry held up at ditch S 10 b, 50 yards from our line. Infantry report impossible to advance.	
5.45.p.m. do.........	9th Brigade reported enemy moving to attack.	
5.55.p.m. do.........	19th Battery reported effect of bombardment very slight, enemy still lining parapet.	
5.56.p.m. do.........	9th Brigade R.F.A. reported forward movement of enemy now reported not taking place.	
6.40.p.m. do.........	O.C. R.A. Southern and Northern Groups informed regarding night lines for Howitzer and Siege Batteries and asking for batteries to be warned we may be going to attack in which case they might be called upon to form distant barrage.	
6.45.p.m. do.........	O.C. R.A. Southern Group reported no signs of counter-attack.	
8.18.p.m. do.........	4th Brigade R.F.A. reported 14th Battery O.O. reports it sounded to him as if the enemy were counter attacking the 4th Corps on our left at 8.p.m.	
10.10.p.m. do.........	Orders received from First Army that every means should be used to prevent the enemy from repairing his wire entanglements or re-erecting fresh wire in front of second lines tonight. Also intermittent Artillery fire to be directed on the communication trenches and cross roads during the night.	

(9 29 6) W 4141—463 100,000 9/14 H W V Forms/C. 2118/10

Army Form C. 2118.

Instructions regarding War Diaries and Intelligence Summaries are contained in F. S. Regs., Part II. and the Staff Manual respectively. Title pages will be prepared in manuscript.

WAR DIARY
or
INTELLIGENCE SUMMARY.
(Erase heading not required.)

Hour, Date, Place	Summary of Events and Information	Remarks and references to Appendices
	GENERAL - 9.5.15.	
At 5.a.m. 9th May 1915........ RUE du PUITS (M 27 a)	Brigadier General F.E. JOHNSON, D.S.O. G.O.C., R.A. LAHORE Division assumed command of all the Artillery of MEERUT and LAHORE Divisions from time of commencement of operations at 5.a.m. Communications with 43rd(Howitzer) Brigade R.F.A., 6th(Siege) Brigade R.G.A.(6" Hows:) and No.1 Group H.A.R. were laid out from "dug-out" of LAHORE Divisional Artillery Signallers, MEERUT Divisional Artillery being only in direct communication with 4th, 9th and 13th Brigades, MEERUT Divisional Ammunition Column and General Staff, MEERUT Division.	
	PIPSQUEAK active all day from near LA RUSSIE. Communications of 4th and 13th Brigades R.F.A. worked well all day, those of the 9th being more exposed were frequently cut, at ~~same~~ one time 9 lines to O.P. being cut at same time. Reports as received during the day were passed to G.O.C., R.A., LAHORE and General Staff, MEERUT Division.	
	The following Officers were killed or wounded during the day as stated:- Major F.N. PARBURY, 20th Battery R.F.A. Killed. Major A.C. LITTLEDALE, 19th ,, ,, Wounded-very seriously. Captain C. HOLLAND, 13th Brigade Ammn Col. Killed. 2/Lieut N.E. FORBES, (Special Reserve). 20th Battery R.F.A. Wounded. (Since dead)	
	Major LITTLEDALE died of his wounds during the night.	[illegible initials]

(9 29 6) W 4141—463 100,000 9/14 H W V Forms/C. 2118/10

Army Form C. 2118.

Instructions regarding War Diaries and Intelligence Summaries are contained in F. S. Regs., Part II. and the Staff Manual respectively. Title pages will be prepared in manuscript.

WAR DIARY
or
INTELLIGENCE SUMMARY.
(Erase heading not required.)

Hour, Date, Place	Summary of Events and Information	Remarks and references to Appendices
4.a.m. 10th May 1915 (typed "19th", corrected "10" above) RUE du PUITS M 27 a.	Certain amount of shelling in vicinity of M 33 d.	
4.30.a.m. do.......	Enemy's howitzers shelled in front of 14th Battery position.	
4.45.a.m. do.......	20th Battery opened fire on roads 46×, V.18×, V.19×, V.15×, V.14×, V.13× firing about 15 rounds every hour, in this vicinity.	×appendix 154
5.a.m. do.......	Batteries of 4th Brigade R.F.A. registered a few points.	
5.20.a.m. do.......	Hostile aeroplane AVIATIK sighted flying high at bearing 90°, engaged with 57 rounds then turned E. over German lines.	
6.50.a.m. do.......	14th Battery had two direct hits on O.P. near 125.×	
11.a.m. do.......	Orders issued for the attack vide Appendix 174, which subsequently/cancelled.	Appendix 174.
11.30.a.m. do.......	PIPSQUEAK had four hits on 7th Battery O.P.	
4.10.p.m. do.......	14th Battery fired at point 120×, house near and in front of it where movement was seen.	
4.40.p.m. do.......	German howitzer shelled LA BASSEE Road about 500 yards South of PONT LOGY.	
6.p.m. do.......	44th Battery O.P. shelled by PIPSQUEAK.	
8.30.p.m. do.......	14th Battery fired at house 140× in combination with heavies.	
	For further information see Tactical Progress Report attached. *	* Appendix 175.

(9 29 6) W4141—463 100,000 9/14 H W V Forms/C. 2118/10

Army Form C. 2118.

Instructions regarding War Diaries and Intelligence Summaries are contained in F. S. Regs., Part II. and the Staff Manual respectively. Title pages will be prepared in manuscript.

WAR DIARY
or
INTELLIGENCE SUMMARY.
(Erase heading not required.)

Hour, Date, Place	Summary of Events and Information	Remarks and references to Appendices
11.p.m. 10.5.15 to 3.a.m. 11.5.15. RUE du PUITS M 27 a	Enemy shelled RUE du BOIS chiefly with PIPSQUEAK.	
5.a.m. 11th May 1915........ RUE du PUITS M 27 a	German heavy howitzer shelled PORT ARTHUR.	
6.30.a.m. do.........	14th Battery fired at party of men at 127, and 7th Battery fired at another party near 130.	
8.15.a.m. do.........	Hostile aeroplane AVIATIK flying high, bearing 100°, was out of range and ~~travelled N.E.~~ disappeared S.E. over German lines.	
9.50.a.m. do.........	Heavy howitzer shelled NEUVE CHAPELLE from BREWERY to M 35 c 3'4.	×Appendix 154
10 to 11.30.a.m. do.........	5'9" Howitzer shelled 44th Battery Headquarters-one man wounded, Headquarters DEHRA DUN Brigade was hit by two shell.	
10.15.a.m. do.........	Hostile aeroplane AVIATIK flying high, bearing 80°, was out of range and travelled N.E.	
11.a.m. do.........	RUE DU BOIS and PORT ARTHUR were shelled and this went on intermittently till 5.p.m. mostly light howitzers and apparently from direction of DISTILLERY.	
11.to 11.30.a.m. do.........	PIPSQUEAK shelled ORCHARD O.P. S 10 b 4'3- 3 direct hits.	
12.5.p.m. do.........	German howitzer shelled trenches in front of PORT ARTHUR.	
12.5 to 12.45.p.m. do.........	WOOLY BEARS shelled vicinity M 32 d and 4'2" Howitzer shelled vicinity M 27 b at the same time.	
1 to 2.30.p.m. do.........	REVOLVER House(S 3 c 5'4) shelled by field guns and 4'2" Howitzers,	
2.45.p.m. do.........	14th Battery shot at group of men behind fire trench between 145 & 146.	
2.50.p.m. do.........	14th Battery fired at O.P. near 120.	
4.p.m. do.........	8th Battery registered points 56 and 59.	
4.30.p.m. do.........	RITZ shelled by 11" Howitzer from direction VIOLAINES-2 shell were blind.	
8.p.m. do.........	G.O.C., R.A., MEERUT Division assumed command of the Artillery of the line from the G.O.C., R.A., LAHORE Division.	
	For further information see Tactical Progress Report attached. *	* Appendix 176.

Army Form C. 2118.

Instructions regarding War Diaries and Intelligence Summaries are contained in F. S. Regs., Part II. and the Staff Manual respectively. Title pages will be prepared in manuscript.

WAR DIARY
or
INTELLIGENCE SUMMARY.
(Erase heading not required.)

Hour, Date, Place	Summary of Events and Information	Remarks and references to Appendices
8.a.m. 12th May 1915.... FOSSE.	German heavy Howitzer shelled vicinity behind LANSDOWNE POST from direction of ILLIES.	
9.10.a.m. do.........	Hostile aeroplane AVIATIK, high, bearing 110°, engaged 55 rounds, then turned in Easterly direction.	
10.a.m. do.........	Heavy howitzer shelled trenches in front of RITZ(S 9 d).	
10.10.a.m. do.........	PIPSQUEAK shelled factory on RUE du BOIS(S 9 d).	
10.20 to 11.15.a.m. do....	German heavy howitzer shelled DOLL's House(M 27 d) several direct hits.	
11.a.m. do.........	2nd Battery registered on the KEEP and approaches to it.	
12 noon. do.........	R.A. Headquarters re-established at FOSSE.	
12.10 & 12.30.p.m. do.....	8th Battery fired at the KEEP and "covered way" in conjunction with 9'2's .	+Appendix 132
12.30.p.m. do.........	2nd Battery fired bursts of fire at "covered way", whilst being engaged by MOTHER, in hopes of catching enemy bolting.	
12.35.p.m. do.........	German "Sausage" up bearing 170° magnetic from M 33 a 3'7.	
12.45.p.m. do.........	PIPSQUEAK fired one shell in vicinity of M 33 b.	
2.30.p.m. do.........	14th Battery fired on house at 151x one direct hit.	
2.35.p.m. do.........	14th Battery fired on working party behind enemy's trench near 146x.	
2.45.p.m. do.........	66th Battery fired on enemy's trenches in reply to PIPSQUEAK shelling our Reserve trenches.	
3.p.m. do.........	A good deal of shelling all the afternoon along LA BASSEE Road down to PONT du HEM and vicinity M 32 and M 33.	
4.15.p.m. do.........	PIPSQUEAK shelled RUE du BOIS(S.10).	
4.45.p.m. do.........	Snipers very active from 68x and 69x 7th Battery fired a few rounds at these houses.	
5.15.p.m. do.........	PIPSQUEAK shelled RUE du BOIS(S.10).	
6.30.p.m. do.........	14th Battery fired at party of men coming out of house at 151x.	
	For further information see Tactical Progress Report attached. *	* Appendix 177.

(9 29 6) W4141—463 100,000 9/14 H W V Forms/C. 2118/10

Instructions regarding War Diaries and Intelligence Summaries are contained in F. S. Regs., Part II. and the Staff Manual respectively. Title pages will be prepared in manuscript.

WAR DIARY
or
INTELLIGENCE SUMMARY.
(Erase heading not required.)

Army Form C. 2118.

Hour, Date, Place		Summary of Events and Information	Remarks and references to Appendices
9 to 12 noon	13th May 1915. FOSSE.	Enemey occasionally shelled the RUE du BOIS.	
9.15 to 9.30.a.m.	do......	PIPSQUEAK shelled 7th Battery O.P.- 2 hits obtained on the house.	
11.10.a.m.	do......	German heavy howitzer shelled old British Salient near S 4 b 2'2.	
From 12 noon	do......	PIPSQUEAK shelled ORCHARD and communicating trench leading to RUE du BOIS.	
12.45.p.m.	do......	PIPSQUEAK shelled vicinity M 33 b and LA BASSEE Road to ROUGE CROIX.	
1.p.m.	do......	WOOLY BEARS shelled 9th Bde R.F.A. Headquarters, firing about 10 rds with good effect-one direct hit.	
2.p.m.	do......	2nd Battery registered 59 tp V.6.x	x appendix 157
From 4.p.m.	do......	Enemey shelled RUE du BOIS heavily.	
4 to 7.p.m.	do......	Vicinity of M 32 and M 33 shelled by heavy and field guns in reply to bombardment.	
4.50.p.m.	do......	F.O.O. 28th Battery R.F.A. reported PIPSQUEAK shelled S 10 b 3'5 all the afternoon- This point is mouth of a communicating trench leading from LANSDOWNE POST to RUE du BOIS, and causing much inconvenience, position of battery not located.	
5.p.m.	do......	8" Howitzer shelled REVOLVER House S 3 c 5'4 obtaining one direct hit and WOOLY BEARS appeared effective on Horse Battery in S 3 a 7'8.	?
5 to 6.p.m.	do......	FORESTERS LANE and LANSDOWNE POST shelled by WOOLY BEARS.	
10.30.p.m.	do......	Orders issued for three short bombardments to take place during 14th in accordance with Appendix 178.	Appendix 178
		For further information see Tactical Progress Report attached.*	* Appendix 179.
		Meerut Division G *439/13 re intensive bombardments to be carried out on nights of 13th/14th & 14th/15th is attached as an appx.	W.L.G. * appendix 179(a)

(9 29 6) W 4141—463 100,000 9/14 H W V Forms/C. 2118/10

Army Form C. 2118.

Instructions regarding War Diaries and Intelligence Summaries are contained in F. S. Regs., Part II. and the Staff Manual respectively. Title pages will be prepared in manuscript.

WAR DIARY
or
INTELLIGENCE SUMMARY.
(Erase heading not required.)

Hour, Date, Place		Summary of Events and Information	Remarks and references to Appendices
8.p.m. 13.5.15) to 4.a.m. 14.5.15.) FOSSE		19th Battery fired 6 rounds per hour on allotted task.	
1.5.a.m. 14th May 1915 FOSSE.	......	Four batteries of R.A. Northern Group fired for two minutes on allotted task.	
2.5.a.m.	do........	28th Battery fired for two minutes(48 rounds) on trench 63 to 51e.	
6.30.a.m.	do........	8th Battery registered 1st and 2nd trenches between V.3 and V.6.	
10.a.m.	do........	2nd Battery fired at KEEP.	
11.15.a.m.	do........	20th Battery registered trench 51e to 63. 28th Battery registered trench 51e to 63, 54e to 53 and roadway 63 to 46.	
11.30.a.m.	do........	2nd Siege Battery bombarded enemy's trenches between points 59 and 56 and on Southern and Eastern faces of KEEP.	x appendix 154
12 noon.	do........	44th Battery fired in conjunction with MOTHER on front line between 59 and 60.	
12.30.p.m.	do........	WOOLY BEAR shelled vicinity M 33 a(Hd Qrs 9th Bde R.F.A.). 8th Battery fired 10 rounds at front line between V.6 and 59.	
1.p.m.	do........	MEERUT Division Operation Order* No.31 received.	*Appendix 180.
2 to 2.15.p.m.	do........	Enemey shelling in RUE du BOIS and near PORT ARTHUR more pronounced.	
2.5.p.m.	do........	2 minutes bomardment by all 18 pr. Batteries as ordered.	
3.p.m.	do........	8th Battery re-registered V 9e, V 10e, V.7 LA TOURELLE Cross Roads-Q 27. Enemey 15 c.m. Howitzer fired a few rounds between PIQUET House and CRESCENT Trench.	
4.p.m.	do........	Operation Order≠ No.19 by G.O.C., R.A., MEERUT Division issued.	≠ Appendix 181.
4.5p.m.	do........	German 8" Howitzer shelled WINDY CORNER.	
5.p.m.	do........	LANSDOWNE POST shelled by WOOLY BEARS.	
5.45.p.m.	do........	14th Battery fired at cross roads near 125.	
		For further information see Tactical Progress Report% attached.	%Appendix 182.

Army Form C. 2118.

Instructions regarding War Diaries and Intelligence Summaries are contained in F. S. Regs., Part II. and the Staff Manual respectively. Title pages will be prepared in manuscript.

WAR DIARY
or
INTELLIGENCE SUMMARY.
(Erase heading not required.)

Hour, Date, Place		Summary of Events and Information	Remarks and references to Appendices
8.p.m.14.5.15.to) 4.a.m.15.5.15.) FOSSE.		20th and 28th Battery's carried out tasks allotted to them.	
		8th Battery fired at slow rate during the night 14th/15th as ordered. 7th and 66th Batteries fired as ordered during night 14th/15th.	
6.45.a.m. to)15th May 1915. 7.5.a.m.) RUE du PUITS M 27 a		Enemy bombarded front trenches of "C" Sub-section with howitzer and PIPSQUEAK.	
9.10.a.m.	do........	LANSDOWNE POST shelled by 10.5.c.m. Howitzer.	
11.a.m.	do........	14th Battery was shelled by large howitzer(6 or 8") from direction of HAUTE POMMEREAU- 12 shell near battery- 3 of them blind.	x appendix 184
2.30.p.m.	do........	2nd Battery fired 3 rounds at PIPSQUEAK which was active from direction just E. of FERME du BIEZ and silenced him- This was repeated at 3.p.m. and 5.15.p.m.	
4.p.m.	do........	66th Battery fired on Machine Gun emplacements near 56x-2 direct hits obtained.	
5.p.m.	do........	Headquarters Divisional Artillery, MEERUT Division established at RUE du PUITS(M 27 a). G.O.C., R.A.,LAHORE Divn assumed command of the Artillery on the line.	
5 to 5.30.p.m.	do........	44th Battery fired as ordered.	
6.p.m.	do........	20th and 28th Batteries fired on wire in front of trenches- 20th on 51ex to 54x, 28th on 53x to 54ex.	
6.12.p.m.	do........	Enemy shelled our trenches in front of PORT ARTHUR(S 10 b 7'10).	
6.20.p.m.	do........	66th Battery fired on enemy's Infantry near 130x to keep down fire on our aeroplane.	
8.p.m.	do........	9th and 13th Brigades R.F.A. opened fire and formed barrages in accordance with schedule of tasks laid down. Points registered by 9th Brigade RFA are shown in appx 182(a) For further information see Tactical Progress Report attached. O.O. No 43 by GOC RA LAHORE DIVISION received	‡ appendix 182(a) * Appendix 183.
11.51.p.m.	do........	13th Brigade R.F.A. reported Germans had shown the Red light denoting attack.	
11.50.p.m.	do........	9th Brigade R.F.A. wired that reported from LANSDOWNE POST Red rockets almost due S. at 11.37.p.m. Memo re signals to be used by 7th Division attached as an appx*	[initials] * appendix 183(a).

(9 29 6) W4141—463 100,000 9/14 H W V Forms/C. 2118/10

Instructions regarding War Diaries and Intelligence Summaries are contained in F. S. Regs., Part II. and the Staff Manual respectively. Title pages will be prepared in manuscript.

Army Form C. 2118.

WAR DIARY
or
INTELLIGENCE SUMMARY.
(Erase heading not required.)

Hour, Date, Place	Summary of Events and Information	Remarks and references to Appendices
12.15.a.m. 16th May 1915 RUE du PUITS M 27 a.	13th Brigade R.F.A. reported rifle fire on the front that was attacked not very severe- but no news as to whether assault successful or not.	
12.37.a.m. do........	Information received from No.1 Group H.A.R. that Observation Officer at RITZ reported Green light gone up in direction of V.6.x	
12.40.a.m. do........	Information received from No.1 Group H.A.R. that F.O.O. reported Red Rocket and green flares being sent up from German lines.	
12.42.a.m. do........	O.C. R.A. Southern Group wired "unofficially reported attack failed and German machine guns still firing".	x appx 154
12.55.a.m. do........	Following information received from MEERUT Division Report Centre:- 2nd Division- Right battalion.. No news. ,, 2nd from Right Battalion.. Taken 2nd line enemy trench. ,, 3rd ,, ,, ,, Taken 1st line enemy trench. ,, 4th ,, ,, ,, No advance. MEERUT Division, Both battalions..........No advance.	
1.38.a.m. do........	9th Brigade R.F.A. reported Inniskillings have captured front line and being supported by Oxfords. Wircesters held up. 7th Liverpools captured R.1.x K.R.R's captured 2nd line.	
1.42.a.m. do........	13th Brigade R.F.A. reported our Infantry failed to reach the enemy's trenches.	
2.23.a.m. do........	13th Brigade R.F.A. wired F.O.O. reported the attack of GARHWAL Brigade will be renewed after a further bombardment.	
2.46.a.m. do........	13th Brigade R.F.A. reported that at 2.40.a.m. White Rocket observed on our right. Advanced MEERUT Division informed accordingly.	
3.4.a.m. do........	9th Brigade R.F.A. reported Red Rocket just gone up-Advanced MEERUT Division informed.	
3.14.a.m. do........	13th Brigade R.F.A. wired that F.O.O. reported that another attack starts at 3.15.a.m.	
3.30.a.m. do........	13th Brigade R.F.A. asked if German field gun at FERME DU BIEZ and S 17 b 5'2 could be engaged by them as firing hard at the time. 13th Brigade ordered to keep on screen and engage guns.	
3.35.a.m. do........	9th Brigade R.F.A. reported Red Rocket with White stars just gone up.	
~~XXXXXXX~~.do do........	No,1 Group wired that GARHWAL Brigade reported Signal lines all broken, all information had been signalled but may not have reached MEERUT Division. Attack failed and renewing it in accordance with orders-	

P.T.O.

(9 29 6) W4141—463 100,000 9/14 H W V Forms/C. 2118/10

Army Form C. 2118.

Instructions regarding War Diaries and Intelligence Summaries are contained in F. S. Regs., Part II. and the Staff Manual respectively. Title pages will be prepared in manuscript.

WAR DIARY
or
INTELLIGENCE SUMMARY.
(Erase heading not required.)

Hour, Date, Place	Summary of Events and Information	Remarks and references to Appendices
	German front line very strongly held both by Infantry and maxims- Very heavy bombardment required.	
3.40.a.m. 16th May 1915.... RUE du PUITS.	13th Brigade R.F.A. reported signal for success of 22nd Infantry Brigade went up at 3.20.a.m.	
3.54.a.m. do.........	13th Brigade R.F.A. reported our attack had failed again.	
4.17.a.m. do.........	13th Brigade R.F.A. reported 44th Battery had fired on field guns at S 17 b 5'2, which have now stopped firing, and 44th Battery ordered to engage them again if they open fire.	
4.37.a.m. do.........	9th and 13th Brigades R.F.A. were ordered to stop firing and come into observation, but should open fire immediately if any favourable opportunity offers.	
4.51.a.m. do.........	4th Brigade R.F.A. wired that Advanced LAHORE Division reported situation at 3.25.a.m. as follows:- 6th Infantry Brigade in position area R.1., R.3., R.5., R.6. 5th Infantry Brigade was about R.7 and V.2. New situation 4.a.m. as follows:- 7th Division had effected lodgment in enemy's front line trenches. GARHWAL Brigade assault failed.	Appendix 15A
5.35.a.m. do.........	13th Brigade R.F.A. reported that at 5.24.a.m. three white stars appeared about S.20.	
6.a.m. do.........	14th Battery shelled O.P. at 121, movement seen near that place.	
6.17.a.m. do.........	13th Brigade R.F.A. reported our Infantry report that Germans moving along the latters front trench from V.6. towards V.3. Advanced MEERUT Division and G.O.C., R.A., LAHORE Division were informed., and 13th Brigade R.F.A. ordered to open fire with one battery at slow rate of careful fire to protect flank of 2nd Division, and remaining batteries ready to deal with reported concentration should need arise.	
6.30.a.m. do.........	8th Battery opened fire on V.3. to V.6. to support attack on our right- this was repeated at 9.20.a.m.	

Army Form C. 2118.

Instructions regarding War Diaries and Intelligence Summaries are contained in F. S. Regs., Part II. and the Staff Manual respectively. Title pages will be prepared in manuscript.

WAR DIARY
or
INTELLIGENCE SUMMARY.
(Erase heading not required.)

Hour, Date, Place	Summary of Events and Information	Remarks and references to Appendices
6.49.a.m. 16th May 1915..... RUE du PUITS.	SIRHIND Brigade reported at 6.20.a.m. to be moving to St VAAST in support of 2nd Division- This was received through 9th Brigade R.F.A. Advanced MEERUT Division and 4th and 13th Brigades R.F.A. informed.	
8.a.m. do..........	Very heavy shelling by enemy of our support trenches near RITZ.	
8.50.a.m. do..........	Enemey heavy howitzer shelled our trenches S. of PORT ARTHUR.	
8.50.a.m. do..........	Information received from 7th Division had reached QUINQUE RUE near M 5 and 2nd Division reached V.2. 4th,9th,13th Brigades R.F.A. were informxxed.	
8.51.a.m. do..........	9th Brigade R.F.A. reported following orders issued to BAREILLY Brigade Infantry. Role of Indian Corps to be defensive. Indian Corps will assist 2nd Division to form a defensive flank. Bareilly Brigade now holding LANSDOWNE POST and road. 4th and 13th Brigades R.F.A. informed.	
9.10.a.m. do..........	14th Battery fired at enemy's batteries near 118 and behind 117-147.	x appendix 154
9.32.a.m. do..........	Situation appeared to be as follows, reading left to right:- GARHWAL Brigade back on its original line. 2nd Division (Worcesters no advance point S 10 c 4'7. (Oxfords point V.2. (Inniskillings point R.7. (60th Rifles point R.5. (Bedfords point R.3. (7th Liverpools point R.1. 7th Division holding sector described P.5., N.9.,M.5.,M.3.,.	
9.40.a.m. do..........	15.c.m. Howitzer shelled 7th Battery position without effect.	
9.50.a.m. do..........	C.R.A. JULLUNDUR ⊕ Brigade reported German Heavy Howitzer shelling LA BASSEE Road S 4 v 3'0. to S 4 b 1'4, from direction of T 2 a or T 3 c at 9.30.a.m. PIPSQUEAK shelling near CROIX BARBEE at 9.30.a.m. and 14th Battery is firing on hostile guns near LA RUSSIE in answer. G.O.C. R.A. LAHORE Division and G.O.C. No.1 Group H.A.R. informed.	⊕ O.C. IV Bde RFA "grouped" with JULLUNDUR Inf Bde.
9.56.a.m. do..........	C.R.A. JULLUNDUR Brigade reported house 157 would appear to be likely O.P. it has good view of all this country. Suggested good shelling by heavies. House 111 might also receive attention. G.O.C. No.1 Group H.A.R. informed.	

Instructions regarding War Diaries and Intelligence Summaries are contained in F. S. Regs., Part II. and the Staff Manual respectively. Title pages will be prepared in manuscript.

WAR DIARY
or
INTELLIGENCE SUMMARY.
(Erase heading not required.)

Army Form C. 2118.

Hour, Date, Place		Summary of Events and Information	Remarks and references to Appendices
10.10.a.m. 16th May 1915. RUE du PUITS		C.R.A. JULLUNDUR Brigade reported trench N. of 61 being enfiladed by Machine Gun from just N. of V.6. and would like it knocked out- 13th Brigade were informed, but possibly too close to our own trenches.	
10.30.a.m.	do	7th Battery fired at suspected O.P. just W. of 68.	
10.34.a.m.	do	13th Brigade R.F.A. reported 2nd Division bombing parties reported moving East from V.3. and V.4., and 44th Battery going to shoot on German 2nd line East of V.6e. MEERUT Division and G.O.C., R.A., LAHORE Division were informed.	
11.a.m.	do	14th Battery fired on O.P. near 125-3 direct hits.	
11.9.a.m.	do	Information received from 1st Army that 2nd Division had captured 3 Officers and 100 men-enemy losses severe.	x appendix 1174
11.20.a.m.	do	4 guns of 2nd Battery fired on LORGIES Road at a point where German Battalion was reported.	
11.28.a.m.	do	One gun 2nd Battery was turned on to KEEP-German movement seen there.	
11.52.a.m.	do	8th Battery ordered to form barrage V.9e, V.10e to R 17 at slow rate of fire.	
12.10.p.m.	do	8th Battery opened barrage on LA BASSEE Road and V.9e to V.7.	
12.35.p.m.	do	O.C., R.A., Southern Group reported Yellow flag can be seen just E. of R.6. No others seen further to the East.	
12.40.p.m.	do	66th Battery fired on the FERME dy BIEZ.	
1.20.p.m.	do	LAHORE Divisional Artillery intimated that it was reported that Germans were retiring along the LA BASSEE Road and asked us to be on the look out. 4th, 9th and 13th Brigades R.F.A. were informed.	
1.45.p.m. and 3.30.p.m.	do	1st Battery position and Headquarters Highland F.A. Brigade shelled- about 70 rounds- no damage done except one water cart smashed.	
2.35.p.m.	do	8th Battery dispersed Germans in open, by gun fire, near DISTILLERY, and got fleeting opportunities till 3.5.p.m.	
2.45 & 5.p.m.	do	7th Battery fired at Red House 160 suspected as O.P.-5 direct hits.	
3.4.p.m.	do	Howitzer and PIPSQUEAK fired on 7th Battery O.P. at slow rate.	
3.30.p.m.	do	Enemy reported to be moving up from N 17 and P 14.	
3.43.p.m.	do	14th Battery fired at trees near 69. Infantry reported snipers at this place.	
3.50.p.m.	do	13th Brigade R.F.A. reported German "Sausage" just come up at 3.35.p.m. the bearing from M 31 b 9'7 being 120°.	

(9 29 6) W4141—463 100,000 9/14 H W V Forms/C2118/10

Army Form C. 2118.

Instructions regarding War Diaries and Intelligence Summaries are contained in F. S. Regs., Part II. and the Staff Manual respectively. Title pages will be prepared in manuscript.

WAR DIARY
or
INTELLIGENCE SUMMARY.
(Erase heading not required.)

Hour, Date, Place	Summary of Events and Information	Remarks and references to Appendices
5.20.p.m. 16th May 1915.... RUE du PUITS.	13th Brigade R.F.A. reported Bareilly Brigade taking over Southern Section of the line at 8.p.m. Headquarters at LANSDOWNE POST. Order of Battalions on front line right to left-58th Rifles, Black Watch and 125th Rifles.	
5.45.p.m. do........	7th Battery fired at German trenches to keep down rifle fire on our aeroplane.	
6.45.p.m. do........	C.R.A. JULLUNDUR Brigade(4th Brigade) informed that G.O.C., R.A., LAHORE Division wishes one section per battery to open fire on night lines every hour during night at the approximate half hours from 8.30.p.m. to 3.30.a.m. Six rounds per battery each time. Highland artillery included if safe to fire. Enemy reported dead beat and much shaken.	
6.52.p.m. do........	9th and 13th Brigades ordered to keep two sections per battery on normal night lines and remaining section or single guns laid out on barrage No.1. Six rounds to be fired at each barrage task once every hour but at half past each hour from 8.30.p.m. to 4.30.a.m. . This in addition to any rounds fired on night lines if necessary to do so.	
7.25.p.m. do........	2nd Battery R.F.A. reported Infantry under impression that Germans are contemplating a retirement tonight. From observation their trenches look beyond repair.	
	For further information see Tactical Progress Report* attached.	*Appendix 184

Army Form C. 2118.

Instructions regarding War Diaries and Intelligence Summaries are contained in F. S. Regs., Part II. and the Staff Manual respectively. Title pages will be prepared in manuscript.

WAR DIARY
or
INTELLIGENCE SUMMARY.

(Erase heading not required.)

Hour, Date, Place		Summary of Events and Information	Remarks and references to Appendices
5.a.m. 6.a.m.) and 8.30.a.m.) RUE du PUITS.	17th May 1915.	2nd Battery fired at PIPSQUEAK.	
6.a.m.	do.	Germans began heavy shelling on RUE du BOIS, Reserve trenches and LANSDOWNE POST.	
7.10.a.m.	do.	9th Brigade R.F.A. reported enemy constantly shelling RUE du BOIS and Reserve trenches with 5'9" and 8" Howitzers.	
7.45.a.m.	do.	15 c.m. Howitzer obtained direct hit on LANSDOWNE POST.	
7.50.a.m.	do.	4th Brigade R.F.A. reported that German parapet had been repaired in places in front of "a" Sub section during the night.	
8.36.a.m.	do.	66th Battery reported 3 white flares sent up from our own trenches on right front. Heavy howitzer battery very active on RUE du BOIS at 8.a.m. Advanced MEERUT Division informed.	Appendix 154
9 to 10.30.a.m.	do.	Several PIPSQUEAK shell fell near 66th Battery.	
9.12.a.m.	do.	4th and 13th Brigades R.F.A. were ordered to keep any known PIPSQUEAKS under observation during the day and neutralize at once if become active .	
9.32.a.m.	do.	Information received from Advanced MEERUT Division that enemy bombing our front heavily from V.6. and asking to turn heavy guns on to this point. LAHORE Divisional Artillery were asked for howitzer fire to be turned on to V.6. 13th Brigade R.F.A. also ordered to turn on 18 pr. battery on to this point.	
9.45.a.m.	do.	8th Battery fired on V.6. to stop bombing.	
9.55.a.m.	do.	13th Brigade R.F.A. were ordered to form barrage V 9e,V 10e, to R 17 and Q 28 at once at section fire 2 minutes- to be made two tasks.	
9.57.a.m.	do.	All Brigades informed that 2nd Division now attacking on line Ferme du BOIS to Q 14.	
10.10.a.m.	do.	14th Battery fired at enemy PIPSQUEAK near 118 and 119.	
10.14.a.m.	do.	9th Brigade R.F.A. ordered to form barrage 53 to FERME du BIEZ and also FERME du BIEZ- two tasks- section fire two minutes.	
10.17.a.m.	do.	C.R.A. JULLUNDUR Brigade reported enemy battery very active from 186 or near 184 firing over 7th Battery O.P.-probably down RUE du BOIS.	O.C. 4th Bde RFA
10.[illegible].a.m.	do.	Battery of Highland F.A. Brigade fired at PIPSQUEAK near 118 and 119.	

Army Form C. 2118.

Instructions regarding War Diaries and Intelligence Summaries are contained in F. S. Regs., Part II. and the Staff Manual respectively. Title pages will be prepared in manuscript.

WAR DIARY
or
INTELLIGENCE SUMMARY.
(Erase heading not required.)

Hour, Date, Place	Summary of Events and Information	Remarks and references to Appendices
10.30.a.m. 17th May 1915.... RUE du PUITS.	BAREILLY Brigade reported through 9th Brigade R.F.A. that enemy surrendering in large numbers to 2nd Division, and thoroughly disorganised also asks for fire on V.6.×	
10.35.a.m. do........	C.R.A. JULLUNDUR Brigade reported he had ordered 7th and 66th Batteries to fire along road 53× to 50× to V.13× forming barrage. C.R.A. JULLUNDUR Brigade informed that 9th Brigade Battery already doing this and would help battery on 65× to 51e× and 53× to 60×.	
11.a.m. do........	9th and 13th Brigades R.F.A. ordered that barrages at section fire 2 minutes to be reduced to 12 rounds per hour per task and battery on V.6× to reduce to slow rate of fire.	
11.5.a.m. do........	9th Brigade R.F.A. wired that F.O.O. reported from Infantry H.Q. that two battalions had surrendered to 2nd Division(This proved to be incorrect).	×Appendix 154
11.12.a.m. do........	13th Brigade R.F.A. ordered that battery firing on V.6.× to turn on to trench from V.6.× to V.6e× - all barrages to be kept up at rate of 18 rounds per hour- this latter order sent to 9th Brigade R.F.A. and 4th Brigade R.F.A. were informed of these orders.	
11.45.a.m. do........	4th,9th and 13th Brigades R.F.A.ordered to put a few H.E. or percussion shrapnel in to all likely enemy O.P's at intervals during the day. Our own fast being made untenable through their PIPSQUEAK fire which must have direct observation.	
12.30.p.m. do........	66th Battery had 6 direct hits on house 50×.	
1.2.p.m. do........	9th Brigade R.F.A. wired that F.O.O. LANSDOWNE POST reports BAREILLY Brigade at 12.45.p.m. joining up with left of 2nd Division at V.1.× 4th and 13th Brigades informed.	
1.5.p.m. do........	Advanced MEERUT Division message received that BAREILLY Brigade left sub-section report enemy, when they vacate their front trenches by day, return after dusk by the communicating trenches running through point 58× to 60× and thence along their trench. 9th Brigade informed and asked to endeavour to register this communication trench to-day with one section and lay up for HUNS to-night.	
1.10.p.m. do........	4th, 9th and 13th Brigades R.F.A. informed that position believed to be as follows:- 2nd Division-left battalion shortly going to advance and right of BAREILLY Brigade will extend to its right and maintain touch with this 2nd Division battalion. BAREILLY Brigade also has order to advance if favourable opportunity offers.	

(9 29 6) W4141—463 100,000 9/14 H W V Forms/C. 2118/10

Army Form C. 2118.

Instructions regarding War Diaries and Intelligence Summaries are contained in F. S. Regs., Part II. and the Staff Manual respectively. Title pages will be prepared in manuscript.

WAR DIARY
or
INTELLIGENCE SUMMARY.
(Erase heading not required.)

Hour, Date, Place		Summary of Events and Information	Remarks and references to Appendices
1.58.p.m. 17th May 1915...... RUE du PUITS.		9th Brigade R.F.A. reported BAREILLY Brigade hold line right to left-58th Rifles, 2nd Black Watch, ½ Bn 125th Rifles and ½ Bn 41st Dogras, remaining half of these two battalions in Reserve with 4th Black Watch. 2nd 8th Gurkha Rifles left LANSDOWNE POST about 1.30.p.m. to connect up 58th Rifles with 2nd Division. 4th and 13th Brigades R.F.A. were informed.	
2.45.p.m.	do........	4th, 9th and 13th Brigades R.F.A. informed that enemy reported to be bringing up two Corps as reinforcements.	
3.38.p.m.	do........	13th Brigade R.F.A. reported 3 white lights observed S.E. of 44th Battery at about one minute interval at 2.34.p.m.	
4.7.p.m.	do........	9th Brigade R.F.A. informed that enemy reported moving down communication trench from 58* to move south, and orders for battery registered on this to stand by to stop this.	*appendix 154
4.20.p.m.	do........	Information received from Indian Corps that enemy reported to be endeavouring to construct trenches from V.2* to R.9* and from V.5* to R.12* along ditch. 13th Brigade R.F.A. were asked if they could turn right battery on to search ditch from V.5* to R.12* with safety to 2nd Division. 8th Battery carried this out.	
4.25.p.m.	do........	9th and 13th Brigades R.F.A. informed that Barrage No*.1 would be required from 8.p.m. to 10.p.m. at rate of 20 rounds per hour per barrage. C.R.A. JULLUNDUR Brigade was also informed accordingly. 13th Brigade R.F.A. were informed that ROOMES trench was being heavily shelled by field guns near LA TOURELLE and were asked to endeavour to neutralize them. 9th Brigade R.F.A. also asked to endeavour to neutralize.	*Appendix ~~[illegible]~~ 181
4.30.p.m.	do........	8th Battery registered front of 58th Rifles with night lines for four guns on front. Enemy shelled RUE du BOIS, FORESTERS LANE and communication trenches between them very heavily with 15.c.m. Howitzer and PIPSQUEAK.	
4.40.p.m.	do........	C.R.A. JULLUNDUR Brigade reported BREWERY NEUVE CHAPELLE heavily shelled between 3.30 and 4.p.m.	
4.45.p.m.	do........	9th Brigade R.F.A. reported 5'9" shelling area RUE du BOIS to RITZ, FORESTERS LANE and communication trench.	
4.50.p.m.	do........	8th Battery opened searching fire on ditch V.5* to R.12* on enemy's trench.	

(9 29 6) W 4141—463 100,000 9/14 H W V Forms/C. 2118/10

Army Form C. 2118.

Instructions regarding War Diaries and Intelligence Summaries are contained in F. S. Regs., Part II. and the Staff Manual respectively. Title pages will be prepared in manuscript.

WAR DIARY
or
INTELLIGENCE SUMMARY.
(Erase heading not required.)

Hour, Date, Place	Summary of Events and Information	Remarks and references to Appendices
5.10.p.m. 17th May 1915..... RUE du PUITS.	One section 8th Battery searched and swept behind LA TOURELLE Cross roads.	
5.17.p.m. do........	9th Brigade R.F.A. ordered to keep one section per battery on roads round FERME du BIEZ and 53×to V.15.× Remaining 2 sections on night lines as required by O.C., R.A., Northern Group. Rate of fire 12 per every two hours- to be fired during period of ten minutes- from 10.p.m. onwards.	
5.25.p.m. do........	20th Battery silenced PIPSQUEAK shelling PORT ARTHUR and again at 6.40.p.m.	
5.40.p.m. do........	O.C. 13th Brigade R.F.A. informed that only barrages required by his Brigade would be V.9e×to V.7×trench and V.9e×to Q.27×road. This should be possible with one section for each task remaining guns being on proper night lines to cover their defensive front. Rate of fire 12 rounds every two hours to be fired in period of ten minutes.	×appendix 184
6.19.p.m. do........	4th,9th and 13th Brigades ordered that true bearings of hostile guns should be noted during hours of darkness from points easily fixed on map.	
6.45.p.m. do........	Orders were received from Indian Corps that enemy to be given no rest day or night and every means to disturb them with bombing, rifle and gun fire to be carried out. Orders were issued accordingly to 9th and 13th Brigades R.F.A. and C.R.A. JULLUNDUR Brigade informed.	
7.32.p.m. do........	66th Battery reported that Huns shelling very heavily whole day, but placing their shell well over the fire trenches of "A" Sub-section- JULLUNDUR Brigade- only casualty believed to be one man of 4th Suffolks.	
8.p.m. do........	MEERUT Division ordered* that Divisional Artillery of Indian Corps would barrage from near ESTAIRES-LA BASSEE Road up to and including communication trench from FERME du BOIS Q 13×FERME TOULOTTES P.19×P 20×to N.23×and all road junctions and communicating trenches in that area. slow continuous fire to be kept up during night-no howitzer or lyddite to be used.	* Appendix. 185
8.25.p.m. do........	Information received from MEERUT Division that 6th Brigade reported enemy again collecting behind COUR d'AVOUE about 7.p.m. and had been heavily shelled.	
	For further information see Tactical Progress Report≠ attached.	≠ Appendix 186

(9 29 6) W 4141—463 100,000 9/14 H W V Forms/C. 2118/10

Instructions regarding War Diaries and Intelligence Summaries are contained in F. S. Regs., Part II. and the Staff Manual respectively. Title pages will be prepared in manuscript.

WAR DIARY
or
INTELLIGENCE SUMMARY.
(Erase heading not required.)

Army Form C. 2118.

Hour, Date, Place		Summary of Events and Information	Remarks and references to Appendices
4.a.m.	18th May 1915. RUE du PUITS.	* MEERUT Division No.G-65 regarding the day's bombardment received and communicated to the 4th, 9th and 13th Brigades R.F.A. under No.664-R.A.(L) also further orders communicated under B.M.205, B.M.206, B.M.207, B.M.208 and B.M.209.	* Appendix 187 Appendix 188 Appendices 189, 190, 191, 192 + 193
7.a.m.	do.	C.R.A. JULLUNDUR Brigade, 9th and 13th Brigades R.F.A. informed that G.O.C., R.A., LAHORE Division wished for fire to be opened on same lines as firing carried out during last night. About 12 rounds on each task. At 9a.m. Barrage No.1 will be formed also special tasks on PIPSQUEAKS enemy's O.P's and special trenches as already indicated.	x appendix 184
9.17.a.m.	do.	4th, 9th and 13th Brigades informed that G.O.C. R.A. LAHORE considered a very slow rate of fire should be maintained on barrages ordered, say 6 or 8 rounds per hour up to time to be fixed later for bombardment on our right when rate would be quickened up.	
1.30.p.m.	do.	Advanced MEERUT Division G-80 ø received regarding assault on FERME du BIEZ to take place at 4.30.p.m. to be preceded by an intensive bombardment the period which would be intimated later.	ø Appendix 194
1.45.p.m.	do.	Advanced MEERUT Division G-77, ≠ received regarding SIRHIND Brigade to organise a bombing party.	≠ Appendix 195
2.20.p.m.	do.	MEERUT Division G-82 % received regarding 3rd Canadian Brigade using Blue Flags 16" square on four foot poles as distinguishing marks- all units were informed.	% appx 196
3.30.p.m.	do.	One gun 2nd Battery fired at new German barricade near 59 obtaining 4 direct hits and destroying left half of barricade.	
3.35.p.m.	do.	4th, 9th and 13th Brigades ordered that from 4.30.p.m. onwards rate of fire 30 rounds per task per hour.	
3.52.p.m.	do.	9th Brigade R.F.A. reported House 51 occupied by snipers and machine guns. House 50 as an O.P. 28th Battery turned on both houses with H.E. with result of 3 direct hits on each.	
4 to 4.35.p.m.	do.	One gun of 2nd Battery was neutralizing battery at S 18 a 4'2.	
4.10.p.m.	do.	MEERUT Division operation order © No.32 received.	© Appendix 197
4.52.p.m.	do.	13th Brigade R.F.A. reported that 44th Battery O.P. state cannot see anything of assault.	
5.13.p.m.	do.	O.O. 14th Battery reported 3 pale green lights seen in direction of PORT ARTHUR making straight line with NEUVE CHAPELLE. Two white lights seen in same direction five minutes later.	

(9 29 6) W4141—463 100,000 9/14 H W V

Instructions regarding War Diaries and Intelligence Summaries are contained in F. S. Regs., Part II. and the Staff Manual respectively. Title pages will be prepared in manuscript.

WAR DIARY
or
INTELLIGENCE SUMMARY.
(Erase heading not required.)

Army Form C. 2118.

Hour, Date, Place	Summary of Events and Information	Remarks and references to Appendices
5.35.p.m. 18th May 1915.... RUE du PUITS.	PIPSQUEAK shelled our trenches near PORT ARTHUR.	
5.46.p.m. do.......	13th Brigade R.F.A. reported could hear little rifle fire at 4.50.p.m. in direction of S 15 d. 5.15.p.m. germans probably leaving FERME du BOIS by communicating trench. Germans shelling their own trenches from V.2x onwards to V.3.x otherwise comparatively little artillery fire. Germans in trenches showing lights which means their guns are shooting short. German O.P's far back now and weather thick.	
5.57.p.m. do........	O.C. 44th Battery reported could see attack moving forward near S 15 d at 5.50.p.m.	
6.4p.m. do.......	O,C, 13th Brigade R.F.A. ordered to turn one section on trench R 8x to Q 14x for 10 minutes and then to return back to Q 18x to P.20.x	x Appendix 154
7.30.p.m. do.......	13th Brigade R.F.A. reported H.L.I. bombing party of SIRHIND Brigade stated to be held up and no news of this Brigade attack. Guards Brigade attack progressing. 44th Battery OMP. stated at 7.p.m. left of 6th Infantry Brigade appeared to be digging themselves in.	
8.20.p.m. do.......	13th Brigade R.F.A. reported wall running along trench between GOOD LUCK House and SNIPER's House broken down to-day by shell fire and anyone passing between these two points in full view of German trenches. Advanced MEERUT Division were asked if R.E. could repair this wall to-night.	
9.30.p.m. do.......	4th, 9th and 13th Brigades R.F.A. informed that should attack by SIRHIND Brigade be carried out during night batteries would increase rate of fire to 60 rounds per hour per barrage for one hour commencing quarter of an hour after time of assault. On expiration of one hour batteries to revert to present slow rate about 12 rounds per hour. Most probably little notice will be given before assault takes place.	
10.10.p.m. do.......	4th and 9th Brigades were ordered to cancel orders issued at 9.20.p.m. as above in spite of any attack of SIRHIND Brigade and to continue firing at normal rate of 12 rounds per battery per hour.	

(9 29 6) W4141—463 100,000 9/14 H W V Forms/C. 2118/10

Army Form C. 2118.

Instructions regarding War Diaries and Intelligence Summaries are contained in F. S. Regs., Part II. and the Staff Manual respectively. Title pages will be prepared in manuscript.

WAR DIARY
or
INTELLIGENCE SUMMARY.
(Erase heading not required.)

Hour, Date, Place	Summary of Events and Information	Remarks and references to Appendices
11.30.p.m. 18th May 1915...... XXX RUE du PUITS	MEERUT Division G-96* received stating SIRHIND Brigade not to attack tonight.	*Appendix 198
	MEERUT Division G-561@ received re consolidation of positions gained etc.	@Appendix 199
	For further information see Tactical Progress Report% attached.	%Appendix 200
		[signature]

Army Form C. 2118.

Instructions regarding War Diaries and Intelligence Summaries are contained in F. S. Regs., Part II. and the Staff Manual respectively. Title pages will be prepared in manuscript.

WAR DIARY
or
INTELLIGENCE SUMMARY.
(Erase heading not required.)

Hour, Date, Place	Summary of Events and Information	Remarks and references to Appendices
12 m.n. 18th/19th May 1915... RUE DU PUITS.	Definite orders received that the attack by the SIRHIND Brigade would not take place.	
4.10.a.m. 19th May 1915...... RUE DU PUITS.	Indian Corps No.G-309 received regarding 2nd and 7th Divisions consolidating the line M.5-LA QUINQUE RUE-P.11, P.10, Q.7, also regarding continuation of operations. Communication to units. *	* Appendices 201, 202
4.35.a.m. do.........	MEERUT Division G-565%regarding Indian Corps Artillery to assist 2nd and 7th Divisions in operations and attack on FERME du BOIS.	% Appendix 203
	Weather very thick, but cleared during the day.	
5.a.m. do.........	13th Brigade R.F.A. were asked if they could get another battery registered on FERME duBOIS and part of communication trench between Q.16 and Q.17 Q.18, and ordered to verify trenches V.4 to R.13 and V.5 to R.12 and road immediately if observation possible.	
5.30.a.m. do.........	Orders sent to the 9th Brigade R.F.A. for one battery to barrage LA BASSEE Road from V.9e to LA tourelle Cross Roads, section fire 5 minutes to commence at once, especially houses that might bring machine gun fire towards the FERME du BOIS.	× appendix 154
5.40.a.m. do.........	Orders sent to 13th Brigade for barrage V.4 to R.13 to be continued at rate of 15 rounds per hour. Point V.4 to be included if possible to locate, also barrage R.8, Q.16, Q.13 and Q.14 at same rate.	
6.30.a.m. do.........	13th Brigade R.F.A. reported trench Mortar situated near V.1. causing good deal of damage to support trenches 300 yards in front of factory.	
8.25.a.m. do.........	9th Brigade R.F.A. were ordered to stp barrage on LA BASSEE Road for present.	
9.50.a.m. do.........	One gun of 2nd Battery opened up a new gap at 59.	
10.25.a.m. do.........	13th Brigade R.F.A. reported that at 10.5.a.m. German H.E. went into German trenches to right of V.2. and white star went up from the trenches.	
10.45.a.m. do.	O.C. 44th Battery reported new trench running from V.2 to R.17 towards R.8., further direction cannot be followed. Advanced MEERUT Division were informed.	
11.15.a.m. do.........	10.5.c.m. Howitzer shelled our support trenches in RUE du BOIS from direction of HAUTE POMMEREAU- 4 shell were blind.	

(9 29 6) W4141—463 100,000 9/14 H W V Forms/C. 2118/10

Army Form C. 2118.

Instructions regarding War Diaries and Intelligence Summaries are contained in F. S. Regs., Part II. and the Staff Manual respectively. Title pages will be prepared in manuscript.

WAR DIARY
or
INTELLIGENCE SUMMARY.
(Erase heading not required.)

Hour, Date, Place	Summary of Events and Information	Remarks and references to Appendices
11.55.a.m. 19th May 1915...... RUE du PUITS.	9th Brigade R.F.A. reported 10.5.c.m. howitzer shelling our support trenches from direction of HAUTE POMMEREAU. 13th Brigade R.F.A. were informed that 2nd Division reported enemy digging on line V.4× to R.13× and ordered to give them a dustingnand increase this barrage to 30 rounds per hour for one hour. Enemy also reported digging from V.2× towards R.7× increase rate of fire of action on V.2× and let fire go about 100 yards towards R.7× from V.2× which should be safe if fire observed. Battery on R.8×, Q.16× to Q.18× to bring fire back 100 yards N. of R.8× in direction of V.2×. R.8× requires dusting. Communication trench R.12× to R.9× also requires 12 rounds.	
12.26.p.m. do.........	9th and 13th Brigades R.F.A. were asked to complete work on wall broken between GOOD LUCK and SNIPER's Houses, as Sappers very hard pressed with work on trenches day and night.	
12.31.p.m. do.........	All units were ordered to post a man to warn batteries not to shoot when anything going across line of fire near adjacent roads during deliberate rate of fire owing to number of prematures that have lately occurred. This order not to obtain during process of an action when firing at quick rate.	
2.p.m. do.........	9th Brigade R.F.A. were asked to neutralize PIPSQUEAKS at FERME du BIEZ and DISTILLERY- in accordance with wishes of G.O.C. No.1 Group H.A.R. These hostile guns were annoying the IRISH Guards.	×appendix 154
2.45.p.m. do.........	PIPSQUEAK shelled 7th Battery O.P..	
2.55.p.m. do.........	PIPSQUEAK at FERME du BIEZ neutralized by 20th Battery.	
3.7.p.m. do.........	20th Battery R.F.A. fired on battery at V.18× and silenced it- DISTILLERY Battery not located.	
3.30.p.m. do.........	14th Battery fired a few rounds at house 100 yards S.W. of 125×.	
3.45.p.m. do.........	9th Brigade R.F.A. reported flashes visible at S 18 a ~~XXX~~ 2'4-20th Battery ordered to search and 28th Battery to observe.	
4.25.p.m. do.........	2nd Battery carried out registration on line R.12× to R.8× to verify line exactly.	
4.28.p.m. do.........	"Flash" Battery at S 18 a ~~XXX~~ 2'4 silenced by 20th and 28th Batteries who fired in conjunction with each other.	

(9 29 6) W4141—463 100,000 9/14 H W V Forms/C. 2118/10

Army Form C. 2118.

Instructions regarding War Diaries and Intelligence Summaries are contained in F. S. Regs., Part II. and the Staff Manual respectively. Title pages will be prepared in manuscript.

WAR DIARY
or
INTELLIGENCE SUMMARY.

(Erase heading not required.)

Hour, Date, Place	Summary of Events and Information	Remarks and references to Appendices
4.45.p.m. 19th May 1915.... RUE du PUITS.	66th Battery fired on working party at S 11 a 5'4.	
5.45 & 6.15.p.m. do.......	PIPSQUEAKS burst near 66th Battery position.	
6.p.m. do.......	MEERUT Division Operation Order No. 33 * received regarding Infantry reliefs.	* Appendix 204
	A few 77 mm. shell fell on each side of 44th Battery.	
6.15.p.m. do.......	One 10.5.c.m. shell fell near 8th Battery.	
6.20.p.m. do.......	4th, 9th and 13th Brigades R.F.A. were informed that under orders of Indian Corps no firing would go on between 8.p.m. and 12 midnight on account of reliefs- except in case of attack. Orders re barrages from midnight onwards to follow. Some PIPSQUEAKS and Howitzer shell fell near 2nd Battery-true bearing of scoop 134½° from M 32 a 4'3- LORGIES indicated.	
6.30.p.m. do.......	13th Brigade R.F.A. were ordered that from midnight to 4.a.m. following barrages would be required at rate of 15 rounds per hour:- One battery:- One section Q.13x to Q.17x, remaining two sections to remain on normal night lines. Remaining batteries on normal night lines- one section being ready to turn on to V.2.x at short notice if required. German Howitzer fired a few shell in to CROIX BARBEE.	x appendix 134
6.35.p.m. do.......	9th Brigade ordered that from midnight to 4.a.m. following barrages would be required at rate of 15 rounds per hour:- Roads round FERME du BIEZ. LA BASSEE Road from V.9e x to R 16.x All guns not required for these tasks to be laid out on normal night lines.	
10.10.p.m. do.......	4th Brigade R.F.A. were ordered that under orders of G.O.C. Division barrage batteries of 9th and 13th Brigades firing short bursts of fire at 12.5.a.m. 20th May 1915. 9th and 13th Brigades R.F.A. were ordered to fire these bursts of 8 rounds and after 12.5.a.m. barrages ordered to be carried on at rates detailed.	
	For further information see Tactical Progress Report ✝ attached.	✝ Appendix 205

(9 29 6) W4141—463 100,000 9/14 H W V Forms/C. 2118/10

Army Form C. 2118.

Instructions regarding War Diaries and Intelligence Summaries are contained in F. S. Regs., Part II. and the Staff Manual respectively. Title pages will be prepared in manuscript.

WAR DIARY
or
INTELLIGENCE SUMMARY.
(Erase heading not required.)

Hour, Date, Place	Summary of Events and Information	Remarks and references to Appendices
5.50.a.m. 20th May 1915..... RUE DU PUITS.	G.O.C. No.1 Group H.A.R. intimated that a good deal of work had been done during the night on new German fire trench running from V.2.x to R.8.x and trench now full of men, and well worth turning a battery on. 13th Brigade R.F.A. ordered to block both ends of trench by turning on Sections registered on above points and then systematically searching the trench itself.	
6.a.m. to 7.a.m. do........	PIPSQUEAK shelled vicinity of M 33 and M 34 and 10.5.c.m. Howitzer shelled PONT LOGY.	
7.a.m. do........	10.5.c.m. Howitzer shelled our trenches near PORT ARTHUR.	
7.15.a.m. do........	14th Battery fired on PIPSQUEAK active from near 147x and on probable O.P's	
7.30.a.m. do........	9th Brigade R.F.A. reported 4.2" howitzer shelling PONT LOGY and PIPSQUEAK roving the country.	
8.20.a.m. do........	13th Brigade R.F.A. were informed that new german breastwork reported running from V.2.x to a point midway between V.2.x and R.9.x- from latter point trench runs across to R.8x, and ordered to verify and register to-day. Section to keep V.2x in observation all day.	x appendix 154
8.51.a.m. do........	G.O.C. MEERUT Division ordered that 50 yards of German trench from V.2.x towards R.9.x and 50 yards of trench from V.2.x towards LA BASSEE Road to be thoroughly hammered with H.E. and shrapnel and properly battered about- fire to be deliberate and observed. 13th Brigade R.F.A. were ordered to do this.(vide Appendix 206 *)	* Appendix 206
9.30.a.m. do........	Following barrages were formed by R.A. Southern Group and continued to dark vide B.M. 260% :- From V.2x along new breastwork half way up to point R.9.x- 150 rounds to be expended on this during the day- partly H.E. and percussion shrapnel. From V.4.x to R.13x both inclusive- 18 rounds per hour. From Q.16x to Q.17,x Q.18x- 18 rounds per hour.	% Appendix 207
9.40.a.m. do........	G.O.C. Division ordered that 50 yards of enemy trench from V.2.x towards V.1.x thoroughly battered by slow deliberate fire during the day. H.E. and percussion shrapnel to be employed- 13th Brigade R.F.A carried out this in accordance with Appendix 208 ≠.	≠ Appendix 208

(9 29 6) W4141—463 100,000 9/14 H W V Forms/C. 2118/10

Instructions regarding War Diaries and Intelligence Summaries are contained in F. S. Regs., Part II. and the Staff Manual respectively. Title pages will be prepared in manuscript.

WAR DIARY
or
INTELLIGENCE SUMMARY.
(Erase heading not required.)

Army Form C. 2118.

Hour, Date, Place		Summary of Events and Information	Remarks and references to Appendices
10.6.a.m. 20th May 1915 RUE du PUITS.		4th and 9th Brigades R.F.A. were ordered to put occasional rounds into any likely O.P's which overlooks ground round the FERME du BOIS at odd intervals- this in addition to neutralizing active PIPSQUEAKS.	
10.45.a.m.	do	66th Battery fired 4 rounds at working party near point 51.x	
11.20.a.m.	do	2nd Battery R.F.A. fired on German reliefs (men in two's and three's) near point 57.x	
11,45.a.m.	do	14th Battery fired a few rounds at house W. of 151x where light was seen (probably signalling lamp) in the roof- 2 hits.	
12noon and 1.45.p.m	do	7th Battery R.F.A. fired 8 rounds at communication trench S.W. of 63x where movement was seen.	x appendix 154
2.p.m. to 5.p.m.	do	14th Battery fired at batteries near 75x at intervals.	
2.40.p.m.	do	19th Battery fired at O.P. of PIPSQUEAK shooting from DISTILLERY obtaining 2 direct hits and desired effect on the battery.	
3.p.m.	do	No.C.R.A. 51* issued to O.C. R.A. Southern Group for certain barrages to be formed.	* Appendix 209
3.45.p.m.	do	"Flash" Battery at S 18 a 4'2 re-opened fire and was silenced by 28th Battery.	
4.45.p.m.	do	German heavy howitzer shelled NEUVE CHAPELLE.	
5.30.p.m.	do	Observation Officer LANSDOWNE POST reported column of reddish smoke in front of LA BASSEE Church- either a church or house on fire.	
6.p.m.	do	O.C. 13th Brigade R.F.A. ordered to form additional barrages vide R.A. Q 10 %.	% Appendix 210
6.58.p.m.	do	PIPSQUEAK shelled 7th Battery O.P..	
7.15.p.m.	do	66th Battery observed 3 red flares sent up from our trench 500 yards S. of LA BASSEE Road.	
8.15.p.m.	do	O.C. R.A. Souther Section reported Heavy Machine Gun fire from direction of SCHOOL House.	
9.23.p.m.	do	BAREILLY Brigade wired to 13th Brigade R.F.A. that all batteries should be warned that patrols of that Brigade would be out reconnoitring German front line to see if vacated or otherwise.	
		For further information see Tactical Progress Report@ attached.	@ Appendix 211

[signature]

(9 29 6) W4141—463 100,000 9/14 H W V Forms/C. 2118/10

Instructions regarding War Diaries and Intelligence Summaries are contained in F. S. Regs., Part II. and the Staff Manual respectively. Title pages will be prepared in manuscript.

WAR DIARY
or
INTELLIGENCE SUMMARY.
(Erase heading not required.)

Army Form C. 2118.

Hour, Date, Place		Summary of Events and Information	Remarks and references to Appendices
1.15.a.m. 21st May 1915...... RUE du PUITS.		O.C. R.A. SOUTHERN Group was informed that Sirhind Brigade requested that no Battery fired to be directed on points V.1. R.7. R.8. Q.18. Q.15. R.4. R.5. as they hoped to occupy trench from R.5. to Q.15. and asked that batteries forming barrages might be warned accordingly. Also informed that CANADIAN Division reported that Canadian 3rd Brigade had taken M.9. and ORCHARD and attacking M.10. It has also taken L.12 and possibly L.11. Canadian attack on K.5 did not succeed. Steps now being taken to consolidate position won. This was received verbally from Advanced MEERUT Division. LAHORE Divisional Artillery was also informed.	
11.15.a.m.	do........	O.C. R.A. SOUTHERN Group reported following received from R.H.A. on our right "As far as known our line runs V.1. R.7. R.5. Q.8.". Advanced MEERUT Division was informed accordingly.	
11.35.a.m. and) 2.50.p.m.)	do.... ...	2nd Battery R.F.A. fired at movement seen near point 58.	appendix 154
12 noon to 12.30.p.m.	do......	10.5.c.m.(? 15.c.m.) howitzer shelled vicinity of ROUGE CROIX- about 6 blind out of 20.	
12.15.p.m.	do.........	10.5.c.m. howitzer shelled vicinity of M 33 a- about 6 rounds-true bearing of scoop 106°.	
12.45.p.m.	do.........	O.C. 13th Brigade R.F.A. intimated that report by R.H.A. that our line appeared to run through R.7. is presumed to be incorrect.	
12.55.p.m.	do.........	7th Battery fired on house between 65 and 68 on party of men seen to enter it_ six hits obtained on the house.	
1.35.p.m.	do.........	44th Battery Observaing Officer reported two yellow flags have been flying in old German front line trench immediately behind V.1.	
2.p.m.	do.........	30th Howitzer Battery shelled V.2. and neighbourhood- several lyddite threw planks and other objects into the air.	
3.15.p.m.	do.........	66th Battery fired on house S 5 d 4'3 which Infantry reported to be O.P. Battery at S 18 a 4'2 active on our support trenches.	
5.20.p.m.	do.........	One gun 2nd Battery fired at battery in S 18a 4'2, which was causing annoyance in our support trenches.	
3.[illegible]0.p.m.	do.........	2nd Battery fired a few rounds at barricade near 59.	
4.p.m.	do.........	14th Battery had three direct hits on GABLE House 100 yds S.W. of 125.	

Army Form C. 2118.

WAR DIARY
or
INTELLIGENCE SUMMARY.
(Erase heading not required.)

Instructions regarding War Diaries and Intelligence Summaries are contained in F. S. Regs., Part II. and the Staff Manual respectively. Title pages will be prepared in manuscript.

Hour, Date, Place	Summary of Events and Information	Remarks and references to Appendices
4.p.m. 21st May 1915...... RUE du PUITS.	28th Battery fired at probable O.P's between 53 and V.12.	
4.30.p.m. do.......	PIPSQUEAK shelled vicinity of M 33 c. MEERUT Division Operation Order No.34 * received and orders were issued accordingly vide C.R.A. 52@ 53@ 54@and 55@	* Appendix 212 @ Appendices 213, 214, 215, 216
7.p.m. do.......	G.O.C. No.1 Group H.A.R. was informed as per R.A.Q.14% regarding Battery shelling LORETTO Road from direction of AUBERS, also re single howitzer shelling "E" Sub-section and knocked out M.G.	% Appendix 217
8.p.m. do.......	9th Brigade R.F.A. were ordered that all three batteries to open fire on night lines from 10.p.m. to 10.30.p.m. except that battery on FERME du BIEZ roads will open on that objective- Rate of fire section fire one minute. From 1a.m. to 2.a.m. battery on FERME du BIEZ will open fire as already ordered.	×Appendix 154
8.10.p.m. do.......	MEERUT Division G-137 ø received regarding attack by ALDERSON's Force. This was communication to 4th, 9th abd 13th Brigades under No.669-R.A.(L)≠.	ø Appendix 218 ≠Appendix 219
8.30.p.m. do.......	MEERUT Division intimated that left flank of 1st H.L.I. would be marked by a Red lamp in to-night's attack when the position was reached.	
9.45.p.m. do.......	Orders received from MEERUT Division that no Artillery fire to take place in vicinity of FERME du BOIS i.e. R.7. R.8. Q.15. and Q.16. after midnight tonight on account of our Infantry patrols working out in that direction- This was communicated to O.C. R.A. Southern Group vide B.M. 273 ##.	##Appendix 220
	For further information see Tactical Progress Report attached*	* appendix 221
	Meerut Division G126 regarding readjustment of the line held by GARHWAL & BAREILLY Bdes is attached as an appx	$ appendix 221(a)

(9 29 6) W4141—463 100,000 9/14 H W V Forms/C. 2118/10

Instructions regarding War Diaries and Intelligence Summaries are contained in F. S. Regs., Part II. and the Staff Manual respectively. Title pages will be prepared in manuscript.

WAR DIARY
or
INTELLIGENCE SUMMARY.
(Erase heading not required.)

Army Form C. 2118.

Hour, Date, Place		Summary of Events and Information	Remarks and references to Appendices
22nd May 1915. RUE du PUITS.		All batteries of the MEERUT Divisional Artillery carried out tasks as ordered.	
5.45.a.m.	do.	Germans bombarded our trenches opposite FESTUBERT heavily for an hour.	
1.15.p.m.	do.	10.5.c.m. Howitzer from direction of BOIS du BIEZ shelled our support trenches behind PORT ARTHUR-about 25% of the shell were blind.	
1.30.p.m.	do.	15.c.m. Howitzer shelled vicinity of M.26.	
2.30.p.m.	do.	Some 10.5.c.m. shell fell over the 2nd Battery-bearing of scoop 121° true from M 32 a 0'10.	
3.30.p.m.	do.	20th Battery registered house near point 53-2 direct hits.	*appendix 154
4.p.m.	do.	20th Battery registered houses near 51.	
4.5p.m. to 5.p.m.	do.	2nd Battery fired at Battery at S 18 a 4'2 which was annoying our Infantry.	
4.10.p.m.	do.	7th Battery fired a few rounds into house 60 yards S.W. of 125.	
4.30.p.m.	do.	14th Battery fired a few rounds at cross roads near 125.	
6.p.m.	do.	10.5.c.m. Howitzer shelled the RUE du BOIS.	
		10.5.c.m. Howitzer shelled GOOD LUCK Corner.	
6.15.p.m.	do.	15.c.m. Howitzer fired one round in vicinity of M 27 a.	
7.p.m.	do.	PIPSQUEAK shelled vicinity of M 27 a and b.	
10.p.m.	do.	PIPSQUEAK dropped a few shell in vicinity of M 27 b.	
		Heavyvhowitzer shelled 7th Battery O.P..	
		For further information see Tactical Progress Report* attached.	*Appendix 222

(9 29 6) W4141—463 100,000 9/14 H W V Forms/C. 2118/10

Army Form C. 2118.

Instructions regarding War Diaries and Intelligence Summaries are contained in F. S. Regs., Part II. and the Staff Manual respectively. Title pages will be prepared in manuscript.

WAR DIARY
or
INTELLIGENCE SUMMARY.
(Erase heading not required.)

Hour, Date, Place	Summary of Events and Information	Remarks and references to Appendices
23rd May 1915....... RUE du PUITS.	All batteries of the MEERUT Divisional Artillery carried out tasks as ordered.	
6.15.p.m. do.........	2nd Battery fired to silence PIPSQUEAK at S 18 a 4'2- this was repeated at 1.40.p.m.	
6.20.a.m. do.........	66th Battery fired a few rounds at working party near 54.x	
10.a.m. to 11.a.m.do.........	LEICESTER LOUNGE(O.P. at S 9 d 5'6) shelled by 10.5.c.m. How- this is new O.P. of 8th Battery R.F.A.	
12.30.p.m. do.........	14th Battery fired on house 50 yards S.W. of 151,x where signalling seen going on- 2 direct hits. This was repeated at 6.5.p.m.- 3 more hits obtained.	x appendix 154
	Howitzer shelled BREWERY- 2 blind shell fell near the 7th Battery O.P..	
1.2.p.m. do.........	20th Battery registered their new zone from ORCHARD Redoubt to V.6.x	
3.45.p.m. to 4.p.m.do.........	7th and 66th Batteries shelled trenches on our front in reply to shelling of road near 7th Battery R.F.A.	
7.p.m.m do.........	19th Battery registered new zone.	
	For further information see Tactical Progress Report* attached.	*Appendix 223

Army Form C. 2118.

Instructions regarding War Diaries and Intelligence Summaries are contained in F. S. Regs., Part II. and the Staff Manual respectively. Title pages will be prepared in manuscript.

WAR DIARY
or
INTELLIGENCE SUMMARY.
(Erase heading not required.)

Hour, Date, Place	Summary of Events and Information	Remarks and references to Appendices
12.30.a.m. to 1.a.m. 24th May 1915........ FOSSE.	19th and 20th Batteries fired on points V.9e, V.6e, and 59(KEEP) at request of BAREILLY Brigade.	
3.a.m. to 4.a.m. do.......	Heavy howitzer shelled vicinity of M 27 d and RUE du PUITS.	
10.a.m. do.......	5th Siege Battery fired with aeroplane observation at Machine Gun near FERME du BOIS- registered this point, also point on this trench on either side- Airman reported fire very effective, trenches flattened and hit on Machine Gun was followed by many violent explosions.	
11.10.a.m. do.......	8th Battery registered German trench East of FERME du BOIS.	
11.35.a.m. do.......	20th Battery registered FERME du BOIS, FERME d'AVOUE, FERME du TOULOTTES- R.10, V.4., V.7., R.17e.	×appendix 152
4.p.m. do.......	Headquarters Divisional Artillery, MEERUT Division re-established at FOSSE.	
5.p.m. do.......	5th Siege Battery fired on trench running N. from FERME du BOIS, in conjunction with 8th Battery R.F.A. 5 out of 6 rounds were hits in the trench.	
	For further information see Tactical Progress Report* attached.	*Appendix 224
	The Indian Corps was allotted a front from point 140 to QUINQUE RUE. The LAHORE Division from point 140 to the ORCHARD Redoubt and the MEERUT Division from the ORCHARD Redoubt to the Highland Division on its right.	[signature]
	The 4th Brigade R.F.A. ceased to be employed with the LAHORE Division for the defence of its Northern Section and orders were issued for its withdrawal to rest. (See appx 224(a) + appx 224(b)	×appendix 224(a). *appendix 224(b).

Army Form C. 2118.

Instructions regarding War Diaries and Intelligence Summaries are contained in F. S. Regs., Part II. and the Staff Manual respectively. Title pages will be prepared in manuscript.

WAR DIARY
or
INTELLIGENCE SUMMARY.
(Erase heading not required.)

Hour, Date, Place	Summary of Events and Information	Remarks and references to Appendices
5.55.a.m. 25th May 1915 ..... FOSSE.	Hostile biplane seen to N.E. from 44th Battery gun position.	
7.a.m. do.........	Farm at M 33 a 8'7(Headquarters 9th Brigade R.F.A.)shelled by 10.c.m. gun for half an hour hitting the farm several times.	
8.30.a.m. do.........	Hostile aeroplane seen travelling East over M 27 and M 28.	
9.40.a.m. do.........	Hostile biplane seen to N.E. from 44th Battery gun position.	
10.a.m. to 11.a.m do.........	PIPSQUEAK shelled RUE du BOIS intermittently.	
1.p.m. to 3.p.m. do.........	28th Battery registered V.7e and RUE du MARAIS.	
2.p.m. do.........	2nd and 8th Batteries carried out registration of the following points:- P.28, Q.18, Q.9, M.20, N.23, Farm 200 yards S.W. of P.18.	
2.30.p.m. do.........	10.5.c.m. shell killed one Corporal and one gunner and wounded one gunner of the 44th Battery R.F.A.	appendix 154
3.p.m. to 3.45.p.mdo.........	20th Battery registered as follows:- (i) German support trench from 59(KEEP) to V.6. (ii) Barricade on LA BASSEE Road to point 60. (iii)Probable machine gun emplacement between 60 and 57.	
4.55.p.m. do.........	"Sausage" up true bearing 108$\frac{1}{2}$° from S 10 b 1'7.	
5.40.p.m. do.........	Two "Sausages" seen true bearings 115° and 150° 55' from S 31 b 8'7.	
6.15.p.m. do.........	PIPSQUEAK shelled road from PONT LOGY to about M 27 d.	
	19th Battery re-registered a few points on their new front during the day. 5th Siege Battery registered trench running N. from Q.15- Airman reported 4 hits on the trench.	
	For further information see Tactical Progress Report attached. *	* Appendix 225
	The 4th Brigade R.F.A. instead of going into rest were ordered to take up positions to cover a portion of the left front of the Highland Division.	[illegible signature]

(9 29 6) W 4141—463 100,000 9/14 H W V Forms/C. 2118/10

Instructions regarding War Diaries and Intelligence Summaries are contained in F. S. Regs., Part II. and the Staff Manual respectively. Title pages will be prepared in manuscript.

WAR DIARY
or
INTELLIGENCE SUMMARY.
(Erase heading not required.)

Army Form C. 2118.

Hour, Date, Place		Summary of Events and Information	Remarks and references to Appendices
9.45.a.m. to 10.15a.m	26th May 1915.... FOSSE.	10.5.c.m. Howitzer shelled vicinity of LA BASSEE Road near PONT du HEM firing one round every 30 seconds from direction of LA RUSSIE.	
10.40.a.m.	do......	2nd Battery fired on DISTILLERY in order to check zero line, corrector etc,*	
10.45.a.m.	do......	8th Battery registered trench midway between V.1. and V.2.	
10.50.a.m.	do......	2nd Battery fired a couple of rounds at screen or notice board seen being put up in German trench near V.2. The screen cam e down when fired at.	
12 noon.	do......	20th Battery registered point V.6e and support trench from V.6 to 59(KEEP).	
2.p.m.	do......	8th Battery fired a few rounds at PIPSQUEAK battery near Q.19.	
2.15.p.m.	do......	LEICESTER LOUNGE(S 9 d 5'6) was shelled.	Appendix 15A
3.20.p.m.	do......	2nd Battery fired 40 rounds H.E. at V.2-R.7-R.8 and knocked the trench about.	
		PIPSQUEAK shelled RUE du BOIS- one direct hit on RITZ.	
4.45.p.m.	do......	8th Battery engaged V.2. with H.E.	
5.p.m.	do......	PIPSQUEAK shelled RUE du BOIS S 9 c and front line trench opposite.	
5.5.p.m.	do......	20th Battery fired at PIPSQUEAK Battery at S 18 a 4'2 and silenced it.	
5.45.p.m.	do......	German biplane passed over 44th Battery position.	
9.30.p.m.	do......	2nd Battery fired at PIPSQUEAK just N. of point Q.65.	

Position of MEERUT Divisional Artillery as follows:-

4th Brigade R.F.A.	7th Battery R.F.A.....S	2 c 4 7.
	14th Battery R.F.A.....S	2 c 8 3.
	66th Battery R.F.A.....S	2 d 5 2.
9th Brigade R.F.A.	19th Battery R.F.A.....M	26 d 5 5.
	20th Battery R.F.A.....M	33 a 3 8.
	28th Battery R.F.A.....M	32 b 10 0.
13th Brigade R.F.A.	2nd Battery R.F.A.....M	32 a 3 8.
	8th Battery R.F.A.....M	31 b 9 7.
	44th Battery R.F.A.....M	31 d 5 7.
	30th How Btty R.F.A....M	32 b 8 3.
	5th Siege Btty R.G.A...M	31 b 6 8.
MEERUT Divl Ammn Column	One section LES LOBES	
	Two Sections ROBECQ.	

Headquarters Divisional Artillery,, FOSSE.

Tactical Progress Report*attached.

* Appendix 226

(9 29 6) W4141—463 100,000 9/14 H W V Forms/C. 2118/10.

Army Form C. 2118.

Instructions regarding War Diaries and Intelligence Summaries are contained in F. S. Regs., Part II. and the Staff Manual respectively. Title pages will be prepared in manuscript.

WAR DIARY
or
INTELLIGENCE SUMMARY.

(Erase heading not required.)

Hour, Date, Place		Summary of Events and Information	Remarks and references to Appendices
7.10.a.m.	27th May 1915.. FOSSE.	10.5.c.m. Howitzer shelled the RUE du BOIS S.9 d and open ground N. of RUE du BOIS.	
8.a.m.	do........	20th Battery fired at working party who were visible sand-bagging second line trench just S. of LA BASSEE Road and dispersed them.	
9.30.a.m.	do........	PIPSQUEAK shelled support trenches in S 9 d.	
11.a.m.	do........	44th Battery billet and Headquarters 13th Brigade R.F.A. was shelled by 15.c.m. Howitzer- no damage.	
12 noon.	do........	About this time several 15 c.m. shells fell near the DEHRA DUN Brigade Headquarters.	
3.p.m.	do........	8th Battery registered road Q.20 to Q.12.	
3.4.p.m.	do........	Heavy howitzer shelled vicinity of WINDY CORNER(S 3 c 6'0)- 2 direct hits on REVOLVER HOUSE(S 3 c 5'4).	
3.30.p.m.	do........	8th Battery obtained 2 direct hits on fortified house 300 yards N.W. of R.28 with H.E.	
		44th Battery searched for PIPSQUEAK about M.18.	
4.p.m.	do........	28th Battery registered N.29.	
4.20.p.m.	do........	15.c.m. Howitzer had two direct hits on the RITZ(S 9 d).	
4.45.p.m. & 6.p.m.	do........	2nd Battery fired at S 11 a 4'2 where PIPSQUEAK was reported active.	x Appendix 154
4.50.p.m.	do........	20th Battery silenced PIPSQUEAK at S 18 a 4'2. which was active.	
5.24.p.m.	do........	20th Battery registered all 6 guns on battery at S 18 a 4'2.	
6.p.m.	do........	44th Battery fired on hostile working party about Q.15, Q.16.	
		For further information see Tactical Progress Report* attached.	*Appendix 227.

Army Form C. 2118.

Instructions regarding War Diaries and Intelligence Summaries are contained in F. S. Regs., Part II. and the Staff Manual respectively. Title pages will be prepared in manuscript.

WAR DIARY
or
INTELLIGENCE SUMMARY.

(Erase heading not required.)

Hour, Date, Place	Summary of Events and Information	Remarks and references to Appendices
10.a.m. 28th May 1915....... FOSSE.	44th Battery fired on German front line in reply to shelling- this was repeated at 5.30.p.m.	
10.45.a.m. do..........	2nd Battery fired two rounds per battery fire on night lines in reply to enemy shelling our support trenches.	
11.a.m. do..........	PIPSQUEAK dropped a few shell in support trenches near V.1.	
11.20.a.m. do..........	20th Battery registered new wire near R.8.	
11.30.a.m. do..........	20th Battery obtained 4 direct hits on house at P.16.	
	19th Battery registered "MOUND" S 17 a 8'0 and searched for PIPSQUEAK near DISTILLERY.	
12 noon. do..........	20th Battery obtained 4 direct hits on house at P.16.	
	2nd Battery fired on enemy's front trench near FERME du BOIS.	
12.26.p.m. do..........	2nd Battery fired 2 battery salvoes on night lines in reply to enemy shelling- this was repeated at 12.30.p.m.	
12.30.p.m. do..........	28th Battery fired 15 rounds a V.2. in conjunction with 13th Bde R.F.A.	
	PIPSQUEAK shelled neighbourhood of RITZ in reply to our shelling of their trenches.	
1.45.p.m. do..........	8th Battery fired 30 shrapnel and 20 H.E. on German trench by FERME du BOIS Orchard from R.8. to 200 yards to the West. This was repeated at 4.p.m.	
2.20.p.m. do..........	44th Battery registered R.8 and Q.16.	
3.26.p.m. do..........	2nd Battery fired 3 salvoes on night lines in reply to enemy shelling.	
	Enemy shelled LEICESTER LOUNGE and neighbourhood.	
3.p.m to 3.20.p.m do..........	2 8th Battery fired on trench at point V.2. with H.E. and shrapnel in conjunction with 2nd Battery firing on trench V.2 to R.8. -parapet a good deal knocked about, also some of the new loopholes in parapet destroyed. The 2nd Battery bombarded this trench from 3.45.p.m. to 5.40.p.m. with good effect.	x Appendix 154
3.30.p.m. do..........	PIPSQUEAK fired on RUE du BOIS for some time and 15.c.m. howitzers also joined in at 3.50.p.m. firing on FACTORY and RITZ- this probably in retaliation of our shelling V.2. and trench V.2 to R.8.	
4.45.p.m. do..........	20th Battery opened fire on German front trench 59 to V.6. ø	
4.50.p.m. do..........	28th Battery opened fire on German front trench V.2 to V.3. ø	
5.p.m. do..........	19th Battery opened fire on German second line trench V.3 to V.6. ø	
	ø This in retaliation to PIPSQUEAKS and 15.c.m. Howitzers shelling the RUE du BOIS, FACTORY and RITZ between 330 and 4.p.m.	

(9 29 6) W4141—463 100,000 9/14 H W V Forms/C.2118/10

P.T.O.

Army Form C. 2118.

Instructions regarding War Diaries and Intelligence Summaries are contained in F. S. Regs., Part II. and the Staff Manual respectively. Title pages will be prepared in manuscript.

WAR DIARY
or
INTELLIGENCE SUMMARY.
(Erase heading not required.)

Hour, Date, Place	Summary of Events and Information	Remarks and references to Appendices
5.p.m. 28th May 1915........ FOSSE.	10.5.c.m. howitzer shelled vicinity of M.27.d intermittently for about an hour.	
5.30.p.m. do...........	28th Battery fired on German observing statione a tree with ladder at S 23 d 2'6. There appears to be eithet a"dug-out" or else a single gun emplacement close to this tree.	
8.15.p.m. do..........	RICHEBOURG was shelled and a large house set on fire.	
	For further information see Tactical Progress Report* attached.	*Appendix 228.

(9 29 6) W 4141—463 100,000 9/14 H W V Forms/C. 2118/10

Instructions regarding War Diaries and Intelligence Summaries are contained in F. S. Regs., Part II. and the Staff Manual respectively. Title pages will be prepared in manuscript.

WAR DIARY
or
INTELLIGENCE SUMMARY.
(Erase heading not required.)

Army Form C. 2118.

Hour, Date, Place		Summary of Events and Information	Remarks and references to Appendices
6.30.a.m. 8.15.a.m & 9.30.a.m.	29th May 1915 FOSSE.	44th Battery fired at German working parties.	
7.a.m.	do.	Slow shelling by enemy of WINDY CORNER, LANSDOWNE POST and vicinity PONT LOGY and up LA BASSEE Road by howitzers and PIPSQUEAK commenced and continued for about 3 hours.	
8.45.a.m.	do.	8th Battery fired on house(probably an O.P.)at S 23 d 8'7, on LA BASSEE Road.	
9.a.m.	do.	Heavy howitzer shelled RUE du BOIS(vicinity S 10 a) and PIPSQUEAK shelled vicinity of ROUGE CROIX.	
9.25.a.m.	do.	8th Battery shelled trench V.2. to R.8. as a retaliatory measure.	
9.30.a.m.	do.	2nd Battery fired 25 rounds at German trenches in retaliation to enemy shelling our support trenches- this was repeated at 10.50.a.m., 2.45.p.m., and 6.10.p.m.	
10.30.a.m.	do.	20th Battery registered a battery S 30 a 5'1 who's flashes were observed during the morning.	
11.a.m. to 1.p.m.	do.	PIPSQUEAK fired on our trenches with bursts of gun fire on RUE du BOIS in vicinity of S 9 d.	
12 noon.	do.	15.c.m. Howitzer shelled our communication trenches in vicinity of S 15 a also vicinity of S 8 b.	
12.15.p.m. to 1.15.p.m.	do.	8th Battery bombarded trench R.8. to Q.15, with 30 shrapnel and 20 H.E.- this was repeated from 5.p.m. to 5.45.p.m.	
12.25.p.m. to 2.30.p.m.	do.	2nd Battery engaged enemy's trench from V.2(exclusive) towards R.8. with deliberate fire- this trench appeared to be well knocked about.	
2.15.p.m.	do.	28th Battery commenced firing on V.2. and on communicating trench connecting V.2. to V.4. with V.2. to V.3., deliberate observed fire employed to batter parapets. A good deal of damage was done, sandbags, timber and cooking pots were seen flying in the air.	× Appendix 15ª
2.45.p.m.	do.	PIPSQUEAK shelled from RITZ to LEICESTER LOUNGE S 9 d 9'8- probably in reply to 28th Battery shelling V.2.	
3.15.p.m.	do.	FACTORY and RITZ shelled by 15.c.m. howitzer in reply to 28th Battery shelling V.2.	
3.50.p.m.	do.	44th Battery searches vicinity of Q.18.	
5.p.m.	do.	PIPSQUEAK shelled ROUGE CROIX with a few rounds.	
5.45.p.m.	do.	PIPSQUEAK shelled cross roads M 32 d 7'8.	

(9 29 6) W 4141—463 100,000 9/14 H W V Forms/C. 2118/10.

Army Form C. 2118.

Instructions regarding War Diaries and Intelligence Summaries are contained in F. S. Regs., Part II. and the Staff Manual respectively. Title pages will be prepared in manuscript.

WAR DIARY
or
INTELLIGENCE SUMMARY.

(Erase heading not required.)

Hour, Date, Place	Summary of Events and Information	Remarks and references to Appendices
5.50.p.m. 29th May 1915. FOSSE.	2nd Battery engaged loopholes near V.2. in retaliation forbfire on our trenches- 6 of the 12 were destroyed.	
6.p.m. do.	PIPSQUEAK shelled vicinity of M 33 d.	
6.15.p.m. do.	10.c.m. gun shelled from M 33 a to M 26 d for ~~half~~ half an hour, searching and sweeping.	
	For further information see Tactical Pr gress Report attached.*	* Appendix 229.

Army Form C. 2118.

Instructions regarding War Diaries and Intelligence Summaries are contained in F. S. Regs., Part II. and the Staff Manual respectively. Title pages will be prepared in manuscript.

WAR DIARY
or
INTELLIGENCE SUMMARY.
(Erase heading not required.)

Hour, Date, Place		Summary of Events and Information	Remarks and references to Appendices
6.a.m. 30th May 1915 FOSSE.		PIPSQUEAK shelled RUE du BOIS, near LEICESTER LOUNGE S 9 d.	
6.5.a.m.,6.30.a.m., 7.50.a.m.,8.35.a.m. and 2.40.p.m.	do	2nd Battery fired salvoes on enemy's front trenches in retaliation.	
6.30.a.m.	do	2nd Battery engaged loopholes near V.2. in retaliation-2 of remaining 6 were knocked out(See Tactical Progress Report of 29th).	
11.a.m.	do	44th Battery registered places where PIPSQUEAKS were suspected.	
12.6.p.m.	do	2nd Battery registered a point in enemy's new earthwork M 16 a 6'5.	
1.15.p.m.	do	2nd Battery registered point where tape runs into new earthwork M 16 b 3'7.	
2.p.m.	do	44th Battery registered for night's shooting- trench from Q.15 along ridge towards Q.10.	
2.25.p.m.to 3.15.p.m	do	2nd Battery fired 100 rounds ~~[struck out]~~ on V.2 towards R.8.- trench a good deal knocked about and 6 germna seen bolting.	
2.45.p.m.	do	PIPSQUEAK shelled trenches in S 10 c.	
3.45.p.m.	do	21.c.m. howitzer shelled vicinity M 33 a, M 33 b, and very active all the afternoon.	Appendix 152
4.p.m.	do	8th Battery fired 100 rounds at slow rate on trench R.8 to Q.16- some damage done.	
4.p.m.	do	10.5.c.m. howitzer shelled vicinity M 26 intermittently for three hours	
4.p.m. to 6.30.p.m.	do	44th Battery position shelled considerably by 15.c.m. howitzer- one aiming post damaged.	* appendix. 229(a).
7.p.m	do	Meerut Division operation Orders No 37 received *	
		For further information see Tactical Progress Report attached.	* Appendix 230.
		The 5th Siege Battery R. G. A. was transferred, with 2nd Siege Battery to 1st Corps and marched to its new billets during the night. One section of each battery of 9th + 18th Brigades R.F.A. relieved each other between 9pm + 11.pm.	[initials]

Army Form C. 2118.

WAR DIARY
or
INTELLIGENCE SUMMARY.
(Erase heading not required.)

Instructions regarding War Diaries and Intelligence Summaries are contained in F. S. Regs., Part II. and the Staff Manual respectively. Title pages will be prepared in manuscript.

Hour, Date, Place		Summary of Events and Information	Remarks and references to Appendices
12.15.a.m. to) 12.45.a.m. and) 2.15.a.m. to) 2.45.a.m.)	31st May 1915. FOSSE.	4 Batteries of the 4th and 9th Brigades R.F.A. bombarded parapets damaged during the day in hopes of catching working parties repairing same.	
12.40.a.m.	do........	PIPSQUEAKS opened fire on our trenches in answer to our bombardment.	
2.20.a.m.	do........	PIPSQUEAKS shelled our trenches hard, in reply to our second bombardment.	
7.30.a.m.	do........	44th Battery shelled DISTILLERY- a house behind it was on fire.	
9.30.a.m.	do........	15.c.m. howitzer shelled St VAAST corner and vicinity.	
10.5.a.m.,2.17.p.m.) 3.23.p.m., and) 4.45.p.m.)	do........	2nd Battery fired on enemy in retaliation for their shelling.	
11.a.m.	do........	Two PIPSQUEAK Batteries whichbwere spotted during the night were seen to be firing repeatedly- an attempt to engage them failed as range was too great.	
11.30.a.m.	do........	20th Batery checked registration on trench Q.16 to Q.13.	
12 noon.	do........	8th Battery registered FERME COUR d'AVOUE and farm at Q.12. * C.R.A. O.O No 20 issued	*appendix 230(a).
1.45.p.m.	do........	2nd Battery registered enemy new earthwork and communication trench.	
2.p.m.	do........	15.c.m. Howitzer shelled REVOLVER HOUSE(S 3 c 5'4) and road up to St VAAST for about 1½ hours, including first aid post- direction believed to be AUBERS Ridge.	
2.10.p.m.	do........	8th Battery retaliated on enemy at R.8. to Q.15. and on new white sandbag parapet 50 yards N. of this.	
3.p.m. to 5.p.m.	do........	Germans heavy guns shelled following vicinities continually for about 2 hours.-M 26 b, M 32 d, S 2 b, S 3 d, M 27 d,- direction believed to be VIOLAINES.	x Appendix 1-4
5.5.p.m.	do........	2nd Battery fired on Germans seen in trenches, about this time same Battery registered REDOUBT N.E. of V.2. where germna working parties were seen.	
6.10p.m.	do........	28th Battery fired on M.G. emplacement 100 yards E. of V. obtaining 2 direct hits.	
6.30.p.m.	do........	BIPSQUEAK shelled vicinity of M 33 b.	
6.45p.m.	do........	15.c.m. Howitzer shelled FORESTER's LANE and WINDY Corner. direction believed to be LORGIES.	
		* For further information see Tactical Progress Report attached.	* Appendix 231.
6.pm	do	H Q Divisional Artillery MEERUT Division moved to the CHATEAU at LA CROIX MARMEUSE	

(9 29 6) W 4141—463 100,000 9/14 H W V Forms/C. 2118/10

APPENDIX 155.

TACTICAL PROGRESS REPORT
1st MAY 1916.

[illegible]

Trench in front of 36 to 35. The same [illegible] apparently [illegible] cut to [illegible] at which point there is a very strong redoubt, but owing to the trees and hedges only small patches of the ground can be seen. Some covered with new wire and new stakes and some with old rusty wire and old stakes.

GENERAL:- The depth of wire appears to be about 20 yards but it is difficult to judge, the height is about 3 feet in nearly every case. Where communication trenches run into the fire trench the wire entanglements are much thicker on the East side. No lanes for passage could be seen through the wire except where communication trenches run into the fire trenches but owing to the height of the fire trench breastworks there may be a number which cannot be observed.

The above report by Lieut GAGE, Forward Observing Officer, 7th Battery R.F.A.

AIRCRAFT:-

6.5.a.m. AVIATIK sighted flying high, bearing 125°, engaged with 34 rounds then turned S.S.E.

7.5.a.m. AVIATIK sighted flying low, bearing 160°, engaged with 17 rounds then turned S.S.E.

7.45.a.m. AVIATIK sighted flying high, bearing 45°, engaged with 31 rounds then turned E.

8.a.m. AVIATIK sighted flying high, bearing 90°, engaged with 33 rounds and turned E.

8.45.a.m. AVIATIK sighted flying high at bearing 120°, engaged with 22 rounds and turned E.

2.30.p.m. to 5.15.p.m. German "SAUSAGE" seen low at bearing 215°

Major R.A.

Brigade Major, Royal Artillery,
MEERUT DIVISION.

APPENDIX 156

SECRET

TACTICAL PROGRESS REPORT
2nd MAY 1915

1(a) ACTION BY OUR OWN ARTILLERY
9.a.m. 14th Battery registered Salient between 137 and 141.
11.20.a.m. 66th Battery fired on working party in Redoubt N. of pt.63.
11.30.a.m. 68th Battery shelled trench between 61 and 63.
11.55.a.m. and 6.30.p.m. 14th Battery fired on house 124, probably an O.P., as men seen leaving there.
12 noon. 44th Battery registered trenches near 57.
12 noon. 7th and 68th Battery retaliated on hostile trenches and point 65 for shelling of NEUVE CHAPELLE and our trenches there.
12.15.p.m. 5th Siege Battery registered V.6.
2.30.p.m. 68th Battery fired on working party S. of 63.
4.30.p.m. 20th Battery registered following cross roads with aeroplane T 12 c 6'8, N 32 a 3'3, N 31 d 9'1.

1(b) ACTION BY HOSTILE ARTILLERY
7.45.a.m. Field Howitzer Battery shelled ground in front of 14th Battery and in rear of 28th Battery. Fuze of this shell was ordinary 10'5 c.m. D.A. type marked H Z 14 SIMSON 15. Body of fuze brass and nose of steel.
12 noon NEUVE CHAPELLE was shelled by Field Battery also the 8th Gurkha trenches.

2 INFORMATION
A very quiet day.
Very little sniping, except in front of NEUVE CHAPELLE during afternoon.

IDENTIFICATION:- 1.25 p.m. Many nautical Germans observed in Redoubt at Salient North of 55. They wore dark navy blue trousers, jerseys and caps, all nautical pattern, and their hands deep in their pockets in true nautical style. Some wore German S.H. pattern trousers but rest blue. These men were obviously working in this Salient.

OBSTACLE:- Between the front line trench and the "covered way", for about 40 yards to the East of V.6. there seems to be some sort of low obstacle for about 30 yards behind the front line, with some newly turned earth at the far side. This is similst to that described in yesterday's Tactical Progress Report about point 63.
This is only just visible near V.6., it being impossible to see over the breastwork further to the left, and it is not easy to make out even there.
In the "covered way" just about the 1 of RICHEBOURG L'AVOUE there is the appearance of emplacements for half a dozen machine guns.
In view of the above it is quite likely the Germans mean to hold the "covered way" strongly against troops that may take their first line trenches.
New Chevaux de Frise discovered just N. of POINT 56 in front of German fire trench. Length 50 yards, and consisting of planks 12 feet long fastened together diagonally with ends sharpened, lying between the wire entanglement and the trenches. Also freshly turned earth at S 10 b 6'0 running S.W. for 100 yards, 50 yards behind German front trench.
There appears to be a new parapet about 50 yards behind the German front line between V.6. and 57.

AIRCRAFT:- None were seen today.

Major
[illegible] Royal Artillery

APPENDIX 157

[illegible]

TACTICAL PROGRESS REPORT
8th MAY 1916.
****

1(a) ACTION BY OUR OWN ARTILLERY

4.10.a.m. 5th Battery fired at [illegible] cross roads [illegible] DISTILLERY, also trench near point 99.
4.30.a.m. 4th Brigade R.F.A. [illegible] registration.
4.45.a.m. 2nd Siege Battery registered on "[illegible]" [illegible] result unsatisfactory.
5.5.a.m. 29th Battery commenced to register on [illegible] from 129 to 140.
5.10.a.m. 30th Battery registered [illegible] between points 17[illegible] and 17[illegible]
1 p.m. 2nd and 5th Batteries fired a few rounds at [illegible] "[illegible]" near point V.6.
Between 1 p.m. and [illegible] p.m. [illegible] were registered by 4th Brigade Batteries.
2.54.p.m. 68th Battery fired on trenches near point [illegible] where movement was seen.
[illegible].p.m. 5th Battery registered hose pipe in German trench [illegible] of pt.5[illegible]
5.15.p.m. 30th Battery registered [illegible] with aeroplane.
5.45.p.m. [illegible] Siege Battery registered V.[illegible] [illegible] rounds into trench.
[illegible].p.m. 2nd Siege Battery registered on Hose Pipe [illegible]
[illegible].p.m. 2nd Siege Battery fired 12 rounds at same position. The Hose Pipe had been removed earlier [illegible] after registration by 30th Howitzer Battery.
[illegible].p.m. 4th Brigade Batteries fired a few rounds at enemy trenches to check hostile rifle fire on our aeroplane.
[illegible].p.m. 5th Siege Battery fired 1[illegible] rounds [illegible] point 130-[illegible] hits within 10 yards of hose pipe [illegible] apparently damaged still [illegible]. At point [illegible] but pipe undamaged. At point V.[illegible] [illegible] hit [illegible]
[illegible].40.p.m. 68th Battery [illegible]
During the afternoon [illegible] Battery registered following points:-
T [illegible] ....[illegible] yards. [illegible] ....[illegible] yards
[illegible] ....[illegible] yards.

1(b) ACTION BY [illegible] ARTILLERY

[illegible] [illegible] and [illegible] LUCK House.
[illegible] [illegible] from direction of [illegible]
11.1[illegible].a.m. [illegible] from [illegible] 20 rounds altogether.
1.[illegible].p.m. [illegible] LUCK House in retaliation for shelling of trenches [illegible] Battery.
[illegible] [illegible] Howitzer.

2. INFORMATION.
[illegible] A good deal [illegible]
[illegible] [illegible]
[illegible]
[illegible]
[illegible]

Brigade Major, [illegible] Artillery,
[illegible]

Copy No. ..7....

APPENDIX 158

OPERATION ORDER NO. 29.

By

Lieutenant-General Sir. C. A. ANDERSON, K.C.B.,

Commanding MEERUT Division.

Reference -Map of FRANCE 1/40000. 4th May 1915.

1. Under orders of the Indian Corps, the LAHORE Division will take over the Northern Section of the Indian Corps' front on the night 5th/6th May 1915.
The LAHORE Divisional Artillery will move into the line on the nights 5th/6th and 6th/7th May 1915.

2. The MEERUT Divisional Area is modified, its northern boundary running through PORT ARTHUR - ROUGE CROIX - Road junction R.29.b. 7.0 inclusive - road junction R.27.c. 1.0, exclusive, road junction Q.24.d. 5.1., inclusive, through PARADIS (road inclusive) to road junction in Q.12.c., and thence due west to CLARENCE River.

3. The GARHWAL Brigade and the Machine Guns of the 107th Pioneers, will be relieved by the JULLUNDUR Brigade under arrangements to be made by Brigade Commanders in consultation with one another. The Battalions holding Sub-Sections (a) and (c) will not be relieved until the reliefs of those holding Sub-Sections (b) and (d) are completed.

4. On being relieved the G.O.C. GARHWAL Brigade will billet and bivouac his troops in the vicinity of the RUE DU PUITS, and in such orchards affording him cover as he can occupy, using LORETTO Road, and the RUE DES BERCEAUX when moving out of the trenches.

5. The present depôts of the Sapper Companies of the MEERUT Division and the billets of the 107th Pioneers, will be retained for the meanwhile. (The 34th Pioneers will re-occupy their billets in "les 8 Maisons", the G.O.C., DEHRA DUN Brigade making arrangements to vacate these by 8.30 p.m. on the 6th May).

Cnore Colonel,

General Staff, MEERUT Division.

Issued to Signal Company for despatch at 10-30 p.m.

Copy No. 1 to	Indian Corps.	Copy No. 12 to	Meerut Signals.
2	Eighth Division	13	Divl. Train
3.	LAHORE Division	14	A.A. & Q.M.G.
4	DEHRA DUN Bde.	15	D.A.A.G.
5	GARHWAL Bde.	16	D.A.A.& Q.M.G.
6.	BAREILLY Bde.	17	
7.	C.R.A. MEERUT	18	
8	C.R.E. "	19	
9	4th Ind. Cavalry	20	Diary & Files.
10	107th Pioneers	21	
11	A.D.M.S. MEERUT		

APPENDIX 139

S E C R E T

TACTICAL PROGRESS REPORT
4th MAY 1915.

****

1(a) ACTION BY OUR OWN ARTILLERY.
11.20.a.m. 80th Battery fired at house 51.
4.p.m. 20th Battery registered the following points:-
Cross roads S 12 a 6' 2. Cross roads S 12 c 6' 6.
Cross roads S 12 c 3' 3. FERME du BIEZ.
4.10.p.m. 19th Battery registered fork roads S 32 a 5'3.
4.45.p.m. 14th Battery fired at working party carrying planks 138 support trench. This party was kept busy for some time trying to retrieve planks.
30th Howitzer Battery carried out registration during the day.
The 2nd, 8th, 28th, 7th and 44th Batteries R.F.A. [illegible] Siege and 5th Siege Batteries did not fire to-day.

1(b) ACTION BY HOSTILE ARTILLERY.
12 noon. 10'5 c.m. Howitzer shelled vicinity of S 9 d 1'5, firing single shots at one minute intervals.
1.40.p.m. 77 mm. field guns shelled cross roads S 9 d 1'5, firing single shots.
2.50.p.m. 15.c.m. Howitzer(from direction of LIGNY LE PETIT) shelled vicinity of S 9 d 1'5.
3.25.p.m. German shell fell in the RUE.

2. INFORMATION. A very quiet day.
BOMBING:- "ORCHARD" at S 10 b was bombed at 1.20.p.m.
COMMUNICATIONS:- Southern Group heavy cable(Emergency wire)was laid to O.P. to-day.
AIRCRAFT:- 10.15.a.m. Enemy bi-plane seen N.E. of 44th Battery, after about 15 minutes it vanished E.
11.5.a.m. AVIATIK high bearing 180° travelling S.E., became obscured by cloud.
GERMAN WORKS:- No.1 Group Heavy A.R. reports that enemy appear to be constructing a high breastwork of timber and earth close to and N.W. of Railway from T 2 d to T 2 a [illegible].

5th MAY 1915.
A good deal of sniping during the night in front of "A" Sub section.
A pump has been placed in German front trench at S 11 a 6'7.

[signature] Major R.A.

Brigade Major, Royal Artillery,
MEERUT DIVISION.

S E C R E T

APPENDIX 161

TACTICAL PROGRESS REPORT
5th May 1915

1(a) ACTION BY OUR OWN ARTILLERY
4th Brigade Batteries fired as usual in the early morning.
44th Battery fired at long range about 11 a.m. [illegible]
10.20 a.m. 14th Battery fired at point 10.
12.5 p.m. 7th Battery fired at working party near point 121.
2.7 p.m. 14th Battery shelled party of Germans near point 121, causing them to take cover.
3.15 p.m. 2nd Battery registered point V. [illegible]
4 p.m. 7th Battery fired at activity near 131.
5.40 p.m. 7th Battery fired a few rounds at point 123, where snipers were reported troublesome.
6.30 p.m. 44th Battery carried out registration.
2nd and 5th Siege Batteries carried out some useful registration during the day, the 6th Siege Battery scoring [illegible] hit on house 51.

1(b) ACTION BY HOSTILE ARTILLERY
4.30 a.m. PIPSQUEAK fired 5 rounds at [illegible]
11 a.m. German Heavy Howitzer shelled [illegible]
11 a.m. 21 c.m. Howitzer put several rounds into PORT ARTHUR.
3.30 p.m. 15 c.m. Howitzer put a few rounds into PORT ARTHUR.
4 p.m. to 5 p.m. 10 c.m. and 15 c.m. Howitzers fired on road PORT ARTHUR, LA BASSEE Road [illegible]
6.40 p.m. 77 m.m. guns shelled [illegible]

2. INFORMATION
WIRE:- New wire entanglement observed 50 yards behind fire trench just E. of V.5
AIRCRAFT:- [illegible]
FIRE:- The fire from [illegible]

APPENDIX 161(a)
(13 pages)

SECRET.

No.G.405/26

Headquarters, Meerut Division.
May 6th 1915.

Memorandum.

Enclosed copy of operation order (serial No. 6) is issued as a guide only, and may have to be modified on receipt of Corps Orders.

The dates are suppositious only and correct dates and timings of bombardment will be forwarded later.

2. Please acknowledge.

P Davies
Major,
General Staff,
Meerut Division.

To,
Dehra Dun Bde
Garhwal Bde
Bareilly Bde
C.R.A. Meerut
C.R.E. Meerut.

SECRET

Copy No. 6

OPERATION ORDER No.30,
by
Lieut:-General Sir Charles ANDERSON, K.C.B.,
Commanding MEERUT Division.

Reference maps:-
6th May 1915.

Map of trenches - 1:10,000.
BELGIUM & Part of FRANCE, Sheet 36, - 1:40,000, & (Third Edition)
FRANCE - BETHUNE Sheet - 1:40,000.

-:-:-:-:-:-:-:-:-:-:-:-:-:-:-

Information. 1. The 1st Army is attacking on the 8th May 1915 with the object of breaking through the enemy's line and gaining the LA BASSEE - LILLE Road between LA BASSEE and FOURNES and then advancing ~~on DON~~. to the line BAUVIN-DON.

The 1st Corps, retaining its right at GIVENCHY, will attack on a broad front in the vicinity of RICHEBOURG L'AVOUE with the object of advancing on RUE DU MARAIS, LORGIES and ILLIES.

The Indian Corps will operate so as to cover the left of the 1st Corps, with the object of capturing the FERME DU BIEZ and of subsequently advancing to the line LIGNY LE GRAND - LA CLIQUETERIE FERME.

The 4th Corps will operate so as to break through the enemy's line in the vicinity of ROUGES BANCS with the object of:-

(i) orgahising a defensive flank from the vicinity of LA CORDONNERIE FARM to FROMELLES.
(ii) Turning the AUBERS defences by an attack from the north-east.

Its subsequent advance will be directed on LA CLIQUETERIE Farm with the object of effecting a junction with the Indian Corps.

The 2nd Cavalry Division will remain in readiness near ESTAIRES to act as the situation developes.

The Lahore Division will hold the front allotted to the Indian Corps, less that portion from which the attack is to be delivered by the Meerut Division. It will engage the enemy with rifle, machine-gun and trench-mortar fire, to assist in protecting the left flank of the Meerut Division from counter--attack from the north.

Lahore Division will also open a communication trench from the advanced listening post at point 61 to connect up with our attack if this becomes desirable.

Intention. 2. The Meerut Division will make (is making) the attack to be delivered by the Indian Corps.

This attack is to be made on the enemy's trenches from the vicinity of the point V.6 to the vicinity of the point 56 as the first objective. On this front the enemy's wire will be cut by artillery fire.

The second objective is the capture of LA TOURELLE and houses in the vicinity of point 50.

The third objective is the capture of the DISTILLERY and FERME du BIEZ.

Subsequent objectives will be the occupation of the BOIS DU BIEZ, LIGNY LE PETIT, LIGNY LE GRAND and LA CLIQUETERIE.

~~ERIE~~ so as to join up with the 4th Corps.

Bodies of infantry are not to halt if portions of the line are held up, but will press on to their further objectives without delay.

Artillery. 3. The Meerut Divisional Artillery, reinforced by that of the Lahore Division, one Section Mountain Artillery, one section of Hotchkiss Motor Battery and certain Heavy and Siege Batteries will support the attack

The attack will be prepared and supported as follows:-

Ist PHASE.-

The assault of the enemy's first line trenches will be preceded by an artillery bombardment, guns being told off to:-

- (a) Destruction of enemy's obstacles.
- (b) Battering of enemy's trenches.
- (c) Battering of enemy's strong points.
- (d) Barrage ~~of~~ against reinforcements advancing from the BOIS DU BIEZ; North-east, the East and the South-east.
- (e) Engaging enemy's batteries by 1st Group Heavy Artillery.

IInd PHASE.

While the infantry are advancing on LA TOURELLE fire will be directed on:-

- (a) LA TOURELLE and the Distillery South of it.
- (b) Houses in vicinity of point 50.
- (c) FERME DU BIEZ.
- (d) South-west edge of BOIS DU BIEZ and approaches from LIGNY and LORGIES.

IIIrd PHASE.

Fire will be concentrated on the FERME DU BIEZ in preparation for the assault on that place.

Barranges will be continued to prevent the approach of reinforcements.

13th Bde RFA

Teams of ~~one Brigade Meerut Artillery~~ will be brought up to a convenient locality in readiness for an advance in support of the infantry at short notice.

9th ~~A second~~ Brigade R.F.A. is alsoto be held in readiness to support this at longer notice.

Lines of advance within our lines are to be reconnoitred and spit-locked and bridges laid out before the day of attack. Light bridges for crossing ditches to be carried, and personnel of each battery must be prepared to rapidly repair roads and remove obstacles encountered in any advance beyond our present lines.

Both Brigades R.F.A. detailed as above will have four miles reserve telephone cable with each battery.

Ammunition to be expended during the bombardment will be dumped previously to avoid congestion of roads during the fight. Special attention will also be directed to ensure that the Brigades R.F.A. detailed to advance will do so with full supply of ammunition.

The section Mountain Artillery will, during the bombardment, operate from a position to be selected near LANSDOWNE POST and will afterwards advance in close support of the infantry attack, taking orders from the G.O.C. Dehra Dun Bde.

No.4 Trench Battery will remain in its present position in the Orchard. It will be at the disposal of the G.O.C. Dehra Dun Bde and will advance under his orders in support of the Brigade.

Dehra Dun Bde
Sect. Mtn.Art.
No.4 Trench Battery R.A.

4. Dehra Dun Bde will, as first objective, carry out the assault on the enemy's front line trenches on a three battalion front.

It will be formed up by 11.0 P.M. on the 7th May, as follows:-

The assaulting battalions in the front line trenches from the junction of the listening post communication trench to in front of the ORCHARD Redoubt inclusive, and in the CRESCENT Trench and ORCHARD Redoubt.

The supporting battalions in BLACKADER Trench and ground in rear of ORCHARD.

The three assaulting battalions will form up in front of our advanced trenches after the wire cutting portion of the bombardment is completed at 5.20 A.M. and before the bombardment of the enemy's trenches ceases at 5.40. A.M.

The assaulting line will, during this bombardment, move up as close to enemy's line as our shell fire permits, and will reach the enemy's front line trenches at the earliest possible moment after this bombardment is lifted to more distant objectives at 5.40 A.M.

The first line will not delay at these trenches but will push on against their further objectives. The capture of the enemy remaining in the trenches and bombing down the trenches to each flank, will be done under Brigade arrangements by succeeding lines.

After taking the first line trenches the battalion on the right will advance with its left on LA BASSEE Road, capturing the houses on the right side of the road, and press on to the Distillery.

The Centre Battalion will advance with its right on the LA BASSEE Road taking houses on the left of the Road, and press on to the LA TOURELLE - FERME DU BIEZ Road.

The left battalion, after crossing the trenches, will sieze the houses at points 52, 53 and on either side of the road leading thence to FERME DU BIEZ. It will also press on and sieze the FERME DU BIEZ.

The battalion in Brigade reserve will be moved up, under orders of G.O.C. Dehra Dun Brigade, into the front line trenches as the assaulting battalions clear them.

Assaulting battalions will, under Brigade arrangements, leave such garrisons as may be necessary to hold them, in the following positions as they are captured. The localities will be strengthened, parties of sappers and pioneers being held in readiness at road junction in M.32.d to be sent forward under orders of C.R.E. to assist in this:-

- (a) ~~North~~ South end of LA TOURELLE Village.
- (b) DISTILLERY.
- (c) Road junction in S.11.a (points 52 & 53)
- (d) Group of houses near point 50.
- (e) FERME DU BIEZ.

The balance of units, after finding the above necessary garrisons, will push on to their further objectives.

Bombing parties will be organised by the G.O.C. Dehra Dun Brigade to bomb outwards along enemy's trenches.

5. The force as per margin will be organised by G.O.C. Garhwal Bde as a complete unit with staff, signalling arrangements and ammunition supply.

Lieut. Col DRAKE-BROCKMAN,
The Garhwal Rifles,
2/8th Gurkha Rifles,
Two bomb-guns of
Garhwal Bde Battery.

It will be formed up in the two eastern blocks of assembly trenches immediately north of RUE DU BOIS, by 1.0 a.m. on 8th May. This force is detailed for the special purpose of securing the eastern edge of the BOIS DU BIEZ and capturing LA RUSSIE. It will move into the front line trenches as they are vacated by Dehra Dun Bde and carry out the above mission under orders of G.O.C. Dehra Dun Bde. It should not be used for the general support of Dehra Dun Bde.

Bareilly Brigade.

6. Bareilly Bde will be formed up as below by 3.0 A.M. on 8th May:-

Three battalions in the three westerly blocks of assembly trenches north of the RUE DU BOIS, one battalion in LANSDOWNE POST and one battalion in breastworks east of that post on north side of FORESTERS LANE.

The Brigade, less 125th Rifles, but including machine gun section of that unit, will be in support of Dehra Dun Brigade, and will, under orders of G.O.C. Bareilly Brigade, occupy

assembly

assembly positions of Dehra Dun Brigade as they become available.

This forward move is to be made in communication with G.O.C. Dehra Dun Brigade as it may either follow, or precede, that of Lieut;Colonel DRAKE-BROCKMAN's detachment.

G.O.C. Bareilly Brigade will detail two Companies, 125th Rifles, as carriers for engineer working parties; to report to C.R.E. at road junction in M.32.d.7/7 at 8.0 P.M. on 7th May.

Hdqrs and two companies 125th Rifles will remain in LANSDOWNE POST till Garhwal Bde has moved into front line trenches, when it will move up into assembly trenches just north of the RUE DU BOIS and await instructions, the C.O. getting into communication with Divisional Headquarters through Dehra Dun Brigade Report Centre on RUE DU BOIS.

Garhwal Brigade.

7. Garhwal Brigade, less two battalions Indian Infantry, will be in Divisional reserve and will be formed up in the second line trenches about CROIX BARBEE by 3.30 a.m. on the day of the attack.

The Brigade will be brought forward by the Brigade Commander to the vicinity of ORCHARD Redoubt on the RUE DU BOIS as the forward movement of Bareilly Brigade makes assembly trenches available for them.

Nos 3 & 4 Coys, S.& M. 107th Pioneers Two Coys 125th Rifles.

8. The troops as in margin will be assembled in shelter trenches north of road junction in M.32.d.7/7 by 3.45 AM on 8th May and will be held in readiness to advance under the orders of the C.R.E..

Five separate working parties, complete with tools, sandbags and carriers, will be organised by the C.R.E. to put localities captured in a state of defence.

Strengths and localities for which required are as below; The balance will remain in reserve under orders of C.R.E. at position of assembly.

Locality for which required.	Strehgth.
~~North~~ South end LA TOURELLE Village and cross roads.	1 Section S. & M. 2 platoons, 107th Pioneers
DISTILLERY	ditto.
Points 52 and 53	ditto.
FERME DU BIEZ	ditto.
Group of houses at points V.10, 50 & 51.	Half Coy., S. & M. One Coy, 107th Pioneers

4th Ind. Cav.

9. The 4th Indian Cavalry will rendezvous in ~~RUE DU PONCH~~ fields, clear of road near cross roads R 20 8/2 at ~~8.0~~ 7.0 a.m. on 8th May, and will remain ready to move mounted at short notice.

Infantry Bde Bomb-guns.

10. Brigade Bomb-gun Batteries will be prepared to advance under orders to be issued by G.O.s C. Brigades.

That of Dehra Dun Bde will be assembled in the ORCHARD on the evening of 7th May.

3 pdr Hotchkiss Battery.

11. The two 3 pdr Hotchkiss guns on lorries will rendezvous at CROIX BARBEE cross roads at 10.0 P.M. on 7th May. The O.C. will report for orders at Divisional Report Centre RUE DU PUITS at 5.0 A.M. 8th May.

That on the trailer will be in position at the barricade at the cross roads at S.5.c.1/8 by the same hour. Its lorry to be concealed on the road about S.4.b.6/3 and the gun run into position by hand.

The motors will move by the ESTAIRES - LA BASSEE Road.

Any subsequent orders to the trailer will be communicated through Lahore Division.

Wire cutting Bridging.

12. Our wire in front of our own trenches will be cut, and necessary bridges placed in position, during the hours of darkness

darkness on the night of the 7th/8th May, under orders of G.O.C. Dehra Dun Bde.
(Moon rises at 2.7 A.M.)

S.A.A.Supply 13. The following advanced depots of S.A.Ammunition have been established.-
1640 boxes in RUE DU BOIS near R.E.Depot.
120 boxes each in dugouts in rear of front trench at junction of communication trenches:-
(a) from south-east corner of ORCHARD,Redoubt,
(b) from North-east corner of ORCHARD Redoubt,
(c) from CRESCENT Trench.

To supplement such arrangements as Brigadiers may make for their own brigades, the supporting and reserve brigades will each detail their rear battalion to carry forward ammunition and establish further advanced depots in the fighting area at such localities as may be found suitable and possible.

Advanced R.E.Depot. 14. Advanced R.E.Depots will be formed at:-
(a) RUE DU BOIS.
(b) Form at M.32.d.7/7.

Bombs & Hand-grenades 15. An advanced depot for bombs (trench gun) and hand-grenades has been established 100 yards in rear of the right of position of assembly of Bareilly Bde.

The Divisional Trench-gun Officer and Divisional Hand-grenade Officer will each arrange that an adequate supply of projectiles is collected.

Medical. 16. A collecting station will be established between LANSDOWNE POST and the tramway line where it crosses FORESTERS LANE. Route for wounded returning from the front will be by the ORCHARD communication trench which runs from RUE DU BOIS to FORESTERS LANE along the north-east side of the tramway and some 100 yards from it. This trench will be reserved for return of wounded only after fighting has commenced, and will be marked accordingly.

Route from collecting station to ST VAAST Corner where an advanced dressing station will be established, will be alongside the tramway line.

A wagon rendezvous in this vicinity will be established and will be marked by the RED CROSS Flag.

Field Ambulances will be opened at VIEILLE CHAPELLE and ZELOBES.. Line of evacuation from wagon rendezvous is <u>via</u> OXFORD Road and WELLINGTON Road.

Distinguishing Marks. 17. Infantry battalions have been provided with red and black flags, 3' X 3', with a white ST Andrew's Cross (see annexed diagram) to assist in showing localities reached by our leading troops.

The distinguishing marks of the Divisions on our right and left, and of the Lahore Division, are as shown in annexure.

Sandbags. 18. Each man of the attacking infantry will carry two sandbags.

Masks. 19. Masks will be kept in readiness soaked in the soda solution by all troops in the front trenches and will be worn by assaulting troops.

Prisoners. 20. Prisoners will be handed by capters to the Lahore Division at Dehra Dun Brigade Report Centre, RUE DU BOIS.

Road Traffic. 21. As per attached sketch.

22.

Supply Depot. 22. An advanced emergency supply depot will be established at house at cross roads in M.32.d near head of tramway line.

Aeroplane Report Centre. 23. A station for receiving messages from aeroplanes will be established in the vicinity of the Divisional Hdqrs, R.15.b 4/5. The Camp Commandant will detail four men (British) to watch the station.

Setting Watches. 24 A Divisional Staff Officer will give the official time to all Brigades, C.R.A. and C.R.E. on the evening of 7th May.

Report Centres. 25.

Meerut Division. & CRA	M.26.d.7/8 after 9.0 p.m. on 7th May.
Dehra Dun Bde.	Ruined house on RUE DU BOIS S.10.a.8/7.
Bareilly Bde.	In close proximity to that of Dehra Dun Bde on RUE DU BOIS.
Garhwal Bde.	LANSDOWNE POST in S.4.a.2/3

Croxie.

Colonel,
General Staff,
MEERUT DIVISION.

Issued at to Signal Coy for distribution,

Copy No.		Copy No	
1 to	Indian Corps,	12	4th Ind. Cavalry
2	1st Division	13	107th Pioneers
3	7th Division	14	Meerut Signals
4	8th Division	15	No. 1 Group H.R.A.
5	Lahore Division	16	Meerut Div. Ammn Col.
6	Meerut Divnl Arty	17	Wing, R.F.Corps
7	Lahore Divnl Arty	18	A.A. & Q.M.G. Meerut
8	Meerut Divnl Engrs	19	A.D.M.S. Meerut
9	Dehra Dun Bde	20	G.S. Meerut
10	Garhwal Bde	21 to 24	War Diary and file
11	Bareilly Bde	25 to 35	Spare

25

FLAGS FOR MARKING POSITION OF ADVANCED TROOPS.

Lahore Division

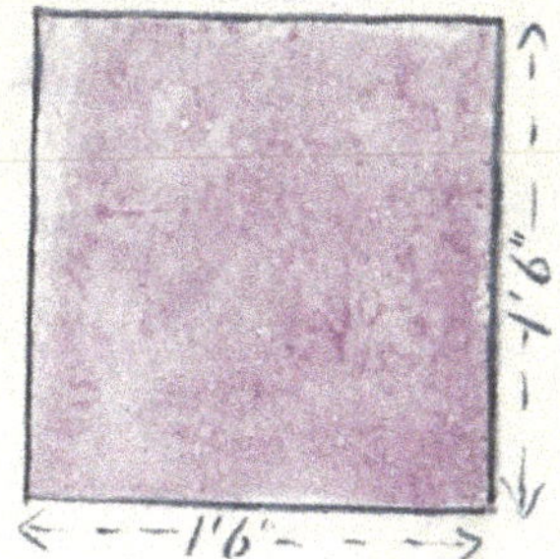

SECRET. No. G.405/36

Headquarters, Meerut Division.

7th May 1915.

Memorandum.

The following corrections are to be made to Meerut Division Operation Order No. 30 issued to you yesterday:-

(i) INFORMATION. Para 1, line 4. Alter "Advancing on DON" to read "Advancing to the line BAUVIN - DON"

(ii) Page 3, line 5. Fill in time - 5.20
line 6. ,, ,, 5.40
line 11. ,, ,, 5.40

Line 37, for "North end" read "South end".

(iii) Page 4, para 8. For "North end" read "South end".

(iv) Page 5, para 13, line 3 - for "164" read "1640"

(v) Page 4, para 9. Alter to read:-

"9. The 4th Indian Cavalry will rendezvous in fields, clear of road, near cross roads in R.20.c.8/2 at 7.0 a.m. on 8th May, and etc. etc. "

Note:- The time given in para 5, line 7, is intended to read "1.0 A.M." Please make this clear in your copy, if not already so.

Major,
General Staff,
Meerut Division.

To,
Dehra Dun Bde
Garhwal Bde
Bareilly Bde
C.R.A. Meerut
C.R.E. Meerut
Lt.-Col. R.Drake-Brockman.

G .405/36 SECRET Headquarters, Meerut Divn

7th May 1915.

Memorandum.

It is of course possible that the enemy might commence a heavy bombardment of our trenches before the at which we are to commence operations. Should this happen, the enemy's artillery would be taken on by our heavy group counter-batteries, but this would have nothing to say to our laid down programme which would still be adhered to. For instance, suppose the enemy began shelling us at 4.15, our counter-batteries will, if called on, take him on - but our wire cutting and other divisional artillery would wait for the laid down hour for their action to commence.

Cowie Colonel,
General Staff,
Meerut Division.

To,

Dehra Dun Bde
Garhwal Bde
Bareilly Bde
C.R.A. Meerut
C.R.A. Lahore
No. 1 Group H.A.R.

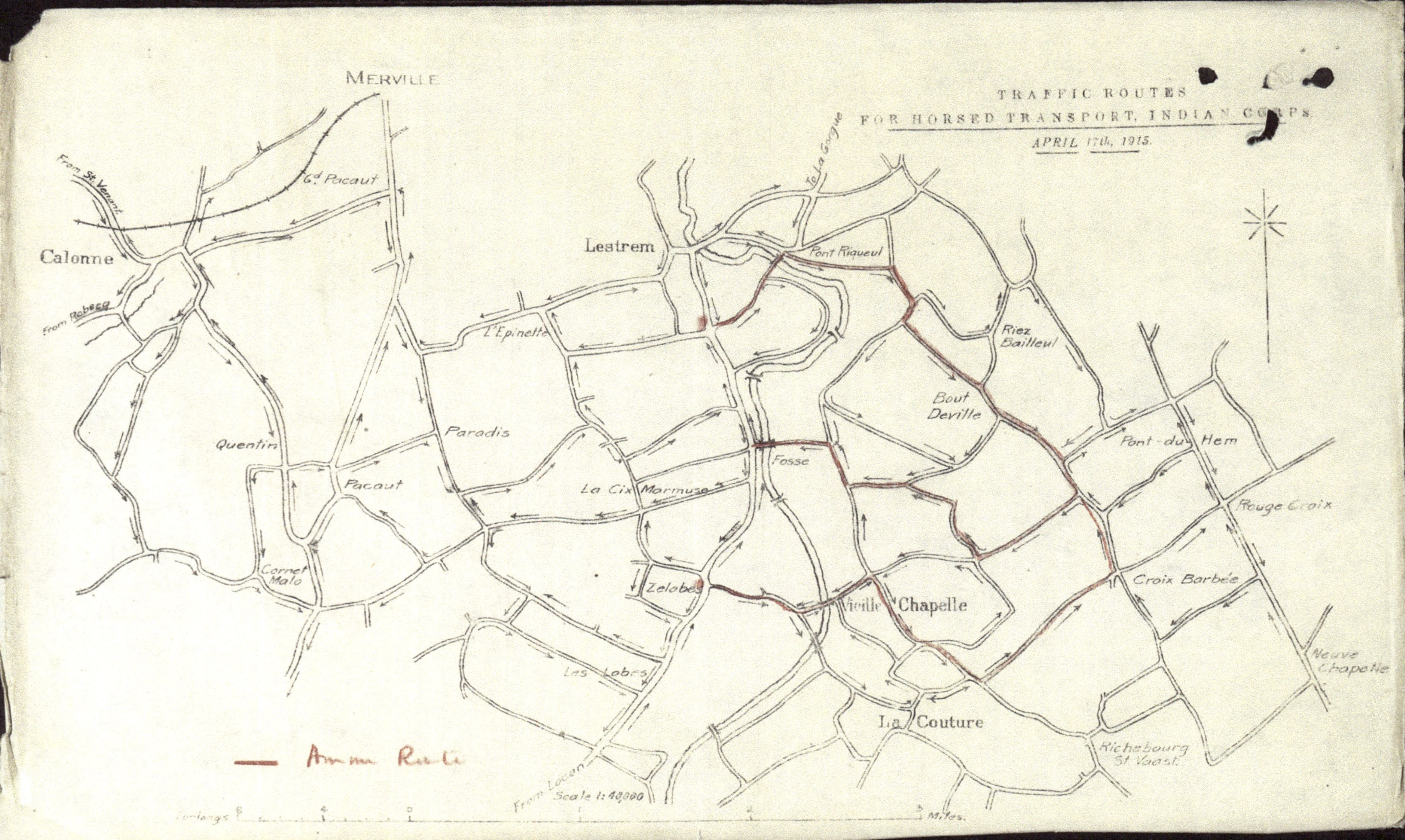
TRAFFIC ROUTES
FOR HORSED TRANSPORT, INDIAN CORPS
APRIL 17th, 1915.
MERVILLE
Gd Pacaut
From St Venant
Calonne
From Robecq
Lestrem
To La Gorgue
Pont Riqueul
Riez Bailleul
L'Epinette
Bout Deville
Paradis
Quentin
Pacaut
Fosse
La Cix Marmuse
Pont-du-Hem
Rouge Croix
Croix Barbée
Cornet Malo
Zelobes
Vieille Chapelle
Neuve Chapelle
Les Lobes
La Couture
Richebourg St Vaast
Ammn Route
From Locon
Scale 1: 40000
Furlongs 8 4 0 1 2 3 Miles.

APPENDIX 162

SECRET.

TACTICAL PROGRESS REPORT
6th May 1915.

****

1(a) ACTION BY OUR OWN ARTILLERY

5th Siege Battery fired on V.3.
10.30.a.m. 66th Battery registered trenches 51 e to 63.
During afternoon 19th Battery registered their new zone 46, 48, 49 to 65 and trench 51 e to 54. 28th Battery registered 46, 48, 49 to 55.
2.p.m. 5th Battery fired on trenches at 54 and V.9.
5.30.p.m. 2nd Battery carried out registration.
6.p.m. 14th Battery registered large shields-probably machine gun shields- near point 128.

1(b) ACTION BY HOSTILE ARTILLERY.

5.a.m. 10'5 c.m. Howitzer dropped 6 rounds in front of 14th Battery.
12.30.p.m. PIPSQUEAK active on houses, communication trench and barricade in RUE du BOIS.
1.p.m. New communicating trench in S 4 c was shelled.
1.30.p.m. and 3.p.m. PIPSQUEAK again active on RUE du BOIS.
3.15.p.m. 10'5 c.m. Howitzer shelled RUE du BOIS from S 10 a 7'7 to S 4 d 0'2.
3.30.p.m. PIPSQUEAK shelled road in M 33 b-attributed to extra traffic and working parties.
3.30.p.m. 15.c.m. Howitzer shelled PORT ARTHUR
Between 4 and 5.p.m. 15.c.m. or 21 c.m. Howitzer shelled PORT ARTHUR.
5.p.m. Neighbourhood of LA COUTURE shelled by 15 c.m. Howitzers.

2 INFORMATION.

FUZE:- Fuze of PIPSQUEAK which fell 60 yards S.E. of GOOD LUCK House on 4th May 1915 from direction of S.E. corner of BOIS du BIEZ, was set at range 3,650 metres.
HOSTILE AIRCRAFT.- N i l
MACHINE GUNS:- 14th Battery registered large shields(? Heavy Machine Guns) just N.W. point 128. They were in two batches of three each.

[signature]

Major R.A.

Brigade Major, Royal Artillery,
MEERUT DIVISION.

APPENDIX 163 4

SECRET. OPERATION ORDER No. 18 Copy No......
by
(6 pages)

Brigadier General R.St.C. LECKY, R.A., C.R.A. MEERUT Division.

Reference maps:- 6th May 1915.
Map of trenches 1/10,000.
BELGIUM and Part of FRANCE, Sheet 36 1/40,000, and
(Third Edition)
FRANCE-BETHUNE, 1/40,000.

INFORMATION. 1. The 1st Army is attacking on the 8th May 1915 with the object of breaking through the enemy's line and gaining the LA BASSEE - LILLE Road between LA BASSEE and FOURNES and then advancing to the line BAUVIN-DON.
The 1st Corps, retaining its right at GIVENCHY, will attack on a broad front in the vicinity of RICHEBOURG L'AVOUE with the object of advancing on RUE du MARAIS, LORGIES and ILLIES.
The Indian Corps will operate so as to cover the left of the 1st Corps, with the object of capturing the FERME DU BIEZ and of subsequently advancing to the line LIGNY LE GRAND-LA CLIQUETERIE FERME.
The 4th Corps will operate so as to break through the enemy's line in the vicinity of ROUGES BANCS with the object of:-
(i) Organising of defensive flank from the vicinity of LA CORDONNERIE FARM to FROMELLES.
(ii) Turning the AUBERS defences by an attack from the North East.
Its subsequent advance will be directed on LA CLIQUETERIE FARM with the object of effecting a junction with the Indian Corps.
The 2nd Cavalry Division will remain in readiness near ESTAIRES to act as the situation developes.
The LAHORE Division will hold the front allotted to the Indian Corps, less that portion from which the attack is to be delivered by the MEERUT Division. It will engage the enemy with rifle, machine-gun and trench-mortar fire, to assist in protecting the left flank of the MEERUT Division from counter-attack from the North.
LAHORE Division will also open a communication trench from the advanced listening post at point 61 to connect up with our attack if this becomes desirable.

INTENTION. 2. The MEERUT Division is making the attack to be delivered by the Indian Corps.
This attack is to be made on the enemy's trenches from the vicinity of the point V.6. to the vicinity of the point 56 as the first objective. On this front the enemy's wire will be cut by Artillery fire.
The second objective is the capture of LA TOURELLE and houses in the vicinity of point 50.
The third objective is the capture of the DISTILLERY and FERME du BIEZ.
Subsequent objectives will be the occupation of the BOIS du BIEZ, LIGNY LE PETIT, LIGNY LE GRAND and LA CLIQUETERIE, so as to join up with the 4th Corps.

ARTILLERY. 3. The MEERUT Divisional Artillery, reinforced by that of the LAHORE Division, one section Mountain Artillery, one section of Hotchkiss Motor Battery and certain heavy and siege Batteries will support the attack.
The attack will be prepared and supported as follows:-
1st PHASE:-
The assault of the enemy's first line trenches will be preceded by an Artillery bombardment, guns of the MEERUT Division performing tasks in accordance with attached schedule.

2nd PHASE.

2nd PHASE:-

While the Infantry are advancing on LA TOURELLE fire will be directed according to schedule.

3rd PHASE:-

Fire will be concentrated on the FERME du BIEZ in preparation for the assault on that place.

Barrages will be continued to prevent the approach of reinforcements.

Teams of the 13th Brigade R.F.A. will be brought up to a convenient locality in readiness for an advance in support of the Infantry at short notice.
9th Brigade R.F.A. is also to be held in readiness XXXXXX XXXXXXX to support this at longer notice.
Lines of advance within our lines are to be reconnoitred and spit locked and bridges laid out before the day of attack. Light bridges for crossing ditches to be carried, and personnel of each battery must be prepared to rapidly repair roads and remove obstacles encountered in any advance beyong our present lines.
Both Brigades R.F.A. detailed as above will have four miles reserve telephone cable with each battery.

Ammunition to be expended during the bombardment will be dumped previously to avoid conjestion of roads during the fight. Special attention will also be directed to ensure that the Brigades R.F.A. detailed to advance will do so with full supply of ammunition.

DEHRA DUN Brigade.

4. DEHRA DUN Brigade is, as first objective, carrying out the assault on the enemy's front line trenches on a three battalion front.

It will be formed up by 11.p.m. on the 7th May.
The three assaulting battalions will form up in front of our advanced trenches after the wire cutting portion of the bombardment is completed at 5.20 A.M. and before the bombardment of the enemy's trenches ceases at 5.40 A.M.
The assaulting line will, during this bombardment, move up as close to enemy's line as our shell fire permits, and will reach the enemy's front line trenches at the earliest possible moment after this bombardment is lifted to more distant objectives at 5.40 A.M.
The first line will not delay at these trenches but will push on against their further objectives. The capture of the enemy remaining in the trenches and bombing down the trenches to each flank, will be done under Brigade arrangements by succeeding lines.
After taking the first line trenches the battalion on the right will advance with its left on LA BASSEE Road, capturing the houses on the right side of the road, and press on to the Distillery.
The Centre Battalion will advance with its right on the LA BASSEE Road taking houses on the left of the Road, and press on to the LA TOURELLE-FERME du BIEZ Road.
The left Battalion, after crossing the trenches, will sieze the houses at points 52, 58 and on either side of the road leadingthence to FERME du BIEZ. It will also press on and sieze the FERME du BIEZ.
The battalion in Brigade reserve will be moved up, under orders of G.O.C. DEHRA DUN Brigade, into the front line trenches as the assaulting battalions clear them.
Bombing parties will be organised bythe G.O.C. DEHRA DUN Brigade to bomb outwards along enemy's trenches.

5. The force as per margin will be organised by G.O.C. GARHWAL Brigade as a complete unit with Staff, signalling arrangements and ammunition supply.

LT Colonel DRAKE-BROCKMAN,
The Garhwal Rifles.
2/8th Gurkha Rifles,
Two bomb guns of
Garhwal Brigade Battery.

It will be formed up in the two eastern blocks of assembly trenches immediately North of RUE du BOIS, by 1.a.m. on 9th May. This force is detailed for the

special

special purpose of securing the Eastern edge of the BOIS du BIEZ and capturing LA RUSSIE. It will move into the front line trenches as they are vacated by DEHRA DUN Brigade and carry out the above mission under orders of G.O.C. DEHRA DUN Brigade. It should not be used for the general support of the DEHRA DUN Brigade.

BAREILLY Brigade.

6. BAREILLY Brigade will be in support of DEHRA DUN Brigade and will, under orders of G.O.C. BAREILLY Brigade, occupy assembly positions of DEHRA DUN Brigade as they become available.
This forward move is to be made in communication with G.O.C. DEHRA DUN Brigade as it may either follow, or precede that of Lieut Colonel DRAKE-BROCKMAN'S detachment.

GARHWAL Brigade.

7. GARHWAL Brigade, less two battalions Indian Infantry, will be in Divisional Reserve and will be formed up in the second line trenches about CROIX BARBEE by 3.30.a.m. on the day of the attack.

3 pr. Hotchkiss Battery.

8. The two 3 pounder Hotchkiss guns on lorries will rendezvous at CROIX BARBEE cross roads at 10.p.m. on 7th May.
The O.C. will report for orders at Divisional Report Centre RUE DU PUITS at 6.a.m. 8th May.
That on the trailer will be in position at the barricade at the cross roads at S 5 c 1 8 by the same hour. Its lorry to be concealed on the road about S 4 b 8 3 and the gun run into position by hand.
The motors will move by the ESTAIRES - LA BASSEE Road.
Any subsequent orders to the trailer will be communicated through LAHORE Division.

WIRE-CUTTING BRIDGING.

9. Our wire in front of our own trenches will be cut, and necessary bridges placed in position, during the hours of darkness on the night 7th/8th May, under orders of G.O.C. DEHRA DUN Brigade. (Moon rises at 2.7.a.m.)

ADVANCED R.E. DEPOT.

10. Advanced R.E. Depots will be formed at:-
(a) RUE du BOIS.
(b) Farm at M 33 d 7 7.

MEDICAL.

11. A collecting station will be established between LANSDOWNE POST and the tramway line where it crosses FORESTERS LANE. Route for wounded returning from the front will be by the ORCHARD communication trench which runs from RUE DU BOIS to FORESTERS LANE along the North East side of the tramway and some 100 yards from it. This trench will be reserved for return of wounded only after fighting has commenced, and will be marked accordingly.
Route from collecting station to St VAAST Corner where an advanced dressing station will be established, will be alongside the tramway line.
A wagon rendezvous in this vicinity will be established and will be marked by the RED CROSS FLAG.
Field Ambulances will be opened at VIEILLE CHAPELLE and ZELOBES.

DISTINGUISHING MARKS.

12. Infantry Battalions have been provided with red and ~~blue~~ black flags 3' X 3', with a white St Andrew's Cross(See annexed diagram) to assist in showing localities reached by our leading troops.
The distinguishing marks of the Divisions on our right and left, and of the LAHORE Division, are as shown in annexure.

MASKS.

13. Masks will be kept in readiness soaked in the soda solution by all troops in the front trenches and will be worn by assaulting troops.

ROAD TRAFFIC.

14. As per attached sketch. (See one attached to APPENDIX 16(a))

SUPPLY DEPOT 15. An advanced emergency supply depot will be established at house at cross roads in M 32 d near head of tramway line

SETTING WATCHES. 16. A Divisional Staff Officer will give the official time to all Brigades, C.R.A., and C.R.E. on the evening of 7th May

REPORT CENTRES. 17.

MEERUT Division and C.R.A.	M 36 d 7 8 after 9.0.p.m. on 7th May.
DEHRA DUN Brigade	Ruined house on RUE du BOIS S 10 a 8 7.
BAREILLY Brigade	In close proximity to that of DEHRA DUN Brigade on RUE du BOIS.
GARHWAL Brigade	LANSDOWNE POST in S 4 a 2'2

Sd R.K. Lynch Staunton
Major R.A.
Brigade Major, Royal Artillery,
MEERUT DIVISION.

Issued at 7.a.m. 7th May 1915
by Motor cyclist.

Copy No. 1 to O.C. 4th Brigade R.F.A.

Copy No. 2 to O.C. 9th Brigade R.F.A.

Copy No. 3 to O.C. 13th Brigade R.F.A.

Copy No. 4 to WAR DIARY.

SECRET.

FLAGS FOR MARKING POSITION OF ADVANCED TROOPS.

MEERUT DIVISION.

LAHORE DIVISION.

1st DIVISION.

7th DIVISION.

8th DIVISION.

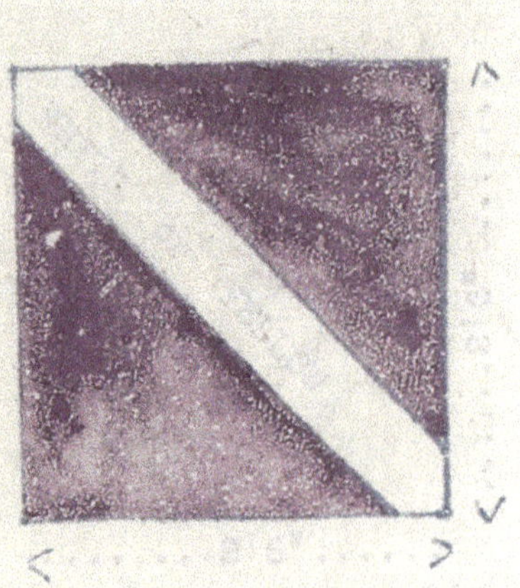

Infantry firing line.

2nd DIVISION.

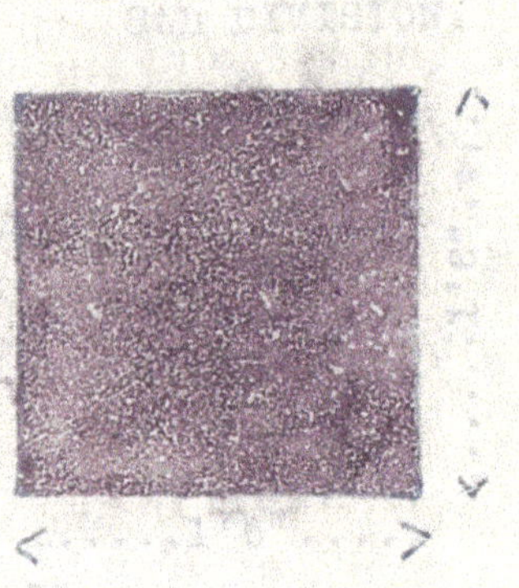

Flanking parties of Bombers.

SECRET

MEERUT DIVISIONAL ARTILLERY

BARRAGES [illegible] TO BE FORMED - REVISED [illegible]

1st PHASE [illegible] to 0.20 [illegible] ASSAULT

4th 1 Battery trench [illegible]
4th 1 Battery trench [illegible]
4th 1 Battery trench 131 to 140 and up communicating trenches to BOIS du BIEZ

(a) (1 Section on road 48, V 18, V 19 [illegible]
9th 1 Battery (1 Section on road V 19, V 15 [illegible]
(1 Section on road V 11, V 13, V 15
9th 2 Batteries trench 48, 48, 49 to 63.

13th 1 Battery (1 Section searches road from Q 27 towards LA BASSEE
(2 Sections on trench LA TOURELLE to V 5 a
13th 1 Battery V 10, V 9 to V 10 a
13th 1 Battery (1 Section searches trench 64 to V 8 a
(2 Sections on trench V 5 to V 9 a employing some H.E. and a rather quick rate of fire.

2nd PHASE 0.20 to 0.40 [illegible] INFANTRY ASSAULT

4th 1 Battery 131 to 63
4th 1 Battery 65 to 51 [illegible]
4th 1 Battery 131 to 140 and up communicating trenches to BOIS du BIEZ

9th 1 Battery on roads round [illegible] du BIEZ as at (a) above
9th 1 Battery trench 48, 49, 48 to 63
9th 1 Battery trench 52 [illegible] to 64

13th 1 Battery (1 Section searches road from Q 27 towards LA BASSEE
(2 Sections on trench from LA TOURELLE to V 5 a
13th 1 Battery V 12, V 9 to V 10 a
13th 1 Battery (1 Section searches trench 64 to V 8 [illegible]
(2 Sections on trench V 8 to V 9 a

3rd PHASE 0.40 to 1.15 [illegible] INFANTRY [illegible] LA TOURELLE [illegible]

4th 1 Battery trench 131, 130 to 63 [illegible] rate of fire
4th 2 Batteries 131 to 140 and up communicating trenches to BOIS du BIEZ

9th 1 Battery road 48 to V 19 [illegible]
9th 1 Battery to remain in observation but prepared to [illegible] 131, 130 to 63 if necessary
9th 1 Battery in observation

13th 1 Battery (2 Sections search LA BASSEE Road from LA TOURELLE [illegible]
(1 Section on trench LA TOURELLE to V 5 a
13th 1 Battery on road and trench V 12, V 9 to LA [illegible]
13th 1 Battery in observation

4th PHASE [illegible]

4th 2 Batteries trench 131, 130 to 63 [illegible]
4th 1 Battery 131 to 140 and up [illegible] BIEZ (to double [illegible])
2 Brigades in [illegible]

When searching or sweeping roads, rounds should be [illegible] side of road, and short or over [illegible]

APPENDIX 163(a)

SECRET

No. 405/45-G

Headquarters, Meerut Division.

7th ~~xxxxx~~ May 1915.

Memorandum.

Operations ordered for tomorrow are postponed. Division Hdqrs will not move to report centre tonight. Acknowledge by wire.

Crowe

Colonel
General Staff,
Meerut Division.

CRA Meerut

S E C R E T.

No. G.405/55

Headquarters, Meerut Division.

8th May 1915.

Memorandum.

The operations ordered in Meerut Division Operation Order No. 39 of 6th/7th instants, and postponed (vide my G.405/45 of yesterday) will be commenced as laid down in the above Operation Order, tomorrow morning 9th May 1915. Please acknowledge by wire.

Crowe

Colonel,
General Staff,
Meerut Division

To,

CRA Meerut

APPENDIX 164.

SECRET.

TACTICAL PROGRESS REPORT

7th May 1915.

1(a) ACTION BY OUR OWN ARTILLERY.
Very thick and misty, observation quite impossible before 7.30.a.m. and for certain objects up to 8 and 9.a.m.
7th Battery scored 6 direct hits on V. 15.
12 noon. 8th Battery fired on trenches V 9e to V 6.
1.10.p.m. and 3.10.p.m. 14th Battery fired on working party in communicating trench.
During the afternoon 9th Brigade Batteries registered their zones.
3.p.m. Two Batteries of Northern Group shelled trenches to keep down rifle fire on our aeroplane.
5th Siege Battery checked registration on FERME du BIEZ, House 50, V.7., obtaining a direct hit on 50.

1(b) ACTION BY HOSTILE ARTILLERY.
11.30.a.m. and 12.15.p.m. 21 c.m. Howitzer shelled houses just behind CRESCENT Trench.
12 noon to 2.p.m. 28th Battery O.P. near SNIPER's House, heavily shelled by PIPSQUEAK, also barricade and trenches at PORT ARTHUR.
1.20.p.m. PIPSQUEAK scored 2 direct hits on 7th Battery O.P. in NEUVE CHAPELLE.
3.p.m. to 5.p.m. At intervals PIPSQUEAK shelled PORT ARTHUR end of RUE du BOIS.
Between 4.p.p.m and 5.p.m. 21.c.m. Howitzer shelled PORT ARTHUR, and CRESCENT Trench, switching until rounds fell between PICKET House and RUE du BOIS.
4.45.p.m. PIPSQUEAK dropped shell close to GOOD LUCK House.

2. INFORMATION.
HOSTILE AIRCRAFT:- None were seen.
VISUAL SIGNALLING:- Carried out during the day by 8th Battery, with good results.

R. V. Lynch-Staunton

Major R.A.

Brigade Major, Royal Artillery,
MEERUT DIVISION.

APPENDIX 165.

Meerut D.A. (2)

TIME TABLE - INDIAN CORPS.

Line to be broken through V.6 to 56.

0:0 -- 0:20.

GUNS	FROM	TO	OBJECTIVES.	REMARKS.
1 15" How:	0:0	0:20	Fme. de BIEZ.	
1 9·2" How:	0:0	0:20	Houses at points 50 &51.	
1 9·2" How:	0:0	0·20	LE TOURELLE and TOULOTTE.	
1 9·2" How:	0:0	0·20	Houses at V9E.	
1 6" How. Secn.	0:0	0:20	Houses at points V10 V11.	
2 6" How. Secns.	0:0	0:20	Points V6 & Keep.	
1 6" How. Secn.	0:0	0:20	Houses at points 63, 64.	
3 18 pr. Bdes.	0:0	0:20	Wire cutting.	
1 bty. 18 pr.	0:0	0:20	Barrage V6, V9E, 54 to V8E.	
1 bty. 18 pr.	0:0	0:20	Barrage V10E to V10.	
1 bty 18 pr.	0:0	0:20	Barrage V5E to LE TOURELLE X Rds. Barrage Q27 along LA BASSEE Rd.	
1 bty. 18 pr.	0:0	0:20	Barrage V11 V15 V19 46.	
2 btys. 18 pr.	0:0	0:20	Barrage 46-49-65.	
1 bty. 18 pr.	0:0	0:20	Barrage 51E-63.	
2 btys. 18 pr.	0:0	0:20	Barrage 63-131-140- and 127.	
1 Bde. 4·5" How.	0:10	0:20	Trenches 58-54-51E-54E- 53.	

TIME TABLE - INDIAN CORPS.

Line to be broken through V.6 to 56.

0:20 -- 0:40

GUNS	FROM	TO	OBJECTIVES	REMARKS
1 15" How.	0:20	0:40	Fme. de BIEZ	
1 9.2" How.	0:20	0:40	V10 and V11	
1 9.2" How.	0:20	0:40	LE TOURELLE.	
1 Secn. 6" How.	0:20	0:40	Houses at points 63 & 64.	
1 Secn. 6" How.	0:20	0:40	Houses at V9E.	
1 6" How.) 1 Bde. 4.5" How.)	0:20	0:40	Bombardment of trenches.	
1 bty. 18 pr.	0:20	0:40	Barrage V6-V9E-54 to V8E.	
1 bty. 18 pr.	0:20	0:40	Barrage V10E to V10.	
1 bty. 18 pr.	0:20	0:40	(Barrage from V5E to (LE TOURELLE X Rds. (Q27 along LA BASSEE (Rd.	
1 bty. 18 pr.	0:20	0:40	Barrage V11-V15-V19 -46.	
2 btys. 18 pr.	0:20	0:40	Barrage 46-49-65.	
2 btys. 18 pr.	0:20	0:40	Barrage 56-53-52-63.	
2 btys. 18 pr.	0:20	0:40	Barrage 58-54-63	
2 btys. 18 pr.	0:20	0:40	Barrage 63-131-140-127	
1 bty. 18 pr.	0:20	0:40	Barrage V7-60.	
1 bty. 18 pr.	0:20	0:40	Barrage 54-58-to West.	
1 bty. 18 pr.	0:20	0:40	Barrage 53-49) 31 to S.E.) 50 to V14.)	
1 bty. 18 pr.	0:20	0:40	Barrage R17,R22 to V15.	
1 bty. 18 pr.	0:20	0:40	Barrage road Fme. du BIEZ to LORGIES.	
1 bty. 18 pr.	0:20	0:40	Barrage road V20 to LIGNY LE PETIT.	

TIME TABLE - INDIAN CORPS.

Line to be broken through V.6 to 56.

At 0:40 Infantry assault and push on to the line running N.E. and S.W. through R of RICHEBOURG L'AVOUE.
It is assumed that the Infantry make good the cross roads at V7 at 1:15.

GUNS	FROM	TO	OBJECTIVES	REMARKS.
1 15" How.	0:40	1:15	BEAU PUITS.	Up till 1:10.
1 9.2" How.	0:40	1:15	Fme. de BIEZ.	Up till 1:45.
1 9.2" How.	0:40	1:15	Distillery.	Up till 1:20.
1 Secn. 6"How.	0:40	1:15	Houses at V7.	
1 Secn. 6"How.	0:40	1:15	Houses at V10 V11.	
1 Secn. 6"How.	(0:40 (0:55	0:55 1:15	Houses at 50 & 51. FERME du BIEZ.	
1 Secn. 6"How.	(0:40 (0:55	0:55 1:15	Houses V9E Distillery.	
1 bty. 4.5" How.	0:40	1:15	(Points 53-52, houses (at 49. Points 63 & (64. Point 46.	Lifting as required.
1 bty. 4.5" How.	0:40	1:15	(Points V10 V9 to (V10E. Points V7, (V8 V12.	Lifting as required.
1 bty. 4.5" How.	0:40	1:15	(V6 to V9E. V5E to (LE TOURELLE X Rds.	Lifting as required.
1 bty. 18 pr.	0:40	1:15	LE TOURELLE X road. Q27 along road.	
1 bty. 18 pr.	0:40	1:15	Barrage V7 V8 V12.	
2 Btys. 18 pr.	0:40	1:15	Barrage R17 R22 V14 V15.	
1 bty. 18 pr.	0:40	1:15	Barrage V11 to LORGIES.	
1 bty. 18 pr.	0:40	1:15	Barrage V7 to V9E.	
1 bty. 18 pr.	0:40	1:15	Barrage 46 to V19.	
1 bty. 18 pr.	0:40	1:15	Barrage from V19 to LIGNY LE PETIT.	
2 btys. 18 pr.	0:40	1:15	Barrage line 46-49-65.	
1 bty. 18 pr.	0:40	1:15	Barrage line S11 b Trench.	
1 bty. 18 pr.	0:40	1:15	Barrage line 63 to 51E.	
2 btys. 18 pr.	0:40	1:15	Barrage line 63-131.	
2 btys. 18 pr.	0:40	1:15	Barrage line 131-140.	

TIME TABLE - INDIAN CORPS.

Line to be broken through V.6 to 53.

From occupation of LE TOURELLE cross roads to capture of Fme. du BIEZ at 1-45 and DISTILLERY at 1-35.

GUNS	FROM	TO	OBJECTIVES	REMARKS.
1 15" How.	1:10	1:45	LIGNY LE GRAND.	
2 9.2" How.	1:20	1:45	FERME du BIEZ.	
1 6" How. bty.	1:15	1:45	FERME du BIEZ.	
1 6" How. bty.	1:15	1:45	Distillery and then Fme. du BIEZ.	
2 4.5"How. btys.	1:15	1:45	House at R17-Trench R22-Fme. du BIEZ.	
1 4.5"How. bty.	1:15	1:45	Trench at 46-49-64E Houses 63-64.	
2 Btys. 18 pr.	1:15		63-131.	
2 Btys. 18 pr.	1:15		131-140.	
2 Btys. 18 pr.	1:15		63-49-46.	
1 Bty. 18 pr.	1:15		46 to V19.	
1 Bty. 18 pr.	1:15		V19 to LIGNY LE PETIT.	
1 Bty. 18 pr.	1:15		V13 to LORGIES.	
1 Bty. 18 pr.	1:15		Q27 to Q30.	
2 Btys. 18 pr.	1:15		Q29 to R23.	

TIME TABLE - INDIAN CORPS.

Line to be broken through V.6 to 56.

1:45 -- 2:10.

GUNS	FROM	TO	OBJECTIVES	REMARKS.
1 15" How.	1:45	2:10	LIGNY LE GRAND.	
1 9.2" How.	1:45	2:10	V10 V20.	
1 9.2" How.	1:45	2:10	LIGNY LE PETIT.	
1 9.2" How.	1:45	2:10	BEAU PUITS.	
1 9.2" How.	1:45	2:10	LORGIES.	

S E C R E T.

No.G.405/38

Headquarters, Meerut Division.

7th May 1915.

*****

<u>MEMORANDUM</u>.

A mortar for firing smoke balls is being sent to you by Captain Stewart who will explain how it is employed.

The signals are to be used by Colonel DRAKE-BROCKMAN to intimate the position of his command as it advances through the BOIS DU BIEZ and to guide the troops of the LAHORE Division, and the artillery supporting him switching their fire forward in front of his advance.

There are three signal bombs:-

(i) Giving out green smoke and white stars.
(ii) Giving out yellow smoke.
(iii) Giving out a single trail of yellow smoke coming down.

When any one of these signals are observed above the trees of the BOIS, fire from our trenches and from the Artillery covering Colonel DRAKE-BROCKMAN'S advance will be carried well forward and clear of the vicinity where the smoke signal has appeared.

It is left to Colonel DRAKE-BROCKMAN to decide when he will show the signals, but he is reminded that they will be more easily seen if fired from his left flank.

Colonel.
General Staff,
MEERUT DIVISION.

To:-
DEHRA DUN BRIGADE.

Copy to:-
LAHORE DIVISION.
C. R. A. LAHORE DIVISION.
C. R. A. MEERUT DIVISION.
No 1 Group. H.A.R.
No II Group H. A. R.
GARHWAL BRIGADE.
BAREILLY BRIGADE.

SECRET.

The following position marking flags will be used by Divisions as under :-

1ST DIVISION.
Flags 5-ft by 3-ft, red with white perpendicular stripe, on 9-ft poles.

2ND DIVISION.
Yellow screens, 1 per coy, 6-ft by 3-ft.
Yellow 3-ft by 5-ft flags on 3-ft poles.
Yellow 5-ft by 3-ft flags on 6-ft - 8-ft poles.

X LONDON DIVISION.
Sandbag cloth disc 2-ft in diameter, black cross in centre, on 12-ft pole.

MEERUT DIVISION.
Flags 3-ft by 3-ft, white diagonal cross, south and eastern triangles red, north and western triangles black.

LAHORE DIVISION.
Large yellow flags, 16-ft square.
16 inches not ft.

S E Holland Major, G.S.,
for B.G.G.S., 1st Corps.

6th May, 1915.

Go. CRA Meerut

APPENDIX 165(a)

Operation Order No.44 Copy No. 3
by
Brig.Genl. F.E.Johnson,C.M.G.,D.S.O.,R.A.,
Commanding Lahore Div. Artillery.

7th May 1915.

Ref.Maps 1/10,000
Sheet 36 S.W.1/20000
1/40,000 Bethune Sheet.

1. The 1st Army will attack tomorrow,with the object of gaining LA BASSEE - LILLE road and advancing to line BAUVIN-DON.
1st Corps will attack with the object of advancing on LORGIES and ILLIES.
Indian Corps will cover left of 1st Corps with object of capturing the FERME du BIEZ and of advancing to LIGNY le GRAND - LA CLIQUETERIE FERME .
4th Corps will attack so as to break through enemy's line at ROUGESBANCS,attacking AUBERS from the N.E. and afterwards effecting a junction with Indian Corps at LA CLIQUETERIE FERME.
2nd Cavalry Division will be in readiness at ESTAIRES.
Lahore Division will hold the front allotted to the Indian Corps less that portion from which the attack is to be made by Meerut Division. It will protect Left flank of Meerut Dvn.by rifle and trench mortar fire.

2. The attack by Meerut Dvn.will be made from V 6 to 56 as first objective .
2nd Objective capture of LA TOURELLE and houses near 50.
3rd Objective Distillery and FERME du BIEZ.
Subsequent objectives BOIS du BIEZ,LIGNY LE PETIT,LIGNY LE GRAND and LA CLIQUETERIE.

3. Lahore and Meerut Dvl.Art.,1 Section Mtn.Art.,1 Sect. Hotchkiss Motor Bty and certain Heavy Art. will support the attack
1st Phase Assault of enemy's first line trenches preceded by Art. bombardment,according to attached schedule. This comprises (a) Destruction of enemy's obstacles,(b) Battering of enemy's trenches;(c) Battering of enemy's strong points;(d) Barrage against reinforcements from BOIS du BIEZ, also from N.E.,E and S.E.;(e) engaging enemy's batteries by Heavy Art.
Second Phase During advance on LA TOURELLE,following will be engaged(a) LA TOURELLE and Distillery;(b) houses near 50, (c) FERME du BIEZ;(d) S.W. edge of BOIS du BIEZ and approaches from LIGNY and LORGIES.
Third Phase Concentration on FERME du BIEZ in preparation for the assault,Barrages to prevent approach of reinforcements.
Section No. 5 Bty. Pack Arty.will during the bombardment operate from a position near LANSDOWNE Post and will afterwards advance in close support of the Ifantry attack taking order from the G.O.C. DEHRA DUN BDE.
Ammtn:to be expended during bombardment will be dumped in accordance with orders already issued.
The Lahore Div. will be supported by certain Batteries of Meerut Dvl.Art. and later by certain Btys. of Lahore Dvl. Art. 1st Highland Bde.will be ready to support Lahore Dvn. if called upon.
Art. Bombardment will commence at 5 a.m.,Ifty. assault at 5.40 a.m.

4. The DEHRA DUN BDE.will carry out the assault on enemy's front line trenches,BAREILLY BDE. will be in support,GARHWAL Bde.,less 2 Btns.will be in Dvl. Reserve.
JULLUNDUR ~~XXXXXXXXXXXXX~~ BDE.will hold the defensive line from PORT ARTHUR northwards . Ferozepore Bde. will be in a position of readiness ,SIRHIND BDE will be in Corps Reserve.

5. A special force of 2 Ind.Ifty. Regts.under Lt.Col Drake Brockman, is detailed for purpose of securing Eastern edge of the BOIS du BIEZ and capturing RUSSIE. An officer of the 11th F.A. Bde. will accompany this special force in order that Art.fire may be stopped or reopened as required.

6. S.A.A.will be dumped on East side of PONT LOGY Road opposite CURZON Post and in CURZON Post. 5th F.A.Bde. will supply Jullundur ,11th Sirhind;and 18th Ferozepore Bdes.

7. Medical No. 8 B.F.A.will open at RUE DU PONCH, No.112 I.F.A, at CROIX MARMUSE,with dressing Station on LORETTO Road,M.27.d.

8. G.O.C.,R.A.,Lahore Divn.will be in command of all the ~~xxx~~. Field Arty.and Siege How Btys. supporting Indian Corpsuntil the time when Meerut Dvl. Art. advance.

9. Reports Centres. Advanced LAHORE - M.14.b.10.0.after 10 p.m.
the 7th inst. MEERUT - M.23.d.7.8. after 9 p.m.
on the 7th inst. Lahore and Meerut Dvl.Art. at
M.23.d.9.9. after
9 p.m.the 7th.
Jullundur Bde. - M.35.c.9.8. after 10 p.m.
the 7th inst. Ferozepore Bde.- M.34.b.5.6. after 5 a.m.
on the 8th inst. Sirhind Bde. CROIX MARMUSE
GARHWAL Bde. LANDSDOWNE POST-S.4.a.8.8.

Issued at 5 p.m.

A M [illegible] Major

Brigade Major RA
Lahore Division.

Copy No. 1 to Lahore Dvn.
2 Meerut Dvn.
3 " " Arty.
4. 7th Dvl. Arty.
5. 5th F.A.Bde.
6 11th F.A.Bde.
7 18th F.A.Bde.
8 43rd How.Bde.
9 6th Siege Bde.
10 L.Dvl. Am. Column
11 1st Highland Bde.
12 Section No. 5 Pack Art.
13 Lt.Col. Drake Brockman
14 3 Spare.

SECRET. LAHORE DIVISIONAL ARTILLERY. Copy No. 3

TIME TABLE.

* * * * * * * * * * *

1st Phase ---------0 to 0.10', 0.10' to 0.20'.

5th Bde. 3 Btys. Wire cutting, 0 to 0.10', 54 to 58 from road to road. 0.10' to 0.20' 56 to V.3.
18th Bde. 3 Btys. Ditto.
11th Bde. 1 Bty. Ditto.
2 Btys. 0.10' to 0.20' 56 to V.6.
43rd Bde. 3 Btys. 0 to 0.10' Observation, 0.10' to 0.20' 58, 54, 51c, 54c, 53.
6th Bde. 1 Siege Bty. 1 Sect. Houses 33,34. 1 Sect. V.10, V.11.
1 Siege Bty. 1 Sect. V.6. 1 Sect - Koop.
1st Highland Bde. 3 Btys. Front from 140 to opposite CHAPIGNY.
Section No. 5 Pack Artillery. 0 to 0.10' Observation 0.10' to 0.20' Houses 52, 53 and road 53 towards V.11.

2nd Phase 0.20' to 0.40'.

5th Bde. 1 Bty. 53, 52 to 63.
1 Bty. Trench 63 towards 131.
1 Bty. Road V.19 - LIGNY le PETIT.
11th Bde. 1 Bty. 49 towards 53, V.14 towards 50.
1 Bty. V.15 along road towards LORGIES up to R.25.
1 Bty. Trench 46,48,49 to 65.
18th Bde. 1 Bty. V.15, R.14, R.22 towards LA TOURELLE and up to R.17.
1 Bty. V.7 to 60.
1 Bty. Trench 54,58 and continuation West of Road.
43rd Bde. 3 Btys. Trenches behind cut wire from 53 (inclusive) - 60 (exclusive) and from 50 yds. of 60 to S.10.d.5.
6th Bde. 1 Siege Bty. 1 Sect. 63,64. 1 Sect. House V.9.c.
1 Siege Bty. Trenches behind cut wire as follows:-
1 Sect. 60 (inclusive) to 50 yds. to right. 1 Sect. from 50 yds. North of 60 to 50 yds. to left.
1st Highland Bde. 3 Btys. Front 140 to opposite CHAPIGNY.
Sect. No. 5 Bty. Pack. Arty. 52,53 road 53 towards V.11.

Phase 3. ....0.40' to 0.55' and 1.15'.

5th Bde. 1 Bty. 63 to 51.c.
1 Bty. 43, 48, 49 - 65.
1 Bty. Road V.19 - LIGNY le PETIT.
11th Bde. 1 Bty. 49 towards 53, V.14 - 50.
1 Bty. V.15 along road towards LORGIES up to R.25.
1 Bty. Trench 46, 48, 49 - 65.
18th Bde. 2 Btys. V.15, R.14, R.22 towards LA TOURELLE and up to R.17.
1 Bty. V.7 to V.9.c.
43rd Bde. 1 Bty. 52,53 Houses 49, 33, 34, 46 lifting as required.
1 Bty. V.9, V.10, V.10.c., V.7, V.8, V.12.
1 Bty. V.6 - V.9.c. and V.5.c. - LA TOURELLE Cross Roads.
6th Bde. 1 Siege Bty. 1 Sect. Houses 50, 51 till 0.55' then Fe. du BIEZ till 1.15'. 1 Sect. V.10, V.11 till 1.15'
1 Siege Bty. 1 Sect. V.7 till 1.15'. 1 Sect. V.9.c. till 0.55' then Distillery till 1.15.

Phase 4. ---------1.15' to 1.45'.

5th Bde. 1 Bty. Roads Q.27. towards LA BASSEE.
1 Bty. Observation.
1 Bty. Road V.19. to LIGNY LE PETIT.
11th Bde. 1 Bty. 46,48,49 - 65.
1 Bty. V.15 along road towards LORGIES up to R.25.
1 Bty. 46,48,49 - 65.
18th Bde. 2 Btys. Q.27. - R.23.
1 Bty. 46 to V.19.
43rd Bde. 1 Bty. 63,64, trench 64.c., 49,48 - 46.
2 Btys. Houses R.17. to trench R.22, V.14. to Fe. du BIEZ.
6th Bde. 1 Siege Bty. Fe. du BIEZ. 1 Siege Bty. Distillery afterwards Fe. du BIEZ.

APPENDIX 166

S E C R E T .

TACTICAL PROGRESS REPORT.
8th May 1915.

1(a) ACTION BY OUR OWN ARTILLERY.

4.30.a.m. 4th Brigade Batteries registered on wire opposite "B", "C", and "D" Sub-sections as a division.
9.30.a.m. 14th Battery fired on houses 123 and 124, where sniping was taking place.
10.10.a.m. 66th Battery scored a direct hit on FERME du BIEZ.
4.30.p.m. 14th Battery fired on house 140, where Infantry had reported Machine Gun concealed in house. Machine Gun located in large hole in lower half of wall of house at N.E. corner- smoke of discharge seen.
In the Afternoon- 20th Battery registered C.R.A's Farm T 2 b 1'6 and HAUTE POMMEREAU.
19th and 28th Batteries carried out useful registration on trenches.
6.45.p.m. 66th Battery fired 3 rounds at working party at S 11 b 2'2.

1(b) ACTION BY HOSTILE ARTILLERY.

Enemy's guns much less active than usual throughout the day.
11.a.m. PIPSQUEAK fired a few rounds near CRESCENT Trench.
5.p.m. PIPSQUEAK shelled East end of RUE du BOIS in direction of ORCHARD and PORT ARTHUR.
5.45.p.m. 10'5 c.m. Howitzer shelled PORT ARTHUR.

2. INFORMATION.

AIRCRAFT:- 8.5.a.m. AVIATIK low, bearing 160°, engaged 15 rounds, then turned E.
8.35.a.m. AVIATIK, low, bearing 160°, engaged 24 rounds turned E. and re-appeared at same bearing re-engaged 7 rounds then disappeared E.
10.30.a.m. AVIATIK, high, bearing 160°, engaged 7 rounds turned S, out of sight.
10.30.a.m. AVIATIK, high, bearing 160°, out of range travelled S.
SNIPING:- A little sniping round about PIQUET House.
FRENCH ATTACK:- An 11.p.m. report from Indian Corps states French attack proceeding well, 2 lines of trenches captured and morale of troops excellent.

H.M. Lynch-Staunton
Major R.A.

Brigade Major, Royal Artillery,
MEERUT DIVISION.

"A" Form. Army Form C. 2121.

MESSAGES AND SIGNALS.

No. of Message________

Prefix SB Code RFG m.	Words 91	Charge	APPENDIX 167	Recd. at 10 557 m.
Office of Origin and Service Instructions.	Sent		This message is on a/c of:	Date 7/G 9/5/15
71GR	At ________ m.		________ Service.	From
Priority	To			
	By		(Signature of "Franking Officer")	By Astaugh[illegible]

TO — CRA Meerut

*Sender's Number	Day of Month	In reply to Number	AAA
G15	9th		

Indian Corps directs that zero will be two pm aaa The assault will take place at two forty PM aaa Bareilly Bde will take over the role of Dehra Dun Bde aaa Gharwal Bde that of Bareilly Bde aaa Dehra Dun Bde will pass into reserve 9th Gurkhas to join the Gharwal Bde aaa Gharwal Bde to take over the Smoke signals from Dehra Dun Bde aaa Composition of Col DRAKE - BROCKMANS detachment to remain unchanged also its role is unaltered

From Advanced Meerut

Place

Time 10.28 am

The above may be forwarded as now corrected. (Z)

Censor. Signature of Addressor or person authorised to telegraph in his name

* This line should be erased if not required.

C27642 P. G. Ltd. Wt. W14142/641—20,000 3/15. Forms C2121/10.

APPENDIX 168

No.646-R.A.(L).

Headquarters Divisional Artillery,
MEERUT DIVISION.

S E C R E T.

9th May 1915.

To,
The Officers Commanding,
4th Brigade R.F.A.
9th Brigade R.F.A.
13th Brigade R.F.A.
MEERUT Divisional Ammunition Column.

The following from MEERUT Division begins:-

"Indian Corps directs that operations will be resumed this afternoon-
ZERO will be 2.p.m.
The assault will take place at 2.40.p.m.. BAREILLY Brigade will take over the role of the DEHRA DUN Brigade. GARHWAL Brigade that of the BAREILLY Brigade. DEHRA DUN Brigade will pass into reserve.
9th Gurkhas to join the GARHWAL Brigade. GARHWAL Brigade to take over the SMOKE SIGNALS from DEHRA DUN Brigade. Composition of Colonel DRAKE-BROCKMAN's detachment to remain unchanged also its ~~xx~~ role is unaltered. Ends.
In accordance with above instructions batteries of MEERUT Divisional Artillery will at 2.p.m. take up the same tasks as were originally arranged for ZERO.
LAHORE Division Batteries will however engage 1st line trenches instead of Wire Cutting and will endeavour to knock out Machine Guns.
No. 1 Group Heavy A.R. are arranging to put one "Mother" on "KEEP" and three "Mother's"(if available) on trench V 9 c, V 6 c, V 6.
Fire will be intense from 2.30.p.m. to 2.40.p.m. This does not apply to MEERUT Division Batteries which will maintain normal rate of fire unless situation seems to demand a more rapid rate.
At 2.40.p.m. the assault will take place, and all batteries will take up tasks assigned for the 3rd Phase.
Ammunition expenditure to be strictly economical up to 2.p.m.

C W Lynch-Staunton

Major R.A.

Brigade Major, Royal Artillery,
MEERUT Division.

"A" Form. Army Form C. 2121.

MESSAGES AND SIGNALS.

No. of Message

Prefix ___ Code ___ m.	Words	Charge	This message is on a/c of: APPENDIX 169	Recd. at ___ m.
Office of Origin and Service Instructions.	Sent		___ Service.	Date
	At ___ m.			From
	To			
	By		(Signature of "Franking Officer")	By

TO { O.C. 4th Bde / O.C. 9th Bde / O.C. 13th Bde

* Sender's Number	Day of Month	In reply to Number	AAA
BM27	9		

Reference my 646 RA (4) of today the following amendment has now been ordered AAA Zero will now be 3-30 p m and the Assault will take place at 4 p.m. AAA Programme as issued will be adhered to with this alteration AAA First Rifles is co-operating

From BMRA
Place
Time 1 p.m.

The above may be forwarded as now corrected. (Z)

Censor. Signature of Addressor or person authorised to telegraph in his name [signature]

* This line should be erased if not required.

C27642 P. G. Ltd. Wt. W14142/641—20,000 3/15. Forms C2121/10.

"A" Form. Army Form C. 2121.

MESSAGES AND SIGNALS. No. of Message

Prefix Code m. | Words | Charge | This message is on a/c of: | Recd. at m.

Office of Origin and Service Instructions. | Sent At m. To By | Service. (Signature of "Franking Officer") | Date From By

APPENDIX 170

TO O.C. 9th Bde RFA

Sender's Number: BM28 | Day of Month: 9 | In reply to Number | AAA

Following amendment to my 646 RA(2) AAA First phase cancel task of battery with section on roads round FERME du BIEZ and instead this battery will shell trench 51E to 54 AAA Also first phase remove one battery from trench 46 48 49 to 65 and put it on trench 54 to 58 to the LA BASSEE road inclusive AAA ~~In second phase remove battery from roads round FERME du BIEZ and instead put it on trench 63 to 54~~ Remove second battery from 46 48 49 to 65 and put it on 54 E

From

Place

Time

The above may be forwarded as now corrected. (Z)

Censor. Signature of Addressor or person authorised to telegraph in his name

* This line should be erased if not required.

C27642 P. G. Ltd. Wt. W14142/641—20,000 3/15. Forms C2121/10.

"A" Form. Army Form C. 2121.

MESSAGES AND SIGNALS.

No. of Message

Prefix Code m. | Words | Charge | This message is on a/c of: | Recd. at m.

Office of Origin and Service Instructions.

Sent At m. To By

Service.

(Signature of "Franking Officer")

Date From By

APPENDIX 171

TO O.C. 13th Bde

* Sender's Number BM 29 | Day of Month 9 | In reply to Number | AAA

Amend phase one as follows AAA Remain battery from V 10 V 9 to V 10 E and put it on trench 54 a 57 across road to N E corner of KEEP AAA Phase three for this battery the same AAA In phases one and two employ up to 100 rounds per gun if necessary and sufficient proportion of HE to thoroughly batter these trenches which must be taken at all costs AAA Phase 3 as in original programme but at very slow rate of fire

From BMRA
Place
Time 2-15 pm

The above may be forwarded as now corrected. (Z)

Censor. Signature of Addressor or person authorised to telegraph in his name

* This line should be erased if not required.

C27642 P. G. Ltd. Wt. W14142/641—20,000 3/15. Forms C2121/10.

"A" Form.

Army Form C. 2121.

MESSAGES AND SIGNALS.

No. of Message APPENDIX 171

Prefix ____ Code ____ m.	Words	Charge	This message is on a/c of:	Recd. at ____ m.
Office of Origin and Service Instructions.	Sent		____ Service.	Date ____
	At ____ m.			From ____
	To ____			
	By ____		(Signature of "Franking Officer")	By ____

TO

* Sender's Number	Day of Month	In reply to Number	AAA

by 57 across road to N of W corner of keep AAA In second phase battery instead of Ferme du Bois will do from 63 to 51 and battery from 4648, 49 to 65 will do from 54 by 58 to the LA BASSEE road in clearing AAA In these two phases you may employ up to 100 rounds per gun if necessary with requisite proportion of H.E to thoroughly batter those trenches which must be taken at all costs AAA Phase 3 as in original programme but with very slow rate rather fire

From	BMRA
Place	
Time	2 pm

The above may be forwarded as now corrected. (Z)

Censor. Signature of Addressor or person authorised to telegraph in his name

* This line should be erased if not required.

C27642 P. G. Ltd. Wt. W14142/641—20,000 3/15. Forms C2121/10.

"A" Form. Army Form C. 2121.

MESSAGES AND SIGNALS.

No. of Message

APPENDIX 172

Prefix	Code	m.	Words	Charge	This message is on a/c of:	Recd. at	m.
Office of Origin and Service Instructions.			Sent		Service.	Date	
			At	m.		From	
			To				
			By		(Signature of "Franking Officer")	By	

TO O. C. 4th Bde RFA

* Sender's Number	Day of Month	In reply to Number	AAA
BM 20	9		

In phases one and two battery on trench 63 to 51E may employ up to 100 rds per gun if necessary with sufficient proportion of HE to thoroughly batter this line of trenches which must be taken at all costs. AAA Remaining two batteries normal rate of fire AAA Other three all batteries may also [illegible] fire

From
Place BMRA
Time

The above may be forwarded as now corrected. (Z)

Censor. Signature of Addressor or person authorised to telegraph in his name [illegible]

* This line should be erased if not required.

C27642 P. G. Ltd. Wt. W14142/641—20,000 3/15. Forms C2121/10.

"A" Form. Army Form C. 2121.

MESSAGES AND SIGNALS.

No. of Message

Prefix Code m. | Words | Charge
Office of Origin and Service Instructions.

Sent
At m.
To
By

This message is on a/c of: APPENDIX 173
Service.
(Signature of "Franking Officer")

Recd. at m.
Date
From
By

TO O.C. 9th Bde

Sender's Number	Day of Month	In reply to Number	AAA
BM 31	9		

Re BM 28 cancel battery ordered on 54 b 58 up to road and substitute for this ~~a~~ trenches 63 b 51 E to 51 AAA This applies to this battery in both phases one and ~~two~~ two

From BMRA
Place
Time 2-22pm

The above may be forwarded as now corrected. (Z)

Censor. Signature of Addressor or person authorised to telegraph in his name

* This line should be erased if not required.

C27642 P. G. Ltd. Wt. W14142/641—20,000 3/15. Forms C2121/10.

Secret

APPENDIX 174

INSTRUCTIONS FOR MEERUT DIVISIONAL ARTILLERY 10th May 1915.

1. The 1st Corps will commence a bombardment with Heavy Howitzers at 11.a.m. and will attack on a 600 yard front with their left on V.6. at 3.p.m.

2. Indian Corps bombardment will commence at 2.p.m. and continue till 3.5.p.m. 18 pounders LAHORE Division will cut wire from 1.50.p.m. till 2.p.m. At 3.5.p.m. the GARHWAL Brigade will attack with its left on the ditch running N.W. from 59 and its right on a ditch parrallel to the above running N.W. from near V.6. It will take first line German trenches and then consolidate its position there.
Note:- Details for further moves will be arranged later. It is possible that in the event of the 1st Corps attack not succeeding the Indian Corps may not deliver an assault.

MEERUT Divisional Artillery will operate as under:-

2.p.m. to 3.5.p.m. 4th Brigade R.F.A. on the enemy's trenches from point 140 to S 5 d 2'4.

9th Brigade R.F.A. (1 Battery along 53, 54e, to 57.
(2 Batteries 51e, 54, 58 to LA BASSEE Road.

13th Brigade R.F.A (1 Battery on KEEP S.E. of 59.
(2 Batteries trench V.9e, V.6e to 150 yards W, of V.6e.

In the above phase the normal rate of fire will be section fire two minutes. B.C's must however use their own discretion in dealing with any situation which may arise.

From 3.5.p.m. onwards. 4th Brigade R.F.A. from 140 to S 5 d 2'4.

9th Brigade R.F.A. (1 Battery 51e to 54 .
(2 Batteries in observation.

13th Brigade R.F.A. (1 Battery (1 Section 54 to V.8e.
(2 Sections trench V.9e to V.6e.
(2 Batteries in observation.

In this phase the rate of fire from 3.5.p.m. to 3.15.p.m. must be accelerated. After 3.15.p.m. a very slow rate should be employed.

[signature]

Lieut R.A.

for Brigade Major, Royal Artillery,
MEERUT DIVISION.

10.a.m.

10th May 1915.

Copy No.6

APPENDIX 174

No. 647-R.A.(L). Headquarters Divisional Artillery, MEERUT DIVISION.

SECRET. 10th May 1915.

To,
The Officers Commanding,

4th Brigade R.F.A.
9th Brigade R.F.A.
13th Brigade R.F.A.

With reference to the Instructions for MEERUT Divisional Artillery dated 10th May 1915, all necessary preparations are to be made but the orders will not be carried into force until further definite orders are issued.

The G.O.C., R.A., directs that the strictest possible economy as regards ammunition be employed.

Batteries at present detailed to shoot intermittently on lines of approach, roads round FERME du BIEZ Etc, will not carry the order out unless they actually see hostile reinforcements coming up.

J.K. Macfarlane
for Lieut
Major R.A.
Brigade Major, Royal Artillery,
MEERUT DIVISION.

APPENDIX 175

S E C R E T .

TACTICAL PROGRESS REPORT
10th May 1915.

1(a) ACTION BY OUR OWN ARTILLERY.

Batteries fired on their front during the night, a few rounds at intervals:-
4.45.a.m. 20th Battery fired on roads and road junctions round the FERME du BIEZ, and fired about 15 rounds an hour at irregular intervals during the morning.
5.a.m. 4th Brigade R.F.A. registered a few points.
5.a.m. 9th Brigade R.F.A. commenced registering new tasks.
6.50.a.m. 14th Battery had 2 direct hits on O.P. near 125.
9.30.a.m. 2nd Battery registered the KEEP, some direct hits on parapet being scored with percussion shrapnel and some Germans bolted.
4.30.p.m. 2nd Battery registered CHATEAU near DISTILLERY, where people were seen.

1(b) ACTION BY HOSTILE ARTILLERY.

4.a.m. A certain amount of shelling in vicinity of M 33 d.
4.30.a.m. Field Howitzer shelled in front of 14th Battery position.
11.30.a.m. PIPSQUEAK scored 4 hits on 7th Battery O.P. in NEUVE CHAPELLE.
4.40.p.m. German Howitzer shelled LA BASSEE Road about 500 yards of PONT LOGY.
6.p.m. 44th Battery O.P. in RUE du BOIS heavily shelled by PIPSQUEAK.

2. INFORMATION.

TRENCHES:- Germans seen to be constructing 3rd line of trenches running through N 31 c and d. Several iron shields visible in parapet also two vehicles(possibly either motor transport or some form of light railway truck) behind main trench in open field in N 31 c (position of trench only approximate).

GALVANIZED IRON TANKS:- There are about 12 Galvanized iron tanks(?) on Hill side near HAUTE POMMEREAU. Tanks appear to be circular and about 4 or 5 feet in diameter. The tanks are placed along the trench and extend from about 200 yards W. of point 160 to about 100 yards W. of point 109. They are plaonly visible and little trouble appears to have been taken to conceal them.

AIRCRAFT:- 7.15p.m. 9.5.15. AVIATIK sighted flying high at bearing 90°, engaged with 26 rounds then turned E. over German lines.
5.20.a.m. 10.5.15. AVIATIK sighted flying high at bearing 110°, engaged with 57 rounds then turned E. over German lines.

W. H. Lynch-Staunton

Major R.A.

Brigade Major, Royal Artillery,
MEERUT DIVISION.

APPENDIX 176

SECRET.

TACTICAL PROGRESS REPORT
11th May 1915.

1(a) ACTION BY OUR OWN ARTILLERY.

6.30.a.m. 14th Battery fired at party of men at point 127.
6.30.a.m. 7th Battery fired at party of men behind fire trench between 145 and 146.
2.45.p.m. 14th Battery shot at group of men behind fire trench between 145 and 146, and at 2.50.p.m. fired at O.P. near 120.
4.p.m. 8th Battery registered 56 and 59.

1(b) ACTION BY HOSTILE ARTILLERY.

Hostile artillery pretty active all day.
11.p.m. 10.5.15 to 3.a.m. 11.5.15:- Enemy shelled RUE du BOIS, chiefly with PIPSQUEAK.
5.a.m. Heavy Howitzer shelled PORT ARTHUR.
9.50.a.m. Heavy Howitzer shelled from BREWERY(NEUVE CHAPELLE) to M 35 c 3'4.
10.a.m. to 11.30.a.m. 15 c.m. Howitzer shelled 44th Battery Headquarters- 1 man wounded. Headquarters DEHRA DUN Brigade hit twice.
11 to 11.30.a.m. PIPSQUEAK shelled ORCHARD O.P.(S 10 b 4'3) obtaining 3 direct hits.
12.5.p.m. Howitzer shelled trenches in front of PORT ARTHUR.
11.a.m. to 5.p.m. Intermittent shelling of PORT ARTHUR and RUE du BOIS, chiefly 10.5.c.m. Howitzer, apparently from the direction of the DISTILLERY.
12.5 to 12.45.p.m. "WOOLY BEARS" shelled vicinity M 32 d and 10.5.c.m. Howitzer shelled vicinity M 27 b.
1 to 2.30.p.m. "REVOLVER" House(S 3 c 5'4) shelled by 77 m.m. guns and 10.5.c.m. Howitzers.
4.30.p.m. "RITZ" was shelled by 30.c.m. Howitzer from direction of ILLIES- 2 were blind.

2. INFORMATION.

AIRCRAFT:- 8.15.a.m. AVIATIK flying high, bearing 100°, was out of range and disappeared S.E. over German lines.
10.15.a.m. AVIATIK flying high, bearing 80°, was out of range and travelled N.E.

OBSTACLES:- The wire and parapets between points 56 and V.6. have been badly knocked about, but Germans have placed Chevaux de FRISE at various points along the line, especially where machine guns have been located, and at point 56 they have placed low wire entanglements.

H.M. Lynch-Staunton
Major R.A.

Brigade Major, Royal Artillery,
MEERUT DIVISION.

APPENDIX 177

S E C R E T.

TACTICAL PROGRESS REPORT
12th May 1915.

1(a) ACTION BY OUR OWN ARTILLERY
8.30.p.m. 11.5.15:- 14th Battery fired at house 140 in combination with the heavies.
12th May 1915.
11.a.m. 2nd Battery registered on the KEEP and approaches to it.
12.30.p.m. 2nd Battery fired bursts of fire at "covered way", whilst being engaged by MOTHER in hopes of catching enemy bolting.
12.10 and 12.30.p.m. 8th Battery fired at the KEEP and "covered way" in conjunction with the 9'2" Howitzers.
2.30.p.m. 14th Battery fired on working party behind enemy's trench near 148.
2.45.p.m. 68th Battery fired on enemy's trenches in reply to PIPSQUEAK shelling our Reserve trenches.
6.30.p.m. 14th Battery fired at party of men coming out of house at 151.
19th and 20th Batteries carried out registration during the afternoon

1(b) ACTION BY HOSTILE ARTILLERY.
9.a.m. Heavy Howitzer shelled vicinity behind LANSDOWNE POST from direction of ILLIES.
10.a.m. Heavy Howitzer shelled trenches in front of RITZ(S 9 d).
10.10.a.m. PIPSQUEAK shelled factory on RUE du BOIS(S 9 d).
10.30 to 11.15 a.m. 10.5 c m howitzer shelled DOLL's House obtaining several direct hits.
12 noon and 4.0.p.m. 15 c.m. shelled houses houses behind CRESCENT trench
4.15 p.m. PIPSQUEAK shelled RUE du BOIS(S.10) from S.E. corner of BOIS du BIEZ.
Intermittent shelling of RUE du BOIS during the day.
Good deal of shelling all the afternoon along the LA BASSEE Road down to PONT du HEM, and vicinity M 32 and M 33.

2. INFORMATION.
SNIPING:- Snipers very active from 63 and 60.
AIRCRAFT:-9.10.a.m. AVIATIK, high, bearing 110°, engaged 55 rounds, then turned in Easterly direction.
German "Sausage" up, bearing 170° magnetic from M 33 a 3'7.

WIRE AND PARAPETS:- There is new Chevaux de Fries in front of 1st line trench, particularly noticeable at point 60. Here 2nd line parapet has been raised with dark damp earth and a few white sandbags, but they are covering these sand-bags up withearth.
A certain amount of new wire has been put up in front of 1st line trench from point 58 to V.6.
German front trenches appear to have been levelled off a little but not repaired. Parapet running N.E. from 58 [illegible] strength-ened with black sand-bags.
MACHINE GUNS:- 150 yards from 60 is a probable M.G. emplacement below some red sand-bags.
Houses between V.15 and 55 [illegible] machine guns firing S.W.
DEFENDED HOUSES:- [illegible] sand-bagged.

13th May 1915.

Enemy shelled RUE du BOIS [illegible]
Considerable sniping [illegible]

[illegible]
Major,
[illegible]

APPENDIX 178

S E C R E T.

1st Army.
G.S.
G.S. 82(a)
13.5.15.

Adv: 1st Corps.
4th Corps.
Indian Corps.

1. Selected localities and a length of first and second line trenches in the German lines will be subjected to short and intensive bombardments tonight and tomorrow. These localities and trenches will be selected by G.O.C. Corps.

The bombardments will take place at the following times:-

1.a.m......14th.
2.p.m......14th.
10.p.m......14th.

Each bombardment will be carried out precisely according to the following programme:-

(a) 2 minutes bombardment by all 4'5" Howitzers, 6" Howitzers and 5" Howitzers available. During this period the Infantry will maintain a heavy rifle fire.

(b) 2 minutes dead silence opposite the portion of the German trenches selected.

(c) 2 minutes fire by all 18 pr. and 13 pr. batteries on the German 1st and 2nd line trenches, accompanied by heavy rifle fire.

2. Rounds allotted for each bombardment:-

13 pr. 18 pr. 4'5" Howitzers....4 rounds per gun per minute-shrapnel only.

6" How: 5" How...................2 rounds per gun per minute-shrapnel or heavy lyddite.

3. During the bombardment certain localities will be shelled by the Heavy Artillery under instructions of the M.G. H.A. who will also indicate to the 4th Corps the localities to be shelled by the 4'7" Batteries.

Sd. - BUTLER, Brig: General,
General Staff, 1st Army.

13.5.15.
844-G.

Trench.....V.6. to S.W. — 43rd Bde
V.6. to KNEP.
Front edge of KNEP. } XIII Bde
60 to N.E. — 15th Bde
51 E to ~~52~~ 63 — 9th Bde
Points 53 V.9 E. — VI Bde RGA
63-150 4th Brigade only. — IV Bde

APPENDIX 179

SECRET.

TACTICAL PROGRESS REPORT
13th May 1915.

1(a) ACTION BY OUR OWN ARTILLERY.

During the morning the following batteries registered as under:-

19th Battery R.F.A. wire between 56-60 and on LA BASSEE Road running N. to S. at LE TOURELLE.

20th Battery R.F.A. wire between 51e-54 and cross roads V.19, V.15, and V.12.

28th Battery R.F.A. wire between 53-54e and on cross roads at LE TOURELLE running N.E. and S.W.

During the day the batteries of the 4th Brigade R.F.A. fired at enemy's wire entanglements and registered a few points.

2nd Siege Battery report several direct hits obtained on trench and parapet 59 to 60.

2.p.m. 2nd Battery R.F.A. registered 59 to V.6.

(b) ACTION BY HOSTILE ARTILLERY.

9.a.m. to 12 noon. Occasional shelling of RUE du BOIS.

9.15 to 9.30.a.m. PIPSQUEAK shelled 7th Battery O.P.-2 hits obtained on the house.

11.10.a.m. Heavy Howitzer shelled old British Salient near S 4 b 2'2.

From 12 noon PIPSQUEAK shelled ORCHARD and communicating trench leading to RUE du BOIS.

12.45.p.m. PIPSQUEAK shelled vicinity M 33 b and LA BASSEE Road to ROUGE CROIX.

1.p.m. "WOOLY BEARS" shelled 9th Brigade R.F.A. Headquarters in LORETTO Road firing about 10 rounds with good effect-one direct hit.

4.p.m. to 7.p.m. Vicinity of M 32 and M 33 shelled by Heavy and Field guns in reply to bombardment.

5.p.m. 21.c.m. Howitzer shelled REVOLVER House S 3 c 5'4 obtaining one direct hit, and "WOOLY BEARS" appeared effective on Horse Battery in S 3 a 7'8.

5.p.m. to 6.p.m. "WOOLY BEARS" fell around FORESTERS LANE and LANSDOWNE POST.

PIPSQUEAK shelled S 10 b 3'8 all the afternoon(This point is mouth of communication trench leading from LANSDOWNE POST to RUE DU BOIS)causing much inconvenience- position of battery not located.

2. INFORMATION.

OBSERVATION:- Very misty morning, observation impossible much before 8.a.m.

AIRCRAFT:- No hostile aircraft seen up to-day.

Major R.A.

Brigade Major, Royal Artillery
MEERUT DIVISION.

SECRET. *Intensive Bombardments* APPENDIX 179(a)

1st Army
General Staff
No. G.S. 82(a)
Dated 13-5-15.

Adv. 1st Corps
4th Corps
Indian Corps

---

1. Selected localities and a length of first and second line trenches in the German lines will be subjected to a short and intensive bombardments to-night and tomorrow. These localities and trenches will be selected by G.Os.C., Corps.

The bombardment will take place at the following times:-

~~9.0 p.m. 13th~~ cancelled.
1.0 a.m. 14th
2.0 p.m. 14th
10.0 p.m. 14th

Each bombardment will be carried out precisely according to the following programme:-

(a) 3 minutes bombardment by all 4.5" Hows., 6" Hows. 5" Hows., available. During this period the infantry will maintain a heavy rifle fire.

(b) 2 minutes dead silence opposite the portion of the German trenches selected.

(c) 2 minutes fire by all 18-pr. and 13-pr. batteries on the German first and second line trenches accompanied by heavy rifle fire.

2. Rounds allowed for each bombardment:-

13-pr., 18-pr., 4.5" How.	4 rounds per gun per minute, shrapnel only.
6" How., 5" How.	2 rounds a gun per minute, shrapnel or heavy lyddite.

3. During the bombardment, certain localities will be shelled by the Heavy Artillery under instructions of the M.G., R.A. who will also indicate to the 4th Corps the localities to be shelled by the 4.7" batteries.

13th May 1915. (Sd) R. Butler, Brig. Genl.

General Staff, 1st Army.

G 439/13

CRA Meerut

Targets selected have already been communicated to you. Acknowledge by wire

Div Major

13/5/15

S E C R E T Copy No. 6

APPENDIX 180 (6 pages)

OPERATION ORDER No.31
by
LIEUTENANT - GENERAL Sir Charles ANDERSON, K.C.B.,
Commanding MEERUT Division.

Reference maps:-
FRANCE - BETHUNE Sheet - 1:40,000.
& Special Map 1:10,000.

14th May 1915.

-:-:-:-:-:-:-:-:-:-:-:-:-:-

Information. 1. The 1st and Indian Corps are to renew the attack and to press forward toward VIOLAINES and BEAU PUITS and to establish a defensive flank along the LA BASSEE Road on the left, maintaining the right at GIVENCHY.

The line to be established in the first instance is the general line of the road FESTUBERT - LA QUINQUE RUE - LA TOURELLE cross roads - PORT ARTHUR, which position is to be consolidated.

The 1st Corps is assaulting with the 2nd Division on the right of the Meerut Division with the object of securing the line R.1 - R.3 - R.5 - R.7 - V.4. The assault of this Division will be simultaneous with that of the Meerut Division. Its subsequent advance will be with the object of securing the FERME D'AVOUE and the line of road P.14 to R.13.

The 7th Division is assaulting the German front trenches between N.1 and P.5 in the early hours of the 15th May.

Intention. 2. The Meerut Division less Dehra Dun Brigade and one Brigade R.F.A., and plus the Sirhind Brigade will make the attack to be delivered by the Indian Corps.

This assault is to be made against the enemy front line trenches included between the ditches running from South-south east to North-northwest through points V.5 and V.6. The first objective is the capture of the enemy's front line of V.6 redoubt and of the trenches behind the first line lying west of the north corner of the redoubt as far as the ditch running through V.5. Communication trenches will then be opened connecting captured trenches with our own line. The easterly one of such trenches will be turned into a fire trench facing east. Every endeavour will be made to accomplish this task and consolidate our position before daylight, getting touch on our right with the 2nd Division troops and bombing outwards along enemy trenches on our left flank to the east and south-east. A fire front facing east will thus be formed with V.6 redoubt as its centre. The second objective is to attack outwards in an easterly direction and secure the line 5 V.E - V.6.E - 59. The third objective; when the above line has been secured, and as the attack of the 2nd Division progresses, our attack is to push on and secure the road from PORT ARTHUR to LA TOURELLE Cross roads inclusive and consolidate itself thereon.

Artillery 3 A deliberate artillery bombardment will precede the assault (it commenced at 12 noon ~~today~~ yesterday) and will be maintained for 36 hours. This bombardment will deal with:-

(a) Wire cutting on front of attack both in front of and behind the German front line parapet.

(b) The first and second German lines on the front of attack.

(c) The redoubt at V.6.

(d) The German front line parapet from just north of point V.6 through points 59 and 60 to a point 30 yards east of the LA BASSEE Road.

(e) The keep in rear of point 59.

(f) The group of houses around point V.9.E on the LA BASSEE Road.

(g) The covered way connecting V.9.E with the south-east corner of V.6. redoubt.

(h)

(h) The houses alongside the LA BASSEE Road about V.10.E and V.7.

(k) The houses about the following points:- R.16.E R.17.E - R.17 - R.19 - R.16 - R.18 including the DISTILLERY.

This bombardment will cease on the front to be attacked at 11.25 P.M. on 14th May, i.e., five minutes before the infantry assault at 11.30 P.M. 14th May, but will continue steadily on points lying east of a line passing immediately west of points 59 - V.6.E and V.5.E. Point 59 itself is to be fired at during and after the assault, also point 60. The maintenance of an accurate fire on these two points during the assault is of great importance.

Section Mountain Artillery.

The Section Mountain Artillery will be held in a state of readiness in the vicinity of ST VAAST to advance if required

No.4 Trench Battery.

No.4 Trench Howitzer Battery is placed at the disposal of G.O.C. Garhwal Bde for the operations.

INFANTRY Garhwal Bde

4. The Garhwal Bde will carry out the assault on the enemy front line trenches as in para 2.

The assault will be made on a two battalion front under detailed arrangements to be made by G.O.C. Garhwal Bde.

The assault will be delivered at 11.30 P.M. on the 14th May.

In order to keep under the enemy's fire from his trenches on the left of our attack, the marginal force will be detailed under the command of Lieut:-Colonel G.MORRIS, 2/8th Gurkhas, to hold the front line parapet east of the communication trench running forward from centre of ORCHARD Redoubt. The trench howitzers, bomb-guns and machine guns will be established close to, or in, our front line trenches. Fire will be distributed along the enemy's front from point 60 on the LA BASSEE Road towards V.6. Great caution is to be exercised to avoid firing into the left of our own attacking line. Fire is to commence as soon as the assault starts.

> 1 Battn Ind. Infantry,
> Machine gun sections of Bareilly Bde.
> No.4 Trench Battery
> Bomb-gun batteries of Dehra Dun, Garhwal & Bareilly Brigades.

No.2 Trench Battery.

No. 2 Trench Howitzer Battery is assisting in this bombardment from a point in the Lahore Division trenches and will fire on points 56 and 60 and their vicinity.

SIRHIND Bde

5. Sirhind Bde will be in support to Garhwal Bde. It will be formed up by ten P.M., 14th May in assembly positions as follows:-

Two battns RUE DU BOIS,
remaining battns in LANSDOWNE POST and the breastwork in the vicinity.

BAREILLY Bde

6. Bareilly Bde is in Divisional Reserve and will be held in a state of readiness in second line trenches at CROIX BARBEE from one A.M. on 15th.

Machine gun sections will be put at disposal of G.O.C. Garhwal Bde and will get into position as in para 4 during night 13th/14th May.

In communication with the C.R.E., one battn Indian infantry will be detailed to proceed on 13th May to tram-head at ST VAAST where it will be held in readiness:-

(a) to provide two companies as carrying parties for engineers; &

(b) two companies to proceed along the tram lines to carry ammunition and receive prisoners etc:, on receipt of orders to do so.

7.

Dehra Dun Brigade. 7. Dehra Dun Brigade is in Corps reserve.

Brigade bomb-gun Batteries. 8. Bomb-gun Batteries of Dehra Dun and Bareilly Brigades will be placed at the disposal of the G.O.C. Garhwal Bde ~~and will go into the trenches on night 12th/13th May~~.

4th Cavalry 9. 4th Indian Cavalry will rendezvous at 5.0 a.m. 15th May in fields and orchards between VIEILLE CHAPELLE and LA COUTURE, and send a liaison officer to Divisional Report Centre RUE DU PUITS.

S. & M. Pioneers 2 Coys Ind.Inf. 10. Nos 3 and 4 Companies S. & M., 107th Pioneers, will rendezvous at ST VAAST on the evening of 14th May at 7.30 p.m.

The C.R.E. will organise the following working parties:-

(i) A small barricading party which will report to G.O.C. Garhwal Bde in the RUE DU BOIS at 10.0 p.m.

(ii) A party for the opening of communication along line of ditch passing through V.5, will be despatched from ST VAAST by the C.R.E. as soon as information is received that the German first line has been carried.

(iii) A party for the opening of communication along ditch passing through V.6 will follow as soon as situation is reported such as to admit of their working.

(iv) A party for the consolidation of V.6 when taken will similarly follow when demanded.

All these parties will, on arrival in the RUE DU BOIS come under the orders of the G.O.C. Garhwal Bde.

Wire cut--ting, bridging. 11. G.O.C. Garhwal Bde will arrange for wire to be cut and bridges to be put in position over the ditch in front of our parapet.

S.A.A. supply. 12. A depot of 840 boxes of S.A.A. has been established in RUE DU BOIS at R.E.depot, and 500 at ST VAAST.

The G.O.C. Garhwal Bde will also place two advanced depots of 100 boxes each, in the forward trench from which the assault will be launched.

To supplement such arrangements as Brigadiers may make for their own Brigades, the supporting and reserve brigades will each direct their rear battalion to carry forward ammunition, and establish ~~xxxxxx~~ further advanced depots in the fighting area as may be found suitable and possible.

Advanced R.E.depots. 13. Advanced R.E.Depots are formed at (a) RUE DU BOIS (b) Farm at M.32.d.7/7.

Bombs & Hand-grenades 14. The depots of bombs and hand-grenades 100 yards in rear of assembly trenches north of R.E.depot, RUE DU BOIS, have been restocked.

Medical. 15. A collecting station will be established between LANSDOWNE POST and the tramway line where it crosses FORRESTERS LANE. Route for wounded returning from the front will be by the

SECRET. No G-439/34

CORRECTION TO OPERATION ORDER NO 31.

MEDICAL. 15. Cancel line 4 from "ORCHARD communication trench", to "some 100 yards from it" in line 6 and substitute :-

"Trench east of ORCHARD and thence by LANSDOWNE communication trench. This trench runs roughly parallel to and 5 0 yards west of the main drain and leads into centre of LANSDOWNE POST".

15th May 1915.

[signature]
Major.
General Staff, Meerut Division.

Dehra Dun Brigade. 7. Dehra Dun Brigade is in Corps reserve.

Brigade bomb-gun Batteries. 8. Bomb-gun Batteries of Dehra Dun and Bareilly Brigades will be placed at the disposal of the G.O.C. Garhwal Bde. ~~and will go into the trenches on night 12th/13th May.~~

4th Cavalry 9. 4th Indian Cavalry will rendezvous at 5.0 a.m. 15th May in fields and orchards between VIEILLE CHAPELLE and LA COUTURE, and send a liaison officer to Divisional Report Centre RUE DU PUITS.

S. & M. Pioneers 2 Coys Ind.Inf. 10. Nos 3 and 4 Companies S. & M., 107th Pioneers, will rendezvous at ST VAAST on the evening of 14th May at 7.30 p.m.

The C.R.E. will organise the following working parties:-

(i) A small barricading party which will report to G.O.C. Garhwal Bde in the RUE DU BOIS at 10.0 p.m.

(ii) A party for the opening of communication along line of ditch passing through V.5, will be despatched from ST VAAST by the C.R.E. as soon as information is received that the German first line has been carried.

(iii) A party for the opening of communication along ditch passing through V.6 will follow as soon as situation is reported such as to admit of their working.

(iv) A party for the consolidation of V.6 when taken will similarly follow when demanded.

All these parties will, on arrival in the RUE DU BOIS come under the orders of the G.O.C. Garhwal Bde.

Wire cut-ting, bridging. 11. G.O.C. Garhwal Bde will arrange for wire to be cut and bridges to be put in position over the ditch in front of our parapet.

S.A.A. supply. 12. A depot of 840 boxes of S.A.A. has been established in RUE DU BOIS at R.E.depot, and 500 at ST VAAST.

The G.O.C. Garhwal Bde will also place two advanced depots of 100 boxes each, in the forward trench from which the assault will be launched.

To supplement such arrangements as Brigadiers may make for their own Brigades, the supporting and reserve brigades will each direct their rear battalion to carry forward ammunition, and establish ~~xxxxxx~~ further advanced depots in the fighting area as may be found suitable and possible.

Advanced R.E.depots. 13. Advanced R.E.Depots are formed at (a) RUE DU BOIS (b) Farm at M.32.d.7/7.

Bombs & Hand-grenades 14. The depots of bombs and hand-grenades 100 yards in rear of assembly trenches north of R.E.depot, RUE DU BOIS, have been restocked.

Medical. 15. A collecting station will be established between LANSDOWNE POST and the tramway line where it crosses FORRESTERS LANE. Route for wounded returning from the front will be by the ~~ORCHARD Communication trench which runs from RUE DU BOIS to FORRESTERS LANE along the northeast side of the tramway and some 100 yards from it.~~ This trench will be reserved for return of wounded only after fighting has commenced, and will be marked accordingly.

Route from collecting station to ST VAAST Corner, where an advanced dressing station will be established, will be alongside the tramway lines.

A wagon rendezvous in this vicinity will be established and will be marked by the RED CROSS Flag.

Field

Field ambulances will be opened at VIEILLE CHAPELLE and ZELOBES: Line of evacuation from wagon rendezvous is via OXFORD Road and WELLINGTON Road.

Sandbags 16. Each man of the attacking infantry will carry two sandbags.

Masks. 17. Masks will be kept in readiness, soaked in solution prepared under the direction of medical officers of units. Assaulting troops will wear theirs.

Disting-uishing marks. 18. 2nd Division troops, at night, are wearing a white bib showing both to front and rear.

By day, position of advanced or flank bombing parties of Meerut Division will be shown by a three feet square flag, the top and left portion being black and the bottom and right portion - red, with a white ST ANDREW's CROSS.

Those of 2nd Division will be marked by a yellow screen, 6' by 28" in case of battalions, and yellow flags 28" x 28" in case of companies.

1st Division:- Red flags - 3' x 3' with white perpendicular stripe.

London Divn - Sandbag cloth disc, 2'' in diameter with black cross in centre.

Lahore Divn. - yellow flag 16" square.

Emergency Supply Depot. 19. An advanced emergency supply depot has been estab-lished at house at cross roads in M.32.d. near ~~???~~ head of the tramway line.

Advanced Report Centres. 20.

Meerut Divn.	RUE DU PUITS.
Garhwal Bde.	~~??~~ PICCADILLY, RUE DU BOIS.
Sirhind Bde.	LANSBOWNE POST
Bareilly Bde.	CROSS Roads CROIX BARBEE.

96

C Norie
Colonel,
General Staff,
MEERUT DIVISION.

Issued to Signal Company for distribution, at 12.30 p.m.

Copy No.1 and 2 to Indian Corps,
3 Lahore Division
4 2nd Divn
5 7th Division
6 Meerut Divnl Artillery
7 Lahore Divnl Artillery
8 Dehra Dun Bde
9 Garhwal Bde
10 Bareilly Bde
11 Sirhind Bde
12 Meerut Divnl Engineers
13 4th Indian Cavalry
14 107th Pioneers
15 Meerut Signals
16 No. 1 Group H.A.R.
17 A.D.M.S. Meerut
18 A.A. & Q.M.G.
19 Garhwal Bde (duplicate copy) by separate orderly
20 G.S.
21 to 26 War Diary and spare.

S E C R E T No.G.439/21

Headquarters, Meerut Division.

14th May 1915 - 3.30 P.M.

Memorandum.

The operations mentioned in Meerut Division Operation Order No. 31 of date are postponed for 24 hours. The report centre will not now open until 5.0 P.M. tomorrow.

Please Acknowledge

Acknowledged by wire

R Davies

Major,
General Staff,
MEERUT DIVISION.

To.

(All concerned informed)

S E C R E T. No.G.439/42

Headquarters, Meerut Division

15th May 1915 - 2.0 P.M.

The operation ordered in Meerut Operation Order No.31 dated 14th May 1915, will commence tonight.
Acknowledge by wire.

R Davies

Major,
General Staff,
Meerut Division.

To,

Garhwal Bde
Bareilly Bde
Dehra Dun Bde
Sirhind Bde
C.R.A. Meerut
C.R.A. Lahore
No. 1 Group
4th Ind Cav.
107th Pioneers
C.R.E.Meerut
Meerut Sigs
A.D.M.S.
A.A.& Q.M.G.

No G-439/32.

S E C R E T.

Headquarters Meerut Division.

15th May 1915.

Copy of a memo. from 1st Corps to Indian Corps, No G-167, dated 14th May 1915. (Received under Indian Corps No G-192, dated 14th May 1915).

-:-:-:-:-:-:-:-:-:-:-:-:-

The following distinguishing flags and marks have been arranged in connection with the operations ordered in 1st Corps Operation Order No 83 of 14th May 1915 :-

2nd Division.

(a) Yellow flag (for daylight)
(b) For night attack each man will wear a white patch on chest and back of shoulders.

7th Division.

Red flags with white horizontal bar.

MEMORANDUM.

Forwarded. The above information is contained in Meerut Division Operation Order No 31, dated 14th May 1915.

[signature]
Colonel.
General Staff,
MEERUT DIVISION.

To:-
DEHRA DUN BRIGADE.
GARHWAL BRIGADE.
BAREILLY BRIGADE.
C. R. A. MEERUT.
C. R. A. LAHORE.
C. R. E. MEERUT.

SECRET.   Copy No. 6......
APPENDIX 181 (4 pages).

OPERATION ORDER No. 19.
by
Brigadier General R.St.C. LECKY, R.A., C.R.A. MEERUT DIVISION.

Reference:-
Map FRANCE-BETHUNE Sheet 1/40,000.
and Special Map 1/10,000.

14th May 1915.

INFORMATION. 1. The 1st and Indian Corps are renewing the attack to-night with the object of pressing forward towards VIOLAINES and BEAU PUITS and establishing a defensive flank along the LA BASSEE Road on the left maintaining the right at GIVENCHY. The line to be established in the first instance is the General line of the road FESTUBERT-LA QUINQUE RUE-LA TOURELLE Cross roads-PORT ARTHUR, which position is to be consolidated.

INTENTION. 2. The Indian Corps attack will take place at 11.30.p.m. on 14th May 1915. The assault will be delivered by the GARHWAL Brigade. The SIRHIND Brigade will be in support to the GARHWAL Brigade with two battalions in the RUE du BOIS and remaining battalions near LANSDOWNE POST. BAREILLY Brigade will be in Divisional Reserve, near CROIX BARBEE. DEHRA DUN Brigade will be in CORPS Reserve.
The assault will be made against the enemy front line trenches between the ditches running from S.S.E. to N.N.W. through points V.5. and V.6. The first objective is the capture of the enemy's front line of V.6. Redoubt and of the trenches behind the first line lying West of the North corner of the Redoubt as far as the ditch running through V.5. Communication trenches will then be opened connecting captured trenches with our line. A fire front facing East will, if possible, be consolidated by daylight consisting of the most Easterly communication trench opened up as above, V.6 Redoubt and trench as far as ditch through V.5.
Bombing parties will bomb outwards along enemy trenches on our left flank to E. and S.E.
The second objective will be the line V.5 e, V.6 e, 59.
The third objective will be the road from PORT ARTHUR to LA TOURELLE Cross roads inclusive, where we will consolidate.
The 2nd Division will assault simultaneously with the MEERUT Division with the primary object of securing the line R.1., R.3., R.5., R.7., V.4. and subsequently the FERME D'AVOUE and the line of the road P.14 to R.13.
The 7th Division is assaulting the German front trenches between N.1 and P.5 in the early hours of 15th May 1915.

ARTILLERY. 3. The general bombardment which commenced at 12 noon yesterday will continue till 11.25.p.m. to-day.
The operations of the MEERUT Divisional Artillery will be as laid down in instructions ~~already~~ issued herewith.

TRENCH HOWITZERS. 4. No.4 Trench Howitzer Battery will be at the disposal of G.O.C. GARHWAL Brigade for the operations.

ADVANCED R.E. DEPOTS. 5. Advanced R.E. Depots are at:-
(i) RUE DU BOIS.
(ii)Farm at M 32 d 7'7.

MEDICAL 6. A collecting station will be established just [illegible] of LANSDOWNE POST [illegible] communicating trench running N.E. of tramway from RUE du BOIS to FORESTERS LANE which trench will be reserved for wounded only after fighting has commenced.
There will be an advanced dressing station at St. VAAST corner.

Amended vide Meerut Div O.O. No 31 para 15 –

MASKS. 7. Masks will be kept in readiness soaked in solution prepared under the direction of Medical Officers of units.

DISTINGUISHING MARKS.	8. 2nd Division troops at night are wearing a white bib showing both to front and rear By day, position of advanced or flank bombing parties of MEERUT Division will be shown by a three feet square flag, the top and left portion being black and the bottom and right portion ~~xxxx~~ red, with a white St.Andrew's cross. Those of 2nd Division will be marked by a yellow screen, 6' by 28" in case of battalions, and yellow flags 28" X 28" in case of companies. 1st Division:- Red flags 3' X 3' with white perpendicular stripe. LONDON Divn:- Sand-bag cloth disc, 2' in diamter with black cross in centre. LAHORE Division:- Yellow flag 16" square.
EMERGENCY SUPPLY DEPOT.	9. An advanced emergency supply depot has been established at house at cross roads in M 32 d near head of the tramway line.
ADVANCED REPORT CENTRES.	10. MEERUT DIVISION.) G.O.C.,R.A., MEERUT DIVISION) RUE du PUITS. GARHWAL Brigade.............. 96 PICCADILLY, RUE DU BOIS SIRHIND Brigade.............. LANSDOWNE POST. BAREILLY Brigade.............. CROSS Roads, CROIX BARBEE.

[signature]

Lieut R.A.

for Brigade Major, Royal Artillery
MEERUT DIVISION.

Issued at 4.p.m. by motor cyclist:-

Copy No. 1 to O.C. 4th Brigade R.F.A.
,, 2 to O.C. 9th Brigade R.F.A.
,, 3 to O.C. 13th Brigade R.F.A.
,, 4 to O.C. MEERUT Divisional Ammunition Column.
,, 5 to G.O.C., R.A., LAHORE Division.
,, 6 to WAR DIARY.

S E C R E T.

REVISED INSTRUCTIONS FOR MEERUT DIVISIONAL ARTILLERY

(Vide paragraph 3, Operation Order No. [illegible]).

Night 15th/16th.

(a) Watch front from LA BASSEE Road to our left.

(b) Barrage roads:-

4th Bde R.F.A. - 53, 50, V.15.

4th Bde R.F.A. - LA TOURELLE to FERME du BIEZ for 30 minutes after assault and then not further W. than V.8(fire on road V.8 to V.12 only).

4th Bde R.F.A. - 65 to 53.

4th Bde R.F.A. - Trench 54 to V 8e.

9th Bde R.F.A. - 63, 49, 48, 46.

9th Bde R.F.A. - V.13, V.15, V.19, V.18 - 46.

13th Bde R.F.A. - V.9e, V.10e to R.17, lifting 15 minutes after assault to R.17 - Q.29.

13th Bde R.F.A. - Trench V.9e to V.7, when assault takes place V.10e to V.7 for 20 minutes then stopping.

13th Bde R.F.A. - Trench V.10, V.8e to V 10e and 20 minutes after assault coming into observation.

B A R R A G E

The preceding barrage has been made out on the assumption that the Infantry attacks proceed rapidly and carry the trenches in quick succession. If however, the attack is held up the following barrages will be formed:-

BARRAGE No.1

(If only first line is carried or second line i.e. line 120 yards in rear of first line).

4th Bde R.F.A.-53, 50, V.15

4th Bde R.F.A.-Road LA TOURELLE to FERME du BIEZ

4th Bde R.F.A.-Road 68 to 53

4th Bde R.F.A.-Trench 54 to V 8e

9th Bde R.F.A.-65, 49, 48, 46

9th Bde R.F.A.-Roads round FERME du BIEZ.

13th Bde R.F.A.-V.9e, V 10e to R.17(i.e. LA BASSEE Road)

13th Bde R.F.A.-Trench V.9e to V.7.

13th Bde R.F.A.-Trench V.10, V.8e to V.10e

BARRAGE No.2

(If Infantry gain line V 8e to V.[illegible])

Same as Barrage No.1 for MEERUT 18 pr. Batteries

BARRAGE No.3

(If Infantry reach line V 5e, V 6e, 59, 60.)

Same as Barrage No.1 for MEERUT 18 pr. Batteries

BARRAGE No.4

(If Infantry reach from 59 to LA TOURELLE)

4th Bde R.F.A.-53, 50 to V 14

4th Bde R.F.A.-Road and trench from V.[illegible] towards V 12(not further West than V.[illegible])

4th Bde R.F.A.-Road 68 to 53

4th Bde R.F.A.-Trench 54 to V 8e and V 8e to V.9 and V 10

9th Bde R.F.A.-46, 48, 49, 64e to 63

9th Bde R.F.A.-Roads round FERME du BIEZ.

9th Bde R.F.A.-Road junction V.22.

Rates of fire:- The following are suggested, but must depend entirely on development of events, and on information received.

From 6 p.m. up to time of assault 8 rounds per hour on each task.

After assault 25 rounds per hour, or section fire [illegible] minutes with irregular intervals.

No. 685-R.A.(L).

Headquarters Divisional Artillery,
MEERUT DIVISION.

SECRET.

14th May 1915.

To,
The Officers Commanding,
4th Brigade R.F.A.
9th Brigade R.F.A.
13th Brigade R.F.A.
MEERUT Divisional Ammunition Column.
G.O.C., R.A., LAHORE Division.

Reference Operation Order No.19 of to-day's date, the operations ordered therein are postponed for 24 hours exactly. With this exception the whole order and all instructions on this subject previously issued hold good.

Report Centre MEERUT Divisional Artillery will open at RUE du PUITS at 5 p.m. 15th May 1915.

[signature]

Lieut R.A.

for Brigade Major, Royal Artillery,
MEERUT DIVISION.

APPENDIX 182

TACTICAL PROGRESS REPORT.
14th May 1915.

[S]E[C]RET

1(a) ACTION BY OUR OWN ARTILLERY.
13th May 1915
7.10 p.m. 8th Battery fired a few rounds to stop bombing at front of 3rd LONDON Regt.
8.p.m. 20th Battery opened fire on point V.28 and points V.12, V.13, V.15, V.19, V.18 firing six rounds per hour.
28th Battery opened fire on road 65-64e-49-48-46 also firing six rounds per hour till 4.a.m.
14th May 1915.
1.5 a.m. 18 pr. Batteries opened fire as ordered for 2 minutes, 4 rounds per gun per minute.
6.30 a.m. 8th Battery registered 1st and 2nd trenches between V.3. and V.6.
10.a.m. 2nd Battery fired at KEEP.
11.15 a.m. 20th Battery registered trench 51e to 63, and 28th Battery registered trench 51e to 63, 54e to 53 and roadway 63-46.
11.30 a.m 2nd Siege Battery bombarded enemy's trenches between points 59 and 56 and on Southern and Eastern faces of KEEP.
12 noon. 44th Battery fired in conjunction with MOTHER on front line between 59 and 60.
12.30.p.m. 8th Battery fired 10 rounds at front line between V.6 & 59
2.5.p.m. 2 minutes bombardment by all 18 pr. batteries as ordered.
3.p.m. 8th Battery re-registered V.9e, V.10e, V.7 LA TOURELLE Cross roads-Q.27.
5.45.p.m. 14th Battery fired on cross roads near 125.

1(b) ACTION BY HOSTILE ARTILLERY.
12.30.p.m. WOOLY BEARS shelled vicinity M 33 a.
2 to 2.15.p.m. Shelling in RUE DU BOIS and near PORT ARTHUR more pronounced.
About 3.p.m. 15.c.m. fired a few rounds between PIQUET House and CRESCENT Trench.
4.5p.m. German 21.c.m. Howitzer shelled WINDY CORNER.
5.p.m. WOOLY BEARS shelled LANSDOWNE POST.
Immediately after our bombardment at 2.p.m. the Germans concentrated heavy gun fire on our trenches and all along RUE du BOIS from about RITZ to PORT ARTHUR.
During afternoon 68th Battery O.P. shelled by heavy Howitzers- 12 rounds 3 direct hits.

2. INFORMATION.
Owing to the good light this evening the HAUTE POMMEREAU Ridge stands up very clearly from 28th Battery position(M 33 a 8'9) and house bearing(true)100° 30' from this position- probably an O.P. as there are holes cut in wall.(LORRETO Road is therefore probably seen from this point
AIRCRAFT:- German "Sausage" sighted at bearing 172° from M 14 d 9'2
GALVANIZED IRON TANKS:-Reference Tactical Progress Report of 10th instant, following further information received:-
These are now seen to be large semi-circular sheets of galvanized iron (such as are used in England to roof hay sheds(). They are being built into the trench apparently for the purpose of revetting a new trench which the enemy are constructing in this locality. The trench appears to run from about N 31 d 8'4 S.S.W. through T 1 b till it crosses the road which runs W.N.W. to E.S.E. through this latter square. Here it is hidden from view by the trees of the BOIS du BIEZ There is a communication trench from the point at which the trench crosses the road which runs approximately West down the hill till lost to view in low ground N.E. BOIS du BIEZ. During past two or three nights enemy have been erecting stakes for wire entanglement in front of main trench 30 or 40 yards distant from it. This trench appears to have excellent field of fire over low ground to N.E. of BOIS du BIEZ. These observations made from 7th Battery O.P. in NEUVE CHAPELLE(S 5 a 5'6). ?(The galvanized tanks might be embedded into the parapet and yet appear to be revetting it.

..........Major R.A.

Brigade Major, Royal Artillery,
MEERUT DIVISION.

APPENDIX 182(a)
Copy 203

Operation Order No. 45
by
Brig.General F.E.Johnson, C.M.G., D.S.O.,
Commanding Lahore Divisional Artillery.

May ~~14th~~ 15th 1915.

Reference $\frac{1}{10000}$ map.

1. 1st and Indian Corps will renew attack with object of gaining line - road FESTUBERT - LA QUINQUE RUE - LA TOURELLE cross roads - PORT ARTHUR.

2. The Meerut Division less Dehra Dun Bde. and one Bde. R.F.A. and plus the Sirhind Bde. will make the attack to be delivered by the Indian Corps.

This assault is to be made against the enemy front line trenches included between the ditches running from South-southeast to North-northwest through points V 5 and V 6. The first objective is the capture of the enemy's front line of V 6 redoubt and of the trenches behind the first line lying West of the North corner of the redoubt as far the ditch running through V 5. Communication trenches will then be opened connecting captured trenches with our own line. The easterly one of such trenches will be turned into a fire trench facing east. Every endeavour will be made to accomplish this task and consolidate our position before daylight, getting touch on our right with the 2nd Division troops and bombing outwards along enemy trenches on our left flank to the east and southeast. A fire front facing East will thus be formed with the V.6 redoubt as its centre. The second objective is to attack outwards in an easterly direction and secure the line V.5.c. - V.6.c. -59 . The third objective; when the above line has been secured, and as the attack of the 2nd Division progresses, our attack is to push on and secure the road from PORT ARTHUR to LA TOURELLE Cross roads inclusive and consolidate itself thereon.

3. A deliberate Artillery Bombardment will proceed the assault and will cease on the front to be attacked at 11.25pm on 15th May.

Tasks and Barrages are set out in accompanying Time Table and list of Barrages.

4. Garhwal Bde. will carry out assault at 11.30pm and will be covered by fire of machine guns, trench mortars, bomb guns and rifles.

5. Sirhind Bde. will be in support
Bareilly Bde. " " " Div reserve.
Dehra Dun Bde. " " " Corps "

6. Field Ambulances will be opened at VIEILLE CHAPELLE and ZELOBES.

7. 2nd Division Troops, at night, are wearing a white bib, showing both to front and rear.

By day position of advanced or flank bombing parties of Meerut Division will be shown by a three foot square flag, the top and left portion being black and the bottom and ~~[illegible]~~ right portion - red, with a white St. ANDREW'S CROSS.

Those of 2nd Division will be marked by a yellow screen, 3' by 28" in case of battalions, and yellow flags 28" by 28" in case of companies.

1st Division - Red flags - 3' x5' with white perpendicular stripe.
London Division - Sandbag cloth disc, 2' in diameter with black cross in centre.
Lahore Division - Yellow flag 18" square.

8. Supply of S.A.A. is as follows :-

5th F.A.Bde. to Jullundur Bde.
11th F.A.Bde. to Sirhind "
18th " to Ferozepore Bde.

9. Advanced Report Centres.

Meerut Division	RUE DU PUITS
Meerut Div. Art.	- do -
Lahore Div Art.	- do -
Garhwal Bde.	96 Picadilly
Sirhind Bde.	Landsdowne Post.

[signature]

Major, R.A.,
Brigade Major, R.A.,
Lahore Division

Issued at 12 noon

Copy No. 1 Meerut Division
2 Lahore "
3 Meerut Div. Art.
4. No. 1 Group Res. Hy. Art.
5. 5th F.A. Bde.
6. 11th F.A. Bde.
7. 18th F.A. Bde.
8. 43rd How. Bde.
9. 6 Coy. R.G.A.
10. Lahore Div. Am. Col.
11)
12) Spare.
13)

TIME TABLE
and
BARRAGES. Issued with Operation Order 45.

15th.

1. Meerut Div. Art.

As already detailed for 15th.

2. Lahore Div. Art.

(a) 11th F.A.Bde. Wire cutting.

(b) 8th Bde. R.G.A.
(1) Portions of first line trench which were not demolished on 15th.
(11) Keep and 59.

Night 15th/16th.

1. Meerut Div. Art.

From dusk to 5 minutes before hour of assault.
(a) Watch front from LA BASSEE road to our left.
(b) Barrage roads.
(1) 35, 49, 48, 43.
(11) 55, 50, V.15.
(111) V.9.c., V.10.c. to R.17.
(1v) LA TOURELLE to Ferme du BIEZ.
(v) V.13, V.16, E V.16, V.18 - 43.
(v1) 35 to 53.
(v11) Trench 54 to V.8.c.
(viii) Trench V.9.c. to V.7.
(ix) Trench V.10, V.8.c. to V.10.c.

2. Lahore Divisional Art.

(a) 5th F.A.Bde.
3 Batteries occasional rounds along front trench 30 to V.6. - then Observation.
1 Battery Observation.

(b) 11th F.A.Bde.
All Batteries from dusk till 5 minutes before assault occasional rounds on first and second line trenches to be assaulted - then Observation.

(c) 18th F.A.Bde.
One Battery - Road LA TOURELLE to R.13 occasional rounds till assault
One Battery - Trench V.7.c. to V.5.c.
One Battery - Whole extent of trench running East and West through 54 and 58 from road to road.

(d) 43rd F.A.Bde.
Will shrapnel first and second line trenches to be assaulted and trench running N.N.E. from V.6. from dusk to five minutes before hour of assault at very slow rate of fire.

(e) 8th Bde. R.G.A.
From dusk till 5 minutes before assault occasional rounds shrapnel from barricade North of 30 to V.6.

B A R R A G E .

~~The preceding Barage has been made out on the assumption that the Infantry attacks proceed rapidly and carry the trenches in quick succession. If, however, the attack is held up the following Barrages will be formed :-~~

BARRAGE No. 1 at 11.25 pm.

(If only the first line is carried or second line, i.e. line 120 yds. in rear of 1st line.)

Lahore Divl. Batteries

18th F.A.Bde.	Trench V 7 e to V 5 e
5th -do-	Trench between Ferme du Biez and La Bassee roads past 54 and 58.
5th -do-	Trench 53, 54e to 58.
18th -do-	Quinque Rue from La Tourelle to a point opposite R 14.

Meerut Divl. Batteries.

✓35, 49, 48, 46 ✓ ? 53-50-V.15 ??
53, 50, V18
✓V 9 e, V 10 e to R 17 (i.e. La Bassee road)
9
✓Road La Tourelle to Ferme du Biez
✓Roads round Ferme du Biez
✓Road 38 to ~~23~~ 53
✓Trench 54 to V 8 e
✓Trench V 9 e to V 7
✓Trench V 10, V 8 e to V 10 e.

43rd How.Bde. Covered way V 9 e V 6 e to point 150 W of V 6e
Trench 51 e to point S 5 d 2 5.
Points 55, 56, 60, 59, and trench between those points up to S.10.d.4.10 - increase rate of fire for 1st ten minutes of assault.

2 - 6" B.L.Hows. on V 9 e)
2 " " " " ~~V7~~ V 7 e) Shrapnel, if lyddite not available, and omitting any points
2 " " " " 53 and 52) known to be done in.
2 " " " " 33 and 34)

1 Mother on 50 and 51) Omitting any point known to be
1 Mother on V 10 and V 11) done in.

BARRAGE No. 2 (If Ifty. gain line V 5e to V 6)

Lahore Divl. Batteries.

5th F.A.Bde.	Trench 54, 58 from La Bassee Road to Ferme du Biez road.
18th "	Trench V 14, R 22 to La Tourelle and up to R 17 (2 Batteries)
" "	Tourelle cross roads along road to S.W. for 150 yds. V 14 to Lorgies.

Meerut Divl Batteries. Same as for Barrage No.1 in so far as Meerut Btys. are concerned.

43rd How.Bde. Trench 59, V 6 e and its continuation to the South to a ~~portion~~ point 100 yds. S of V 6 e (This must not be assigned to a Bty. E of La Bassee road, or Ifty. may be fired into)
Trench V 6 e V 9 e (front and rear trenches)
Points 55, 56, 60, 59.

2 - 6" B.L.Hows on V 9 e
2 " " " " V 7 e
2 " " " " R 13 e and R 17 e
2 " " " " R 17
1 Mother on V 10 and V 11
1 Mother on 50, 51

BARRAGE No. 3.

(If Infantry reach line V 5 o, V 3 o, 59, 30)

Lahore Divl. Batteries.

5th F.A.Bde. Trench 54,58 from the La Bassee Road to Ferme du Biez road.

18th F.A.Bde. Trench V 15, V 14, R 22 to La Tourelle and up to R. 17.

18th F.A.Bde. Tourelle cross roads along road S.W. for 150 yds V 14 to Lorgies.

Meerut Divl. Batteries. Same as for Barrage No. 1 in so faras Meerut Btys are concerned.

43rd How.Bde.

Points 55,53,54 o.
Communicating trench East side of La Bassee road from 30 to V 9 o (with Lyddite if available)
Trench 53,54 o,55.

2 - 3" B.L.Hows. on V 7, V 7 o
2 -do- R 16 o and R 17 o
2 -do- 50,51
2 -do- R 17
1 Mother Distillery
1 Mother V 10, V 11.

BARRAGE No. 4.

(If Infantry reach from 30 to LA TOURELLE)

Lahore Divl. Batteries.

18th F.A.Bde. 54 to 51 o.
5th F.A.Bde.(2 Btys) V 15, V 14, R 22, along trench for 120 yds. S.W. of 122 and then through 21 to La Bassee road.
5th F.A.Bde. Road V 14 to Lorgies
18th F.A.Bde. La Bassee road from opposite R 17 towards Q 29

Meerut Divl. Artillery.

43, 48, 49, 34 o to 33
53, 50 to V 14
Roads round Ferme du Biez
Road Junction V 26
Road and trench from V 8 towards V 12 (not further West than V 8)
Road 38 to 53
Trench 54 to V 8 o and V 8 o to V 9 and V 10.

43rd How. Bde.

Points 55 to 54 o and trench between 53 and 54 o V on to 53
Points 52, 53, 35, 34
House between 49 and 49 o.

8th Bde. R.G.A. 2 - 3" B.L.Hows on Distillery
2 -do- 50 and 51
2 -do- V 10 and V 11
2 -do- 65, 64

9.2 How. on Ferme du Biez.

APPENDIX 182(2)

POINTS REGISTERED.

Index letter.	Description.	
	LIGNY LE PETIT	(19th Battery R.F.A. (20th Battery R.F.A. (28th Battery R.F.A.
	LIGNY LE GRAND	(19th Battery R.F.A.(Out of range). (20th Battery R.F.A. (28th Battery R.F.A.
	FERME DU BIEZ	(19th Battery R.F.A. (20th Battery R.F.A. (28th Battery R.F.A.
"P"	Fork Roads T 7 d 3 ' 6.	(20th Battery R.F.A. (28th Battery R.F.A.
"M"	Fork Roads T 1 c 9 ' 7.	(19th Battery R.F.A. (20th Battery R.F.A. (28th Battery R.F.A.
"Q"	Road junction N 31 d 9 ' 1.	(19th Battery R.F.A. (20th Battery R.F.A. (28th Battery R.F.A.
"W"	Farm T 2 b 1 ' 7.	(19th Battery R.F.A. (20th Battery R.F.A. (28th Battery R.F.A.
"R"	Fork roads N 32 a 6 ' 3.	(19th Battery R.F.A. (20th Battery R.F.A. (28th Battery R.F.A.
"O"	ARRET T 2 d 3 ' 4.	(19th Battery R.F.A.(out of range) (20th Battery R.F.A. (28th Battery R.F.A.
	LA TOURELLE	(19th Battery R.F.A. (20th Battery R.F.A. (28th Battery R.F.A.(1 Section only).

The above points have been registered by the above batteries of the 9th Brigade R.F.A. by aeroplane and visual observation, and are prepared to turn on to them at short notice.

APPENDIX 183

SECRET

TACTICAL PROGRESS REPORT
15th May 1915.

1(a) ACTION BY OUR OWN ARTILLERY.
8th Battery fired at slow rate during night 14th/15th as ordered.
7th and 66th Battery's fired as ordered during night 14th/15th
8.p.m. 14.5.15 to) 20th and 28th Batteries carried out
4.a.m. 15.5.15) tasks allotted to them.
2.30.p.m. 2nd Battery fired 3 rounds at PIPSQUEAK which was active silencing him, also again at 3.p.m. and 5.15.p.m. (See 1(b) below).
4.p.m. 66th Battery fired on Machin Gun emplacements near 56- 2 direct hits obtained.
5 to 5.30.p.m. 44th Battery fired as ordered.
6.p.m. 20th and 28th Batteries fired on wire in front of trenches- the 20th on 51e to 54- the 28th on 53 to 54e.
6.20.p.m. 66th Battery fired on enemy's Infantry near 130 to keep down their fire on our aeroplane.
8.p.m. 9th and 13th Brigades R.F.A. opened fire and formed barrages in accordance with schedule of tasks laid down- this fire was kept up during the whole night 15th/16th.
44th Battery carried out registration during the afternoon.
All Batteries of the 9th Brigade R.F.A. fired a few registering rounds on their allotted tasks during the day.
Double House S.W. of 125 was hit and set on fire by one of the batteries of the 1st Highland Brigade R.F.A.

1(b) ACTION BY HOSTILE ARTILLERY.
6.45.a.m. to 7.5.a.m. Enemy bombarded front trenches of "C" Sub-section with Howitzer and PIPSQUEAK.
9.10.a.m. LANSDOWNE POST was shelled by 10.5.c.m. Howitzer.
11.a.m. 14th Battery shelled by large howitzer(8 or 9") from direction of HAUTE POMMEREAU.-13 shell near Battery-5 of them blind.
2.30.p.m. PIPSQUEAK very active on RUE du BOIS from direction just E. of FERME du BIEZ, also at 3.p.m. and 5.15.p.m. (see 1(a) above).
6.12.p.m. Enemey shelled our trenches in front of PORT ARTHUR- (S 10 b 7.10).
44th Battery O.P. was shelled during the day by PIPSQUEAK.
RUE du BOIS was shelled continually during the day in reply to our shelling.
REVOLVER House shelled continually during the afternoon with PIPSQUEAKS.

2. INFORMATION:-
Shooting of 9'2" Howitzers reported to be pretty accurate- this was reported from 44th Battery O.P..
SNIPING:- No sniping from front trenches during the day.
WORK:- 66th Battery report that second line trench from barricade 133 to point 130 has been strengthened with sandbags-two shields visible. Trenches from point 63 to 53 show considerable amount of new earth on them, also shields at short intervals from each other have been newly put in.
FUZE:- The fuze of a heavy shell which fell near the 14th Battery yesterday was marked 42 KZ G Z 14 .
MA 15

[signature]

Major R.A.

Brigade Major, Royal Artillery,
MEERUT DIVISION.

APPENDIX 183(a)

S E C R E T.

ROCKET SIGNALS.

Two rocket guns have been placed in our front line trenches and will be used to signal the result of the preliminary ~~xxxxxx~~ assault of the 7th Division on the morning of May 15th.

The following signals will be employed:-

White stars to indicate the success of the assault of the 22nd Infantry Brigade.

Green smoke mixed with white stars to indicate the success of the assault of the 20th Infantry Brigade.

Red smoke to indicate the failure of the 22nd Infantry Brigade.

Red smoke with white stars to indicate the failure of the 20th Infantry Brigade.

All observing and other officers should be on the look-out for these signals and at once report them.

They may be expected to appear about 8.20.

14th May 1915. (Sd) F.Gathorne-Hardy, Lieut.Col.
General Staff, 7th Division.

No G-439/31. 15th May 1915.

MEMORANDUM.

Forwarded for information.

Colonel.
General Staff,
MEERUT DIVISION.

To:-

DEHRA DUN BRIGADE.
GARHWAL BRIGADE.
BAREILLY BRIGADE.
C. R. A. MEERUT.
C. R. A. LAHORE.
C. R. E. MEERUT.

APPENDIX 184

S E C R E T. TACTICAL PROGRESS REPORT
16th May 1915.

1(a) ACTION BY OUR OWN ARTILLERY.
15.5.15-8.p.m. All batteries of the MEERUT Divisional Artillery opened fire on tasks allotted.
During the night 15th/16th 2nd Battery turned one gun on to PIPSQUEAKS at FERME du BIEZ and LA TOURELLE.
16th May 1915:-
6.a.m. 14th Battery shelled O.P. at 121-movement seen near this house.
6.30.a.m. 8th Battery opened fire on V.3 to V.6 to support attack on our right-this was repeated at 9.20.a.m.
9.10.a.m. 14th Battery fired at enemy's batteries near 118 and behind 117 to 147.
10.30.a.m. 7th Battery fired at suspected O.P. just W. of 68.
11.a.m. 14th Battery fired on O.P. near 125- 3 direct hits.
11.20.a.m. 4 guns of 2nd Battery fired on the LORGIES Road at a point where a german battalion was reportedz
11.28.a.m. One gun of 2nd Battery was turned on to KEEP- German movement being seen there.
11.43.a.m. 66th Battery fired on house V.8.
12.10.p.m. 8th Battery opened barrage on LA BASSEE Road and V.9e to V.7.
12.40.p.m. 66th Battery fired on FERME du BIEZ.
2.35.p.m. 8th Battery dispersed Germans in the open by gun fire near DISTILLERY, and got fleeting opportunities till 3.5.p.m.
2.45.p.m. and)7th Battery fired at RED House 130 which is suspected
5.p.m.)as an O.P.-5 direct hits obtained.
3.43.p.m. 14th Battery fired at trees near 69-Infantry reported snipers at this place.
5.45.p.m. 7th Battery fired on German trenches to keep down rifle fire on our aeroplane.
1st Highland Brigade Batteries registered certain points- Houses 121, 123 and 124 had direct hits put on them.

1(b) ACTION BY HOSTILE ARTILLERY.
15.5.15-9.30.p.m. PIPSQUEAK shelled our communication trench from LANSDOWNE POST to RUE du BOIS.
16th May 1915:-
8.a.m. Very heavy shelling of our support trenches near RITZ.
8.5.a.m. Heavy howitzer shelled British trenches S. of PORT ARTHUR.
9.40.a.m. 15 c.m. How: shelled 7th Battery position without effect.
1.45 to 3.30.p.m. 1st Battery position and Brigade Headquarters of Highland F.A. Brigade shelled- about 70 rounds- no damage done except one water cart smashed.
3 to 4.p.m. Howitzer and PIPSQUEAK fired on 7th Battery O.P. at slow rate.
3.20.p.m. PIPSQUEAK active about N 31 c 4'4-14th Battery fired a few rounds at him.
The following points were shelled constantly during the whole day:-
RUE du BOIS from S 15 a to S 10 b, with 15 and 21.c.m. Howitzers.
Communication trenches from LANSDOWNE POST to RUE du BOIS and Road S 9 a 5'9 by PIPSQUEAK and "H.E."(very heavy all day).
Road from WINDY CORNER to St VAAST and vicinity by 15 and 21.c.m. Hows.

2. INFORMATION.
GALVANISED IRON TANKS:- There is a Galvanised Iron Tank at T 21 a 3'9.
AIRCRAFT:- 7.45.a.m. AVIATIK, low, bearing 130°, out of range and disappeared S.E. over German lines.
10.55.a.m. AVIATIK, high, bearing 120°, engaged with 69 rounds then turned N.N.E. over German lines.
3.55.p.m. AVIATIK, high, bearing 150°, out of range and disappeared S.E. over German lines.
German "Sausage" Balloon seen from 7th Battery O.P.(S 5 a 5'6) true bearing 128°, also visible in direction of FERME du BIEZ true bearing 118½° from bend in road N 31 b 3'2.

Major R.A.
Brigade Major, Royal Artillery,
MEERUT DIVISION.

"A" Form. Army Form C. 2121.

MESSAGES AND SIGNALS. No. of Message

Prefix Code m. | Words | Charge

Office of Origin and Service Instructions.

Sent
At m.
To
By

This message is on a/c of:

APPENDIX 185

Service.

(Signature of "Franking Officer.")

Recd. at m.
Date
From
By

TO Meerut Divl Art

Sender's Number. | Day of Month | In reply to Number | AAA

The Divisional Artillery of Indian Corps will barrage from the main ESTAIRES-LA BASSEE Road up to and including the communication trench from FERME du BOIS Q13 FERME TOULOTTES P19 P20 to N23 and all road junction and communicating trenches within that area some continuous fire to be kept up during the night no Howitzer Lyddite to be used

From Adv Meerut Division
Place
Time 8 pm

The above may be forwarded as now corrected. (Z)

Censor. Signature of Addressor or person authorised to telegraph in his name.

* This line should be erased if not required.

(632) —McC. & Co. Ltd., London.— W 11400/2045. 100,000. 2/15. Forms C 2121/10.

APPENDIX 186

S E C R E T .

TACTICAL PROGRESS REPORT
17th May 1915.

1(a) ACTION BY OUR OWN ARTILLERY.
All batteries of MEERUT Divisional Artillery carried out tasks allotted during the day.
5.a.m.,6.a.m.,and 8.30.a.m. 2nd Battery fired at PIPSQUEAK.
9.45.a.m. 8th Battery fired on V.6 to stop Bombing.
10.10.a.m. 14th Battery fired at enemy's PIPSQUEAK near 118 and 119.
10.30.a.m. Battery of Highland Brigade F.A. fired at PIPSQUEAK near 118 and 119.
12.30.p.m. 66th Battery had 6 direct hits on house 50.
4.30.p.m. 8th Battery registered front of 58th Rifles,(with whom in touch),with night lines for 4 guns on front.
4.50.p.m. 8th Battery opened searching fire on ditch V.5 to R 12 on enemy's trench.
5.10.p.m. One section 8th Battery searched and swept behind LA TOURELLE cross roads.
5.35.p.m. 20th Battery silenced PIPSQUEAK shelling PORT ARTHUR.
6.40.p.m. 20th Battery again silenced PIPSQUEAK shelling PORT ARTHUR.
House at 160 was fired on three times during the day by the 7th Battery- 2 direct hits obtained.

1(b) ACTION BY HOSTILE ARTILLERY.
6.a.m. Germans began heavy shelling on RUE du BOIS, Reserve trenches and LANSDOWNE POST.
7.45.a.m. 15.c.m. Howitzer obtained direct hit on LANSDOWNE POST- heavy shelling still going on.
9 to 10.30.aam. Several PIPSQUEAK shell fell near 66th Battery.
4.30.p.m. Enemey shelling vicinity RUE du BOIS, FORESTERS LANE and communication trenches between them very heavily with 15.c.m. Howitzers and PIPSQUEAKS.
During the day the enemy shelled line RUE du BOIS-PORT ARTHUR-NEUVE CHAPELLE- their fire was kept up practically all day, but most of their shell fell behind our trenches.

2. INFORMATION.
TRENCHES:- New German communication trenches reported from V.5 to V.12 and V.2 to R.9.
ASPHYXIATING GASSES:- It is reported that Germans using Asphyxiating Gasses against our 1st Corps.

[signature]

Major R.A.

Brigade Major, Royal Artillery,
MEERUT DIVISION

"A" Form. Army Form C. 2121.

MESSAGES AND SIGNALS. No. of Message

Prefix Code m. Words. Charge.

Office of Origin and Service Instructions.

APPENDIX 187

This message is on a/c of: Recd. at m.

Sent

At m. Date

To 885 Service. From

By (Signature of "Franking Officer.") By

TO CRA Meerut
~~CRA Lahore~~

Sender's Number	Day of Month	In reply to Number	AAA
* G 65	18th		

Following from Second Divn for information The line gained by the attacks at dusk on 17th will be further consolidated and troops reorganised AAA Artillery bombardment will begin this morning as soon as there is sufficient daylight for accurate observation AAA Dividing line for artillery areas as on 17th AAA 1st Group HAR is bombarding buildings of COUR D'AVOUE Q11 buildings P13 P14 P15 P16 buildings M9 N12 in the first instance AAA Infantry of the Seventh Divn is to gain the line of the road from M3 to road junction at LA QUINQUE RUE AAA 4th Guards Bde will gain the

From line LA QUINQUE RUE P(?) FME

Place COUR D'AVOUE inclusive AAA 6th

Time

P15

The above may be forwarded as now corrected. (Z)

Censor. Signature of Addressor or person authorised to telegraph in his name

* This line should be erased if not required.

(24473). M.R.Co.,Ltd. Wt.W4843/541. 50,000. 9/14. Forms C2121/10.

"A" Form. Army Form C. 2121.

MESSAGES AND SIGNALS. No. of Message

Prefix Code m. | Words. | Charge. | This message is on a/c of: 885 Service. (Signature of "Franking Officer.") | Recd. at m. Date From By

Office of Origin and Service Instructions. Sent At m. To By

TO 2

Sender's Number | Day of Month | In reply to Number | AAA

6th Bde will maintain touch with 4th Bde as latter moves forward AAA 5th Bde will be in Divnl Reserve AAA Infantry attacks of 7th Divn and 4th Bde will take place at 9 am but advantage must be taken of any weakening of enemy in the immediate front to advance under cover of the bombardment AAA 3rd Canadian Bde arrives in position of readiness in area RU de L'EPINETTE LE TOURET CSE du RAUX by 8.30 AM this morning — ends

From Adv Meerut Divn
Place
Time 3.30 AM

The above may be forwarded as now corrected. (Z)

Censor. Signature of Addressor or person authorised to telegraph in his name

Major
G.S.O.(2)

* This line should be erased if not required.

(24473). M.R.Co.,Ltd. Wt.W4843/541. 50,000. 9/14. Forms C2121/10.

"A" Form. Army Form C. 2121.

MESSAGES AND SIGNALS. No. of Message

Prefix Code m. | Words | Charge | This message is on a/c of: APPENDIX 188 Service. | Recd. at m.

Office of Origin and Service Instructions. SECRET

Sent At m. To By

(Signature of "Franking Officer.") Date From By

TO
4th Brigade R.F.A.
9th Brigade R.F.A.
13th Brigade R.F.A.

Sender's Number.	Day of Month	In reply to Number	AAA
* 664 RA (L)	19		

Following from 2nd Division for information: The line gained by the attacks at dusk on 17th will be further consolidated and troops reorganised AAA Artillery bombardment will begin this morning as soon as there is sufficient daylight for accurate observation AAA Dividing line for Artillery areas as on 17th AAA 1st Group H.A.R is bombarding buildings of COUR D'AVOUE Q11 buildings P13 P14 P15 P16 buildings M9 N12 in the first instance AAA Infantry of the Seventh Division is to gain the line of the road FROM M3 to road junction at LA QUINQUE RUE AAA 4th Guards Brigade will gain the line LA QUINQUE RUE ~~P11~~ FME COUR D'AVOUE ~~including~~ inclusive

From
Place
Time

The above may be forwarded as now corrected. (Z)

Censor. Signature of Addressor or person authorised to telegraph in his name.

* This line should be erased if not required.

(632) —McC. & Co. Ltd., London.— W 11400/2045. 100,000. 2/15. Forms C 2121/10.

"A" Form. Army Form C. 2121.

MESSAGES AND SIGNALS. No. of Message

Prefix ... Code ... m.	Words	Charge	This message is on a/c of:	Recd. at ... m.
Office of Origin and Service Instructions.	Sent		... Service.	Date
	At ... m.			From
	To			By
	By		(Signature of "Franking Officer.")	

TO (2)

Sender's Number.	Day of Month	In reply to Number	AAA
*			

AAA 6th Bde will maintain touch with 4th Bde as latter moves forward AAA 5th Bde will be in Divisional Reserve AAA Infantry attacks of 7th Division and 4th Bde will take place at 9.a.m. but advantage must be taken of any weakening of enemy in the immediate front to advance under cover of the bombardment AAA 3rd Canadian Brigade arrives in position of readiness in area RV de L'EPINETTE LETOURET Cse du RAUX by 8.30 a.m. this morning ends

From Brigade Major RA
Place Meerut Division
Time 4-50 a.m.

The above may be forwarded as now corrected. (Z) [illegible] Major RA

Censor. Signature of Addressor or person authorised to telegraph in his name.

* This line should be erased if not required.

(632) —McC. & Co. Ltd., London.— W 11400/2045. 100,000. 2/15. Forms C 2121/10.

"A" Form. Army Form C. 2121.

MESSAGES AND SIGNALS. No. of Message______

APPENDIX 189

Prefix ___ Code ___ m.	Words	Charge	This message is on a/c of:	Recd. at ___ m.
Office of Origin and Service Instructions.	Sent		___ Service.	Date
	At ___ m.			From
	To			By
	By		(Signature of "Franking Officer")	

TO: O.C. 9th Bde RFA

Sender's Number	Day of Month	In reply to Number	AAA
BM 205			

Ref my Secret 664 RA (L) now being delivered by hand it will be of great assistance to the 2nd Div if the hostile PIPSQUEAK battery near FERME du BIEZ is kept well neutralised during their bombardment and afterwards during their [illegible] AAA [illegible] be prepared to [illegible] the [illegible] [illegible] [illegible] RA [illegible] OC [illegible] 2nd [illegible] [illegible]

From	BMRA
Place	
Time	4-30 a m

The above may be forwarded as now corrected. (Z) [illegible signature]

Censor. Signature of Addressor or person authorised to telegraph in his name

* This line should be erased if not required.

C27642 P. G. Ltd. Wt. W14142/641—20,000 3/15. Forms C2121/10.

"A" Form. Army Form C. 2121.

MESSAGES AND SIGNALS.

No. of Message________

Prefix ____ Code ____ m.	Words	Charge	This message is on a/c of:	Recd. at ____ m.
Office of Origin and Service Instructions.	Sent		APPENDIX 190	Date
	At ____ m.		____ Service.	From
	To			
	By		(Signature of "Franking Officer")	By

TO O C 13th Bde

* Sender's Number	Day of Month	In reply to Number	AAA
BM 206	18		

Ref my secret 664 RA(2) ~~[illegible] being [illegible] by [illegible]~~ result it will be of great assistance to 2nd Div during their bombardment and especially during their assault if hostile [illegible] battery or battery near LA [illegible] are kept well neutralised AAA Please be prepared to carry out this in addition to any other tasks which G.O.C. R.A. [illegible] may assign to your Bde AAA These batteries may possibly include [illegible] LA [illegible] [illegible] V[illegible] to R 13 or VA to VLE also shelling of any hostile O.Ps. for bringing fire from North and East towards 2nd Div

From B M R A
Place
Time

The above may be forwarded as now corrected. (Z)

Censor. Signature of Addressor or person authorised to telegraph in his name

* This line should be erased if not required.

C27642 P. G. Ltd. Wt. W14142/841—20,000 3/15. Forms C2121/10.

"A" Form. Army Form C. 2121.

MESSAGES AND SIGNALS.

No. of Message

Prefix Code m. Office of Origin and Service Instructions.	Words	Charge	This message is on a/c of: APPENDIX 191 Service. (Signature of "Franking Officer")	Recd. at m.
	Sent			Date
	At m.			From
	To			
	By			By

TO: C R A JULLUNDUR

Sender's Number	Day of Month	In reply to Number	AAA
B.M. 227	[illegible]		

Ref my Secret 664 RA(2) orders being delivered by hand it will be of the [illegible] [illegible] to [illegible] [illegible] during [illegible] and [illegible] [illegible] [illegible] [illegible] [illegible] [illegible] [illegible] [illegible] [illegible] [illegible] [illegible] [illegible] [illegible] [illegible] [illegible] [illegible] [illegible] LA [illegible] [illegible] [illegible] [illegible] with [illegible] at 5 6 [illegible] [illegible] [illegible] [illegible] [illegible] AAA This is [illegible] [illegible] [illegible] [illegible] [illegible] [illegible] [illegible] [illegible] [illegible] [illegible] [illegible] 6 0 0 LAHORE [illegible] or JULLUNDUR [illegible]

From	B M R A		
Place			
Time	5 a.m.		

The above may be forwarded as now corrected. (Z)

Censor. Signature of Addressor or person authorised to telegraph in his name

* This line should be erased if not required.

C27642 P. G. Ltd. Wt. W14142/641—20,000 3/15. Forms C2121/10.

"A" Form. Army Form C. 2121.

MESSAGES AND SIGNALS.

No. of Message______

Prefix ____ Code ____ m.	Words	Charge	This message is on a/c of:	Recd. at ____ m.
Office of Origin and Service Instructions.	Sent		APPENDIX 192 ____ Service.	Date
	At ____ m.			From
	To			
	By		(Signature of "Franking Officer")	By

TO: O. C. 1st Coln

Sender's Number	Day of Month	In reply to Number	AAA
B M 208	18		

Continuation my B M 206 there [illegible] [illegible] [illegible] [illegible] at [illegible] [illegible] [illegible] [illegible] [illegible] [illegible] [illegible] [illegible] R 25 and [illegible] AAA [illegible] [illegible] be [illegible] [illegible] [illegible] [illegible] [illegible] [illegible] [illegible] should be [illegible]

From: B. M. R. A.
Place
Time: [illegible]

The above may be forwarded as now corrected. (Z)

Censor. Signature of Addressor or person authorised to telegraph in his name

* This line should be erased if not required.

C27642 P. G. Ltd. Wt. W14142/641—20,000 3/15. Forms C2121/10.

"A" Form. Army Form C. 2121.

MESSAGES AND SIGNALS.

No. of Message ______

Prefix ____ Code ____ m. Office of Origin and Service Instructions.	Words / Charge — Sent At ____ m. To ____ By ____	This message is on a/c of: APPENDIX 193 ____ Service. (Signature of "Franking Officer")	Recd. at ____ m. Date ____ From ____ By ____

TO: D C [illegible] Bde

* Sender's Number	Day of Month	In reply to Number	AAA
BM 204	18		

Ref my [illegible] and V.M. [illegible] and possible [illegible] V 5 [illegible] 12 shall be included in probable objectives.

From	B.M.E.A.
Place	
Time	5-35 am

The above may be forwarded as now corrected.

Censor.

(Z) [illegible]

Signature of Addressor or person authorised to telegraph in his name

* This line should be erased if not required.

C27642 P. G. Ltd. Wt. W14142/641—20,000 3/15. Forms C2121/10.

"A" Form. Army Form C. 2121.

MESSAGES AND SIGNALS. No. of Message

APPENDIX 194

Code m.	Words. Charge.	This message is on a/c of:	Recd. at m.
and Service Instructions.	Sent	1038 Service.	Date
	At m.		From
	To		By
	By	(Signature of "Franking Officer.")	

TO { CRA Meerut CRA Lahore

Sender's Number	Day of Month	In reply to Number	AAA
* G 80	18		

The assault this afternoon on the Ferme du ~~Bois~~ Bois will take place at 4.30 pm. It will be preceded by an intensive bombardment the period of which will be intimated later AAA Till then a slow bombardment to overcome any special points & registering will be carried on by Artillery

From Advanced Meerut Division
Place
Time 1.30 pm

The above may be forwarded as now corrected. (Z) C Norie

Censor. Signature of Addressor or person authorised to telegraph in his name

* This line should be erased if not required.

(24473). M.R.Co.,Ltd. Wt.W4843/541. 50,000. 9/14. Forms C2121/10.

"A" Form. Army Form C. 2121.

MESSAGES AND SIGNALS.

No. of Message

Prefix Code m. | Words | Charge | APPENDIX 195 | Recd. at m.

Office of Origin and Service Instructions.

Sent At m. To By

This message is on a/c of: Service. 10 38

(Signature of "Franking Officer")

Date From By

TO ~~Sirhind Bde~~ CRA Meerut ~~CRA Lahore~~

Sender's Number	Day of Month	In reply to Number	AAA
G 77	18		

Organise a bombing party to work NE along front German trench from V1 towards trench junction V2 AAA Block front trench between that junction and V3 AAA If you can work on into German Second trench V2 – V4 so much the better but look out for our artillery shelling line V2 – R9 AAA This bombing party can commence operations as soon as possible AAA Be careful to show your distinguishing flag AAA Eighth Gurkhas have been warned Addressed Sirhind Bde repeated CRA's Lahore & Meerut for information

From
Place Adv Meerut Div
Time 1-30 P.M.

The above may be forwarded as now corrected. (Z) R Davis Major GSO(2)

Censor. Signature of Addressor or person authorised to telegraph in his name

* This line should be erased if not required.

C27642 P. G. Ltd. Wt. W14142/641—20.000 3/15. Forms C2121/10.

"A" Form. Army Form C. 2121.

MESSAGES AND SIGNALS.

No. of Message

APPENDIX 196

Prefix Code m.	Words Charge	This message is on a/c of:	Recd. at m.
Office of Origin and Service Instructions.	Sent		Date
	At m.	1050 Service.	From
	To		
	By	(Signature of "Franking Officer")	By

TO ~~Sirhind Bde~~ ~~C.R.A. Lahore~~
~~Bareilly Bde~~ ~~C.R.E. Meerut~~
C.R.A. Meerut ✓ ~~107th Pioneers~~

Sender's Number	Day of Month	In reply to Number	AAA
G82	18th.		

The Canadian third Brigade are using blue flags sixteen inches square on four foot poles as distinguishing marks

From Adv. Meerut Divn.
Place
Time 2.10 P.m

The above may be forwarded as now corrected. (Z)

Censor. Signature of Addressor or person authorised to telegraph in his name

Crone Col GSO1

* This line should be erased if not required.

C27642 P.G. Ltd. Wt. W14142/641—20,000 3/15. Forms C2121/10.

APPENDIX 197

SECRET Copy No. 9

OPERATION ORDER No.32
by
Lieutenant General Sir Charles ANDERSON, K.C.B.
Commanding MEERUT DIVISION.

Reference maps:- 18th May 1915.
FRANCE - BETHUNE Sheet - 1:40,000
& Special Map 1:10,000.

-:-:-:-:-:-:-:-:-:-:-:-:-:-

Information. 1. Germans are holding FERME DU BOIS and trenches about and to east of it, also the COUR D'AVOINE.

The Indian Corps will attack the FERME DU BOIS at 4.30 P.M. today, in conjunction with an attack ~~from~~ on COUR D'AVOINE by the Guards Brigade.

Meerut Division, reinforced by the SIRHIND Brigade, is to carry out the attack.

Dehra Dun Brigade has again come under orders of Meerut Division.

Intention. 2. The intention is to obtain possession of the FERME du BOIS and of the trench Q.16 - Q 13 - Q.14 up to the LA TOURELLE - QUINQUE RUE Road in conjunction with the progress of the attack on the COUR D'AVOINE by the Guards Brigade with whom touch will be obtained at Q. 12.

Artillery 3. Artillery will co-operate as below.

A slow and deliberate bombardment till 4.0 P.M. when fire will quicken up to 4.20 P.M.

An intensive bombardment from 4.20 P.M. to 4.30 P.M.

Objectives as below:-

9.2" Hows. Two hour bombardment of FERME DU BOIS ending with a salvo, after which 9.2 will work along trench from Q.16 to FERME DE TOULOTTE.

60 Pdrs & 18 pdrs: Shrapnel fire on trench Q.17 - P.19 - P.20 - N.25 N.22 - N.23.

6" & 4.5 Hows. FERME DU BOIS and trenches between there and ESTAIRES - LA BASSEE Road.

18 Pdrs Trench Q.17 - P.19 - P.20 - N.25 - N.22 - N.23.
Trench R.2 - R.9 ; Trench V.3 - V.4 - R.10 - R.11 to R.9 and R.13 & R.12.
Trench V.6.E - R.17.E and also all other trenches between this trench and the ESTAIRES - LA BASSEE Road.

SIRHIND Bde 4. Sirhind Bde will make the attack on the FERME DU BOIS, and will capture it and points Q.15 and Q.16. It will push forward by bombing along the trenches from R.5 to Q.15, so as to establish a front whence the attack can be launched against the FERME DU BOIS from the East and south east, the position being kept under heavy fire from the front V.1 - R.5, and any opportunity for attack even across the open being seized.

The Brigade will establish itself at the FERME DU BOIS and then push southwest along the trench Q.15 - Q.11 - Q.12, in conjunction with the progress of the attack on the COUR D'AVOINE by the Guards Brigade, with whom touch will be obtained at Q.12. The trench Q.15 - Q.11 - Q.12 will be turned into a fire trench, facing northeast, and the line V.1 - R.7 - R.8 - FERME DU BOIS - Q.16 - Q.15 - Q.11 - Q.12 thoroughly consolidated and held as a defensive flank, in connection with the left of the Guards Brigade. Subsequently the trench Q.16 - Q.13 - Q.14 is to be seized.

Bombing parties will also be organised to work northeast from V.1 towards V.2 and V.3 at the earliest possible moment prior to the main attack.

BAREILLY Bde 5. Bareilly Brigade plus 2/8th Gurkha Rifles will hold
their

will hold their present line of trenches from the ESTAIRES-LA BASSEE Road to the point where the new communication trench from our old line near CINDER Track to the captured German trenches takes off. Full use to be made of fire to assist the attack of SIRHIND Brigade.

GARHWAL BRIGADE. 6. GARHWAL Brigade less 2/8th Gurkha Rifles, will be in support of Bareilly Brigade and will remain in its present location.

DEHRA DUN BDE. 7. Dehra Dun Brigade will be in Divisional Reserve, and will remain in its present location.

DISTINGUISHING FLAGS. 8. Advanced portion of Sirhind bombing parties will be marked by YELLOW Flags.

Colonel.
General Staff,
MEERUT DIVISION.

Issued to Signal Company
for distribution at 4-0.P.M.

Copy No 1 & 2 to Indian Corps.
" 3 Lahore Division.
4 2nd Division.
5 Dehra Dun Brigade.
6 Garhwal Brigade.
7 Bareilly Brigade.
8 Sirhind Brigade.
9 Meerut Divisional Artillery.
10 Lahore Divisional Artillery.
11 C. R. E. MEERUT.
12 No 1 Group H.A.R.
13 107th Pioneers.
14 4th Indian Cavalry.
15 A.D.M.S. MEERUT.
16. A. A. & Q. M. G. Meerut
17 Meerut Signals.

"A" Form.

Army Fo

MESSAGES AND SIGNALS.

No. of Message

Prefix Code m. | Words | Charge | This message is on a/c of: | Recd. at m.

Office of Origin and Service Instructions.

APPENDIX 198

Sent At m. To By

1329 Service.

(Signature of "Franking Officer")

Date From By

TO C.R.A. Meerut ~~CRE Meerut~~ ~~CRA Lahore~~

Sender's Number	Day of Month	In reply to Number	AAA
* G 96	18		

Continuation my G 561 of date. Sirhind Bde will not attack tonight aaa addressed CRA Lahore repeated CRA Meerut and CRE Meerut and Bareilly Bde.

From
Place 11.30pm
Time

Adod Meerut

The above may be forwarded as now corrected. (Z) R Davis

Censor. Signature of Addressor or person authorised to telegraph in his name

* This line should be erased if not required.

C27642 P. G. Ltd. Wt. W14142/241—20,000 3/15. Forms C2121/10.

"A" Form. Army Form C. 2121.

MESSAGES AND SIGNALS. No. of Message

Prefix Code m. | Words | Charge | This message is on a/c of: 1327 Service. | Recd. at m.

Office of Origin and Service Instructions. | Sent At m. To By | (Signature of "Franking Officer") | Date From By

APPENDIX 199

TO ~~BAREILLY BRIGADE~~ ~~SIRHIND BRIGADE~~ C.R.A. LAHORE C. R. A. MEERUT.

Sender's Number	Day of Month	In reply to Number	AAA
G-561	18th		

Indian Corps wires begins continue consolidation of positions gained AAA reliefs as arranged to be continued AAA snipers posts to be established and small parties to sieze any opportunity of gaining ground where protection can be obtained or can be made AAA Slow deliberate bombardment of the enemys positions and approaches to be maintained throughout the night on same objectives as last night modified to suit the offensive operation contemplated by the MEERUT Division tonight AAA Objectives of heavy artillery as ordered for last night except 15 inch howitzer which will not fire ends

aaa

From
Place ADVANCED MEERUT DIVISION 11.25 p m
Time

The above may be forwarded as now corrected. (Z) Censor.

P Davies Major, G.S.

Signature of Addressor or person authorised to telegraph in his name

* This line should be erased if not required.

C27642 P. G. Ltd. Wt. W14142/641—20,000 3/15. Forms C2121/10.

APPENDIX 200

S E C R E T .

TACTICAL PROGRESS REPORT
18th May 1915.

1(a) ACTION BY OUR OWN ARTILLERY.

All batteries of the MEERUT Divisional Artillery carried out tasks allotted.

3.20.p.m. 28th Battery fired on houses at points 50 and 51 obtaining 3 direct hits on each house with H.E.

3.30.p.m. One gun 2nd Battery fired at new German barricade near 59 obtaining 4 direct hits and destroying the left half of barricade.

4 to 4.35.p.m. One gun 2nd Battery neutralizing battery at S 18 a 4'2.

1(b) ACTION BY HOSTILE ARTILLERY.

Very little activity of enemy's artillery during the day.

4.45.p.m. LANSDOWNE POST shelled by PIPSQUEAK-too misty to observe anything in this locality.

4.55.p.m. 10.5.c.m. howitzer shelled communicating ~~xxxxx~~ trench from LANSDOWNE POST to RUE du BOIS.

5.35.p.m. PIPSQUEAK shelled our trenches near PORT ARTHUR.

2. INFORMATION.

HOSTILE BATTERIES:- Flashes observed night 17th/18th show that battery at S 18 a 4'2 is well located. It also appears that the RUE des TRONCHANTS battery is still where located by aeroplane. Bearing taken from line of unexploded 10.5.c.m. shell close to farm at S 3 c 8'5, 94° magnetic.

MACHINE GUNS:- Point 50 contains machine guns.

OBSERVATION POST:- 51 is probably an Observation Post.

SNIPING:- 50 is used by snipers.

[signature]

Major, R.A.

Brigade Major, Royal Artillery.
MEERUT DIVISION.

APPENDIX 204

G.105 nineteenth AAA

Operation Order No. thirtythree AAA (i) Garhwal Brigade will relieve Bareilly Brigade on the Indian Corps Front from CINDER TRACK exclusive to front of ORCHARD REDOUBT inclusive tonight AAA Bomb guns now in position on above front will be taken over by Garhwal Bde and remain in position AAA Brigadiers will arrange between themselves details of relief and will ~~xxxxxx~~ report to Advanced Meerut Division when they are completed AAA Billets at CROIX BARBEE for two battalions are placed at disposal of Garhwal Brigade AAA At CROIX BARBEE REDOUBT for one battalion and at LANSDOWNE POST for two battalions at disposal of Bareilly Brigade AAA Garhwal Bde Headquarters at CROIX BARBEE AAA Bareilly Brigade headquarters LANSDOWNE POST AAA Addressed Indian Corps 2nd and Lahore Divisions Meerut and Lahore Arty Dehra Dun Garhwal Bareilly and Sirhind Brigades Meerut Engineers 4th Ind Cavalry 107th Pioneers Meerut Signals No. 1 Group H.A.R A.D.M.S. and A.A. & Q.M.G. Meerut

Advanced Meerut Division
6.0 P.M.

PRIORITY

[signature] Colonel,
G.S.O.(i)

APPENDIX 205

SECRET.

TACTICAL PROGRESS REPORT
19th May 1915.

1(a) ACTION BY OUR OWN ARTILLERY.
All batteries of the MEERUT Divisional Artillery fired as ordered during day and night-barrages.
7.5.p.m. 18.5.15. One gun 2nd Battery fired on gap in parapet near 59, where Germans were at work. This gap was repaired during the night.
19th May 1915:-
9.50.a.m. One gun opened up a new gap at 59-this by 2nd Battery.
2.55.p.m. PIPSQUEAK at FERME du BIEZ neutralized by 20th Battery.
3.30.p.m. 14th Battery fired a few rounds at house 100 yards S.W. of 125.
4.25.p.m. 2nd Battery carried out registration on line R.12 to R.8. to verify line exactly.
4.28.p.m. (Flash) Battery at S 18 a 2'4 silenced by 20th and 28th Batteries who fired in conjunction with each other.
4.45.p.m. 66th Battery fired on working party at S 11 a 5'4.

1(b) ACTION BY HOSTILE ARTILLERY.
11.15.a.m. 10.5.c.m. Howitzer shelled our support trenches in RUE du BOIS from direction of HAUTE POMMEREAU(4 shell were blind).
2.45.p.m. A PIPSQUEAK shelled 7th Battery O.P..
5.45.p.m. PIPSQUEAK and 10.5.c.m. Howitzer shelled M 33 intermittently for an hour.
5.45.p.m. and 6.15.p.m. PIPSQUEAKS burst near 66th Battery position.
6.p.m. A few 77 mm. shell fell on each side of 44th Battery.
6.15.p.m. One 10.5.c.m. shell fell near 8th Battery.
6.20.p.m. Some PIPSQUEAKS and Howitzer shell fell near 2nd Battery-true bearing of scoops $134\frac{1}{2}^{\circ}$ from M 32 a 4'3.-LORGIES indicated.
6.30.p.m. A German Howitzer put a few shell into CROIX BARBEE.
A few shell reported to have fallen in FOSSE and VEILLE CHAPELLE during the evening.

2. INFORMATION.
OBSERVATION:- Very wet misty morning, observation impossible, slight improvemement during the day.
ROCKETS:- 10.a.m. White Rocket light seen-true bearing 141° 10" from M 31 d 8'6.
HOSTILE BATTERIES:- Flashes of battery at S 18 a 2'4 were visible.

O.H. Lynch-Staunton

Major R.A.

Brigade Major, Royal Artillery,
MEERUT DIVISION.

"A" Form. Army Form

MESSAGES AND SIGNALS. No. of Message

APPENDIX 201

Prefix Code m. | Words | Charge | This message is on a/c of: | Recd. at m.

Office of Origin and Service Instructions. | Sent At m. To By | Service. (Signature of "Franking Officer") | Date From By

SECRET

TO C.R.A. Lahore
C.R.A. Meerut

Sender's Number	Day of Month	In reply to Number	AAA
G	19th		

Indian Corps wires begins G309 of date the 2nd and 7th Divisions are consolidating the line M5 LA QUINQUE RUE P11 · P10 - Q7 aaa Operations continue this morning under cover of deliberate artillery bombardment as early as light permits aaa Objective of 2nd Division is to capture line P14 - Q12 - Q11 aaa Time for assault will be arranged by G.O.C. 2nd Division aaa Artillery of Indian Corps will assist 2nd Division attack by bombarding FERME DU BOIS and communication trench running thence by Q16 - Q13 and Q17 to FERME de TOULETTE aaa 4.5 and 6 inch howitzer ammunition is to be husbanded aaa Addressed Meerut repeated 1st Corps & 1st Army ends aaa For action

From
Place Meerut Divn
Time 4.0 AM

The above may be forwarded as now corrected. (Z) [signature] Major GSO (II)

Censor. Signature of Addressor or person authorised to telegraph in his name

* This line should be erased if not required.

C27642 P. G. Ltd. Wt. W14142/641—20,000 3/15. Forms C2121/10.

"A" Form.

Army Form C. 2121.

MESSAGES AND SIGNALS.

APPENDIX 102

No. of Message

Prefix ... Code ... m.	Words	Charge	This message is on a/c of:	Recd. at ... m.
Office of Origin and Service Instructions.	Sent		... Service.	Date
SECRET	At ... m.			From
	To			
	By		(Signature of "Franking Officer.")	By

TO: OC 2nd Brigade RFA; 9th Brigade RFA; 13th Brigade RFA

Sender's Number.	Day of Month	In reply to Number	AAA
* 672-RA(L)	19th		

Indian Corps wire begins Q309 of date the 2nd and 7th Divisions are consolidating the line M5 LA QUINQUE RUE P11-P10-Q7 and operations continue this morning under cover of deliberate artillery bombardment as early as light permits AAA Objective of 2nd Division is to capture line P14-Q12 Q11 AAA Time for assault will be arranged by G.O.C. 2nd Division AAA Artillery of Indian Corps will assist 2nd Division attack by bombarding FERME DU BOIS and communication trench running thence by Q16-Q13 and Q17 to FERME DE TOULOTTE AAA 4.5 and 6 inch howitzer ammunition is to be husbanded AAA addressed Meerut Div repeated 1st Corps and 1st Army ends

From: B M R A MEERUT Division

Place

Time: 4.20 am

The above may be forwarded as now corrected.

(Z) [illegible] Brigade Major RA

Censor. Signature of Addressor or person authorised to telegraph in his name.

* This line should be erased if not required.

Brigade Major RA Meerut Division

(632) —McC. & Co. Ltd., London.— W 11400/2045. 100,000. 2/15. Forms C 2121/10.

"A" Form. Army Form C. 2121.

MESSAGES AND SIGNALS.

No. of Message

Prefix Code m. | Words | Charge | This message is on a/c of: | Recd. at m.

Office of Origin and Service Instructions.

Sent At m. To By

Service.

(Signature of "Franking Officer")

Date

From

By

APPENDIX 203

S E C R E T.

TO C.R.A. LAHORE.
C.R.A. MEERUT.

* Sender's Number	Day of Month	In reply to Number	AAA
G-565	19th.		

Advanced 2nd Division wires begins G-624 of date aaa The result of yesterday afternoons attacks was to gain the line M5-LA QUINQUE RUE -P11-P10-Q7 aaa This line is being consolidated aaa A deliberate artillery bombardment will begin today as early as light permits aaa dividing line for artillery of 2nd and 7th Divisions Q5-P10-M12 aaa G.O.C. R.A. will arrange for artillery of Indian Corps to assist 2nd Division attack by bombarding FERME DU BOIS and communication trench running thence by Q16-Q13 and Q17 to FME DE TOULOTTE aaa 4.5 and six inch howitzer ammunition is to be husbanded and five inch howitzer utilized in preference aaa 1st Group H.A.R. is to bombard COUR D'AVOUE buildings P13-P14-P15-P16-Q11 aaa Under cover of the bombardment 4th and 6th Bdes will seize every opportunity of gaining ground with object of capturing the line P14-Q12-Q11 aaa Hour of

From

Place

Time

The above may be forwarded as now corrected. (Z)

Censor. Signature of Addressor or person authorised to telegraph in his name

* This line should be erased if not required.

C27642 P. G. Ltd. Wt. W14142/641—20,000 3/15. Forms C2121/10.

"A" Form. Army Form C. 2121.

MESSAGES AND SIGNALS.

No. of Message

Prefix Code m.	Words	Charge	This message is on a/c of:	Recd. at m.
Office of Origin and Service Instructions.	Sent		Service.	Date
	At m.			From
	To			
	By		(Signature of "Franking Officer")	By

TO 2/-

Sender's Number	Day of Month	In reply to Number	AAA

assault will be notified later aaa Infantry of 7th Division is to gain ground similarly towards L8-L10-L12-M9 aaa 2nd Division will be relieved during night 19th/20th by Highland Division under arrangements which will be notified later aaa 4th and 6th Brigades will therefore take advantage of and opportunity to withdraw units not required in front line aaa Addressed 4th and 6th Brigades R.A. repeated A.D.M.S. advanced 7th and Meerut Divisions 1st H.A.R. and Highland Division. ends For information in continuation of my G-564 of date.

From MEERUT DIVISION.

Place

Time 4-25.A.M.

The above may be forwarded as now corrected. (Z)

Censor. Signature of Addressor or person authorised to telegraph in his name

Major. G.S.O.2

* This line should be erased if not required.

C27642 P. G. Ltd. Wt. W14142/641—20,000 3/15. Forms C2121/10.

"A" Form.

Army Form C. 2121

MESSAGES AND SIGNALS.

No. of Message

Prefix Code m. | Words | Charge

Office of Origin and Service Instructions.

Sent: At m. To By

APPENDIX 206

This message is on a/c of: Service.

(Signature of "Franking Officer")

Recd. at m. Date From By

TO [illegible]

Sender's Number	Day of Month	In reply to Number	AAA
BM259	25		

[illegible] V 2 towards R 9 [illegible] fifty yards of front from V 2 towards [illegible] with HE [illegible] Forage

From [illegible]
Place
Time [illegible]

The above may be forwarded as now corrected. (Z)

Censor. Signature of Addressor or person authorised to telegraph in his name

* This line should be erased if not required.

C27642 P. G. Ltd. Wt. W14142/641—20,000 3/15. Forms C2121/10.

"A" Form. Army Form C. 2121.

MESSAGES AND SIGNALS.

No. of Message

APPENDIX 207

Prefix	Code	m.	Words	Charge	This message is on a/c of:	Recd. at	m.
Office of Origin and Service Instructions.			Sent		Service.	Date	
			At	m.		From	
			To				
			By		(Signature of "Franking Officer")	By	

TO O.C. R.A. [illegible] Group

* Sender's Number	Day of Month	In reply to Number	AAA
B M 260	20		

Following barrages required by your Group commencing [illegible] and continuing [illegible] [illegible] AAA From V 2 [illegible] [illegible] [illegible] [illegible] to point [illegible] 9 150 rounds to be spent in the [illegible] day [illegible] [illegible] [illegible] [illegible] AAA From V [illegible] to [illegible] [illegible] in [illegible] AAA [illegible] [illegible] Q 17 & 18 AAA 16 rounds for three or two last [illegible] tanks

From	[illegible] R A
Place	
Time	9-30 [illegible]

The above may be forwarded as now corrected. (Z)

Censor. Signature of Addressor or person authorised to telegraph in his name

* This line should be erased if not required.

C27642 P. G. Ltd. Wt. W14142/341—20,000 3/15. Forms C2121/10.

"A" Form. Army Form C. 2121.

MESSAGES AND SIGNALS.

No. of Message______

APPENDIX 208

Prefix ____ Code ____ m. Office of Origin and Service Instructions.	Words / Charge	This message is on a/c of:	Recd. at ____ m.
	Sent At ____ m. To ____ By ____	____ Service. (Signature of "Franking Officer")	Date ____ From ____ By ____

TO [illegible] 1st Bde

* Sender's Number	Day of Month	In reply to Number	AAA
BM261	22		

In connection with [illegible] AAA [illegible] from V2 towards V1 and thoroughly followed by [illegible] deliberate fire during the day [illegible] shrapnel [illegible] from point V1 [illegible] towards V2 [illegible] be [illegible] in this case AAA [illegible]

From			
Place			
Time			

The above may be forwarded as now corrected. (Z)

Censor. Signature of Addressor or person authorised to telegraph in his name

* This line should be erased if not required.

C27642 P. G. Ltd. Wt. W14142/641—20,000 3/15. Forms C2121/10.

"A" Form. Army Form C. 2121.

MESSAGES AND SIGNALS.

No. of Message ____

Prefix ____ Code ____ m.	Words	Charge	This message is on a/c of:	Recd. at ____ m.
Office of Origin and Service Instructions.	Sent		____ Service.	Date ____
	At ____ m.			From ____
	To ____			
	By ____		(Signature of "Franking Officer")	By ____

TO [illegible]

* Sender's Number	Day of Month	In reply to Number	AAA

the tanks [illegible]
V [illegible]
[illegible] AAA [illegible]
first [illegible]
NE from V2 AAA [illegible]
believe that [illegible]
well able to [illegible]
V2 [illegible]
[illegible]
AAA [illegible]

From	BARA [illegible]			[illegible] 260
Place		[illegible]		
Time	9.40a			

The above may be forwarded as now corrected. (Z)

Censor. Signature of Addressor or person authorised to telegraph in his name

* This line should be erased if not required.

C27642 P. G. Ltd. Wt. W14142/641—20,000 3/15. Forms C2121/10.

CRA 51 <u>SECRET</u> 20/5/15 66

OC R.A. Southern Group APPENDIX 209

<u>Instructions for Artillery fire</u>

Re. my B.M. 260 of today barrages mentioned therein are to be continued until 8 p.m. this evening.

1. From 7 p.m. to 8 p.m. battery firing at V.2 and vicinity and towards R.9. will increase its rate of fire to Section fire one minute – some H.E to be used.

2. at 8 p.m. this battery is to lift its fire from V.2. and vicinity and form a barrage across the three German trenches 150 yds to the N.E. of V.2 i.e. half way between V.2 and V.4 and V.2 and V.3.

Rate of fire for this barrage 40 rounds per hour.

During this time our Infantry will be bombing down to V.2. from V.1.

3. At 8 p.m. barrage on Q16 to Q18 will lift and will form barrage from Q 13 to Q.18.

Rate of fire 30 rounds per hour.

During this time our Infantry will capture FERME du BOIS.

4. Barrage from V4 to R13 will increase to 30 rounds per hour at 8 p.m. Fire should be brought short of V.4 towards V.3.

5. Orders as to rate of fire from 9 p.m. onwards will issue later, but batteries should be prepared to fire all night.

[illegible]
Major R.A.
Brigade Major R.A.
Meerut Division

3pm

"A" Form. Army Form C. 2121.

MESSAGES AND SIGNALS. No. of Message

Prefix ..... Code ..... m. | Words | Charge

Office of Origin and Service Instructions.

Sent At ..... m. To ..... By .....

This message is on a/c of: ..... Service. APPENDIX 210

(Signature of "Franking Officer.")

Recd. at ..... m. Date ..... From ..... By .....

TO 17th Bde.

Sender's Number.	Day of Month	In reply to Number	AAA
RA Q 10	26		

in	addition	to	my	CRA 51
a	Barrage	will	be	maintained
on	trench	Q11	Q12 Q17	aaa
12	rounds	per	hour	till
8 pm	aaa	30	rounds	per
hour	8 pm	to	9 pm	aaa
9 pm	onwards	12	rounds	per
hour	aaa	Refer	para	5
of	CRA 51	rate	of	fire
after	9 pm	will	be	12
rounds	per	hour	per	Barrage
aaa				

From BMRA Murat
Place
Time 6 pm

The above may be forwarded as now corrected.

Censor.

(Z) [signature] CRA

Signature of Addressor or person authorised to telegraph in his name.

* This line should be erased if not required.

(632) —McC. & Co. Ltd., London.— W 11400/2045. 100,000. 2/15. Forms C 2121/10.

APPENDIX 211

S E C R E T .

TACTICAL PROGRESS REPORT
20th May 1915.

1(a) ACTION BY OUR OWN ARTILLERY.

All batteries of the MEERUT Divisional Artillery fired during night and day on tasks allotted.

7.15.a.m. 14th Battery fired on PIPSQUEAK active from near 147, and on probably O.P's.

10.45.a.m. 66th Battery fired 4 rounds at working party near 51.

11.20.a.m. 2nd Battery fired on German reliefs(men in two's and three's) near point 57.

11.45.a.m. 14th Battery fired a few rounds at house W. of 151, where light was seen(probably signalling lamp)in the roof-2 hits obtained.

12 noon and 1.45.p.m. 7th Battery fired 8 rounds at communication trench S.W. of 63 where movement was seen.

2 to 5.p.m. 14th Battery fired at batteries near 75 at intervals.

2.40.p.m. 19th Battery fired at O.P. of PIPSQUEAK, shooting from DISTILLERY obtaining 2 direct hits and the desired effect on the battery.

3.45.p.m. "Flash" Battery at S 18 a 4'2 re-opened fire and was silenced by 28th Battery.

Highland F.A. Brigade Batteries fired at houses 122, 123, 124 and house N. of 120. House 124 reported on fire-two hits on 122.

3rd Highland Battery fired at Battery near 116,118.

1(b) ACTION BY HOSTILE ARTILLERY.

6.a.m. to 7.a.m. PIPSQUEAK shelled vicinity of M 33 and M 34 and 10.5 c.m. Howitzer shelled PONT LOGY.

7.a.m. 10.5.c.m. Howitzer shelled our trenches near PORT ARTHUR.

7.15.a.m. PIPSQUEAK active from near 147.

2.40.p.m. PIPSQUEAK active from neighbourhood of DISTILLERY.

3.45.p.m. "Flash" Battery at S 18 a 4'2 was active.

4.45.p.m. German Heavy Howitzer shelled NEUVE CHAPELLE.

6.58.p.m. PIPSQUEAK shelled 7th Battery O.P.

2. INFORMATION.

AIRCRAFT:- 11.15.a.m. German "Sausage" seen 182° from S 10 b 2'8.

1.15.p.m. AVIATIK sighted flying high at bearing 170°, engaged with 49 rounds then turned S.E. over German lines.

3.55.p.m. AVIATIK sighted flying high at bearing 125°, was out of range and disappeared E.

4.10.p.m. RUMPLER flying high at bearing 200°, was out of range and disappeared in clouds.

5.40.p.m. AVIATIK flying high at bearing 90°, out of range and travelled N.N.E.

7.51.p.m. German aeroplane passed over RUE du PUITS going S. and then E.

Major R.A.

Brigade Major, Royal Artillery,
MEERUT DIVISION.

SECRET

O P E R A T I O N   O R D E R   No.34.

Copy No. 12

APPENDIX 212

by

Lieutenant- General Sir Charles ANDERSON, K.C.B.,
Commanding MEERUT DIVISION.

21st May 1915.

(3 pages)

Reference maps:-
FRANCE-BETHUNE - 1:40,000
& Special map 1:10,000.

Information. 1. ALDERSON's Force will make an intensive bombardment on COUR D'AVOINE from 1.10 A.M. to 1.25 A.M., 22nd May.
The bombardment will include area inside points P.14 through Q.9, just east of Q.8, the FERME COUR D'AVOINE (D'AVOUE), north corner of moat Q.12 and trench Q.17 - Q.18.

Intention. 2. The German position Q.15 - Q.16 and R.8 FERME DU BOIS is to be captured tonight.

SIRHIND Bde 3. Sirhind Brigade will carry out the attack and consolidate the position.
The assault will take place at 1.0 A.M., 22nd May.

Garhwal Bde 4. The G.O.C. Garhwal Bde will detail an organised bombing party, supported by a platoon of infantry, to support the attack of Sirhind Bde by bombing along German trench from V.1 to V.2, with the object of establishing themselves there.
This party will not start operations until ten minutes after the Sirhind attack starts, unless enemy opens fire on our attacking troops, in which case it will commence immediately enemy opens fire
G.O.C. Garhwal Bde will also detail a platoon to occupy part of the trench running from his right towards V.1 with the object of assisting the bombing party by their fire.

Artillery 5. The following bombardment has been arranged by C.R.A. This programme commenced at 1.0 P.M. today, and will continue till five A.M. on 22nd May.-

(a) 18 pdr shrapnel, with occasional H.E., on trenches V.2, R.7, R.8, round FERME DU BOIS up to South-west corner of FERME DU BOIS. [Meerut / Lahore]

(b) 4.5" howitzer: 90 rounds lyddite during today at V.2, and also along trenches as in (a); also on the trench which connects German first and second line a short way east of V.2.

(c) 6" howitzer: commencing at 5.0 P.M. tonight will expend 60 rounds lyddite at V.2 and trenhhes round FERME DU BOIS from south-west corner round north-east corner to R.8 and on trench connecting German first and second lines east of V.2.

(d) All above trenches will be shrapnelled to prevent repairs being carried out after the bombardment by lyddite.

(e) Barrages will be formed along trenches:-

i. Q.11, Q.12, Q.17 - P.19 and Q.13, Q.14, Q.18 - P.19 to N.33.
At half an hour after the assault fire will be lifted and no fire will be directed north of line FERME DU TOULOTTE - Q.17 - or ~~east~~ W of line Q.17 - M.13. Rate of fire to be quickened ten minutes after hour of assault, and maintained for twenty minutes, when it will again be slowed down.

ii. R.13 to R.10. [Meerut]

iii. V.5 to line of German second line trench north of V.5. [Meerut]

iv. LA BASSEE Road from V.9.E to R.17.

v. Q.12 to Q.20 till half an hour after our assault, then from LA TOURELLE cross roads along QUINQUE RUE towards R.13 [Meerut]

6.

Bomb-guns. 6. Except in case of getting a really good target, no bomb-gun will fire at vicinity V.2 till 6.0 P.M. to avoid interference with artillery observation.

From 6.0 P.M. to 8.30 P.M. a steady fire will be maintained on this vicinity.

From 8.30 P.M. to within fifteen minutes of hour of assault, an occasional round only will be fired.

From fifteen minutes to the hour of assault till ten minutes past that hour, no firing.

Ten minutes past the hour fixed for the assault, one salvo of all bomb-guns is to be fired at V.2 and vicinity, after which no bomb-gun fire will be directed nearer than 100 yards to the east and to the south of V.2.

Sappers & Pioneers. 7. C.R.E. will hold a working party of one company S. & M. and two companies 107th Pioneers, in readiness to proceed at short notice from R.E. Depot ST VAAST to assist in putting the captured position in a state of defence.

Crorie.
Colonel,
General Staff,
MEERUT DIVISION.

Issued to Signal Coy for distribution at 4.0 P.M.:-

Copy Nos.	
1 & 2	Indian Corps
3	Alderson's Force
4	Lahore Divn
5	Highland Divn
6	No. 1 Group H.A.R.
7	Sirhind Bde
8	Garhwal Bde
9	Bareilly Bde
10	Dehra Dun Bde
11	C.R.A. Lahore
12	C.R.A. Meerut
13	C.R.E. Meerut
14	107th Pioneers
15	A.D.M.S. Meerut
16	A.A. & Q.M.G.
17	Signals - Meerut
18 to 24	War Diaries and files.

"A" Form. Army Form C. 2121.

MESSAGES AND SIGNALS. No. of Message

Prefix Code m. / Office of Origin and Service Instructions.	Words / Charge / Sent At m. To By	This message is on a/c of: Service. (Signature of "Franking Officer")	Recd. at m. Date From By
SECRET			

TO: GOC Sirhind CRA Lahore
Garhwal — " — Meerut
Bareilly CRE — " —

Sender's Number	Day of Month	In reply to Number	AAA
G 131	21		

Reference Operation Order No 34 of todays date aaa Aldersons force is not attacking COUR D'AVOINE tonight aaa The bombardment of that locality is intended to confuse the German and lead them to expect an attack there aaa Aldersons force is actually attacking K5

From
Place 3.45 pm
Time

Adod Meerut

The above may be forwarded as now corrected. (Z) B Davies Maj GS

Censor. Signature of Addressor or person authorised to telegraph in his name

* This line should be erased if not required.

C27642 P. G. Ltd. Wt. W14142/641—20,000 3/15. Forms C2121/10.

SECRET

APPENDIX 213

C.R.A. 52   21/5/1915.   68

O.C. 4th Brigade R.F.A.
" 9th Brigade R.F.A.
" 13th Brigade R.F.A.

SIRHIND Brigade will continue attack on FERME DU BOIS tonight. Hour of assault not yet fixed, but will probably be some time after 11 p.m. - This will be notified later.

2. At the same time GARHWAL Brigade will bomb down the trench from V.1 towards V.2 and will endeavour to establish itself at V.2.

3. Separate orders as to barrages to be formed will issue direct to units concerned - commencing 7. p.m.

4. All advanced posts and Saps etc held by us will be marked with yellow flags (e.g. V.1, machine gun T Head 100x N.E. of R.5, advanced post at S 15 b 9.0 etc).

5. The Highland Division on our right will assault FERME COUR D'AVOUE simultaneously with the assaults of SIRHIND and GARHWAL Brigades.

W.M. Lynch-Staunton
Major RA
Brigade Major RA
Meerut Division

∴ See BM. 273 (amendment)
(1am)

✗ See CRA 54

~~Q 20 to rd gate from Sam de Tonlette — from 7pm to 10 mins after Arrival, at 18 rds per hr.; from 0.10 to 0.30, rate fire 20 rds; then stops.~~

(?) Verbal orders to pause rate from 1.10 to 1.30 am

SECRET

C.R.A. 53

APPENDIX 21/5/15 69

O.C. R.A. Southern Group

The following are the tasks to be carried out by your batteries reference my C.R.A. 52 of date:-

1. One battery will commence a slow deliberate bombardment on V.2. the immediate vicinity of V.2- and trench V.2 - R7 - R8 - to S.W. corner of FERME du BOIS. 30 rds per hour to be fired - which should include a proportion of H.E. This bombardment will continue without cessation from 1 p.m. today until time of assault.

2. ~~One battery will form barrage Q13 Q14 Q17 Q18 commencing at 7 p.m. at rate of 18 rds per hour - 10 minutes after time of assault this rate will be doubled - 30 minutes after time of assault fire will cease altogether.~~

3. One battery will form barrages as follows:-

   (a) 2 Sections V4 to R.13, lifting at time of assault to R10 to R13

   (b) 1 Section will barrage German 2nd line trench 100 yds N.N.W. of point V.5. where small communicating trench is shown on 1/10,000 map.

Barrage (a) + (b) commence at 7 p.m and cease at 5 a.m. Rate of fire 18 rds per hour on each

By Orderly
1-20 pm

[illegible] Hamilton Major RA
Brigade Major RA MEERUT

'X'

Q 20 to Q 12

SECRET APPENDIX 215

C.R.A 54 21/5/1915 70

O.C. R.A. Southern Group

In continuation of my C.R.A 53 of todays date, cancel para 2 of thereof and substitute the following:–

(a) 2 Sections will form barrage Q13, Q14 Q17 Q18 commencing at 7 p.m. at rate of 18 rounds per hour. 10 minutes after time of assault this rate will be increased to Section fire ~~at~~ 40 seconds until 30 minutes after time of assault when fire will cease altogether.

X (b) One section on that portion of the LATOURELLE – LA QUINQUE RUE Road between point Q 20 and road junction 100x SW of Q14 commencing at 7 p.m. and continuing at the rate of 18 rounds per hour until 10 minutes after the hour of assault, when rate of fire will be increased to section fire 20 seconds until 30 minutes after the hour of assault, when fire will cease altogether.

W. Seyd – Henderson
Major R.A
Brigade Major R.A.
Meerut Division

72

SECRET

N.C.R.A. 55.   21/5/15

APPENDIX 216

O.C. 4th Bde R.F.A.
9th Bde R.F.A.
13th Bde R.F.A.

In continuation of my N.C.R.A. 52 of to day's date the German position Q.15 - Q.16 and R.8 FERME du BOIS is to be captured tonight.
The assault will take place at 1. a.m. 22/5/15.
ALDERSON'S FORCE will make an intensive bombardment on COUR d'AVOUE from 1.10. a.m. to 1.25 a.m., this is intended as a "blind" as this Force will not attack this farm tonight, but will attack K.5 tonight.
GARHWAL Brigade's bombing operations do not commence until 1.10 a.m., unless enemy opens fire on SIRHIND Brigade's advance, in which case it will commence immediately the enemy opens fire.

R.M. Lynch-Staunton
Major R.A.
Brigade Major R.A.
Meerut Division

"A" Form. APPENDIX 217 Army Form C. 2121.

MESSAGES AND SIGNALS.

No. of Message

Prefix Code m. | Words | Charge

Office of Origin and Service Instructions.

PRIORITY

Sent At m. To By

This message is on a/c of: Service.

(Signature of "Franking Officer.")

Recd. at m. Date From By

TO hot Group H A R

Sender's Number.	Day of Month	In reply to Number	AAA
* RAQ 14	21		

Battery	shelled	LORETTO	road	today
from	direction	AUBERS	aaa	Definitely
identified	as	10 cm	gun	aaa
fuze	set	at	18.5	aaa
Single	howitzer	shelled	E	subsection
this	evening	and	knocked	out
MG	aaa	located	E	of
45	between	LIGNY LE	PETIT	and
SE	edge	of	BOIS du	BIEZ
aaa	Following	urgent	aaa	In
operation	order	34	of	MEERUT
Div	Para	5	subpara	(e)
line	7	for	east	read
west	7 aaa	Please	acknowledge	and
state	if	understood		

From
Place Meerut D A
Time 7 pm

The above may be forwarded as now corrected. Censor.

(Z) Signature of Addressor or person authorised to telegraph in his name.

* This line should be erased if not required.

(632) —McC. & Co. Ltd., London.— W 11400/2045. 100,000. 2/15. Forms C 2121/10.

"A" Form. Army Form C. 2121

MESSAGES AND SIGNALS.

No. of Message

Prefix ____ Code ____ m. | Words | Charge | This message is on a/c of: | Recd. at ____ m.

Office of Origin and Service Instructions.

APPENDIX 218

SECRET

Sent At ____ m. To ____ By ____

____ Service.

(Signature of "Franking Officer")

Date ____ From ____ By ____

TO			
	CRA	Lahore	Sirhind Bde
			Bareilly Bde
	CRA	Meerut	Garhwal

Sender's Number	Day of Month	In reply to Number	AAA
G 137	21		

Indian Corps wires that Alderson force is attacking K 5 and M10 tonight aaa Infantry attack on K5 takes place at 8-30pm tonight aaa Aldersons force is also arranging to throw forward and entrench a line from left of Canadian Div on QUINQUE RUE through the two advanced posts east of P9 and Q7 and is to be ready to throw the left forward to conform with the right of the Indian Corps Ends

Lahore Div has also arranged to open a heavy fire along its front from 10 to 10.30 pm tonight

From
Place
Time 7-30pm

The above may be forwarded as now corrected. (Z)

Censor. Signature of Addressor or person authorised to telegraph in his name

[signature]
Meerut Div

* This line should be erased if not required.

C27642 P. G. Ltd. Wt. W14142/641—20,000 3/15. Forms C2121/10.

"A" Form. Army Form C. 2121.

MESSAGES AND SIGNALS. No. of Message

Prefix Code m. | Words | Charge | This message is on a/c of: | Recd. at m.

Office of Origin and Service Instructions. — SECRET

Sent At m. To By

APPENDIX 219

Service. Not to be telephoned

(Signature of "Franking Officer.")

Date From By

TO: 2nd, 4th, 9th + 13th Brigades RHA

Sender's Number.	Day of Month	In reply to Number	AAA
* 669RA(2)	21st		AAA

Meerut Division message begins Indian Corps wires that Alderson's force is attacking K 5 and M 10 tonight AAA Infantry attack on K 5 takes place at 8.30 p.m. tonight AAA Alderson's force is also arranging to throw forward and entrench a line from left of Canadian Division on QUINQUE RUE through the two advanced posts East of P 7 and Q 7 and is to be ready to throw the left forward to conform with the right of the Indian Corps ends LAHORE Division has also arranged to open a heavy fire along its front from 10 to 10.30 p.m. tonight ends AAA 9th Brigade RHA also opens fire from 10 to 10.30 pm on its night lines

From: Brigade Major RA
Place: Meerut Division
Time: 8.20 pm

The above may be forwarded as now corrected. (Z) [signature] Major RA Brigade Major RA Meerut Division

Censor. Signature of Addressor or person authorised to telegraph in his name.

* This line should be erased if not required.

(632) —McC. & Co. Ltd., London.— W 11400/2045. 100,000. 2/15. Forms C 2121/10.

"A" Form. APPENDIX 220 Army Form C. 2121.

MESSAGES AND SIGNALS.

No. of Message

Prefix ____ Code ____ m.	Words	Charge	This message is on a/c of:	Recd. at ____ m.
Office of Origin and Service Instructions.	Sent		____ Service.	Date
	At ____ m.			From
	To			
	By		(Signature of "Franking Officer")	By

TO — O.C. R.A. Southern Group (1st Bde)

* Sender's Number	Day of Month	In reply to Number	AAA
BM [illegible]	21		

Orders [illegible] [illegible] [illegible] that there [illegible] no artillery fire [illegible] [illegible] [illegible] [illegible] the [illegible] of [illegible] [illegible] in [illegible] [illegible] [illegible] [illegible] Q 15 and 21 [illegible] of [illegible] midnight [illegible] [illegible] a [illegible] account of our infantry patrols working [illegible] or in that direction AAA [illegible] CRA 53 [illegible] date [illegible] [illegible] should [illegible] [illegible] [illegible] R.A. [illegible] [illegible] [illegible] [illegible] [illegible] [illegible] [illegible] [illegible] [illegible] [illegible] until [illegible] [illegible] [illegible] [illegible]

From			
Place			
Time			

The above may be forwarded as now corrected. (Z)

Censor. Signature of Addressor or person authorised to telegraph in his name

* This line should be erased if not required.

C27642 P. G. Ltd. Wt. W14142/641—20,000 3/15. Forms C2121/10.

APPENDIX 221

S E C R E T .

TACTICAL PROGRESS REPORT
21st May 1915.

1(a) ACTION BY OUR OWN ARTILLERY.
All batteries of the MEERUT Divisional Artillery carried out tasks allotted to them.
11.35.a.m. and 2.50.p.m. 2nd Battery fired at movement seen near 58.
12.55.p.m. 7th Battery fired on house between 65 and 68 on party of men seen to enter it- six hits obtained on the house.
2.p.m. 30th Howitzer Battery shelled V.2. and neighbourhood-several lyddite threw planks and other objects into the air.
3.15.p.m. 66th Battery fired on house S 5 d 4'3 which Infantry reported to be an O.P.
3.20.p.m. One gun of 2nd Battery fired at battery in S 18 a 4'2, which was causing annoyance in our support trenches.
3.30.p.m. 2nd Battery fired a few rounds at barricade near 59.
4.p.m. 14th Battery had 3 direct hits on GABLE House 100 yards S.W. of 125.
4.p.m. 28th Battery fired at probable O.P's between 53 and V.12.

1(b) ACTION BY HOSTILE ARTILLERY.
20th May 1915,
10.10.p.m. Heavy howitzer battery shelled NEUVE CHAPELLE from BREWERY to 7th Battery O.P.
21st May 1915.
12 noon. About 30 shell of various kinds fell near 14th Battery- a large proportion were blind.
12 to 12.30.p.m 10.5 c.m.(? 15 c.m.) howitzer shelled vicinity ROUGE CROIX- about 6 blind out of 20.
12.15.p.m. 10.5.c.m. howitzer shelled vicinity of M 33 a- about 6 rounds- true bearing of scoop 106°.
3.15.p.m. Battery at S 18 a 4'2 active on our support trenches.
4.30.p.m. PIPSQUEAK shelled vicinity M 33 c.
10.c.m. gun from direction of AUBERS shelled LORETTO Road.

2. INFORMATION.
OBSERVATION POSTS:- Windows in the DISTILLERY and Chateau at LA TOURELLE have lately been sand-bagged and it is thought they are still used as O.P's.
TRENCHES:- Trench V.2. to V.3. reported held by enemy at 9.45.a.m. and strengthened during the night.
IDENTIFICATION:- Enemy seen moving about 58 at different times throughout the day- they wore grey uniforms with Red bands round cap.

[signature]

Major R.A.

Brigade Major, Royal Artillery,
MEERUT DIVISION.

APPENDIX 221(a)

No G-126

Headquarters Meerut Division.

21st May 1915.

MEMORANDUM,

Consequent on the re-adjustment of the line now held by the GARHWAL and BAREILLY Brigades that front will, until further orders, be sub-divided as follows:-

"A" SUBSECTION.- CINDER TRACK exclusive to COPSE Communication trench inclusive.

"B" SUBSECTION.- COPSE Communication trench exclusive to ORCHARD exclusive.

"C" SUBSECTION.- The ORCHARD and trench in front of it.

"D" SUBSECTION.- ORCHARD exclusive to trench running from centre of CRESCENT Trench to the front line inclusive.

"E" SUBSECTION.- Thence to LA BASSEE Road inclusive.

C.W. Jacob(?) Colonel.
General Staff,
MEERUT DIVISION.

To:-
DEHRA DUN BRIGADE.
GARHWAL BRIGADE.
BAREILLY BRIGADE.
C. R. A. MEERUT.
C. R. A. LAHORE.
C. R. E, MEERUT.
107th PIONEERS.

Copy for information to:-

INDIAN CORPS.

T.A.M.

Circulate copy to 3 Bdes 45th Bde and 6th Sign Bde.
[illegible] 21

APPENDIX 222

S E C R E T .

TACTICAL PROGRESS REPORT
22nd May 1915.

1(a) ACTION BY OUR OWN ARTILLERY.
All batteries of the MEERUT Divisional Artillery carried out tasks allotted.
8.p.m. 21.5.15. 2nd Battery fired a few rounds at a battery at LIGNY le PETIT at request of Infantry.
22nd May 1915.
3.30.p.m. 20th Battery registered house near point 53-2 direct hits.
4.p.m. 20th Battery registered houses near 51.
4.10.p.m. 7th Battery fired a few rounds into house 60 yards S.W. of point 125 from which enemy were suspected of sniping at 7th Battery O.P.
4.5p.m. and 5.p.m. 2nd Battery fired at battery at S 18 a 4'2 which was annoying our Infantry.
4.30.p.m. 14th Battery fired a few rounds at cross roads near 125.
30th Battery shelled back trench connecting V.2 and V.4- Hit it 3 times, breaching it in two places, but not quite to the ground.
30th Battery shelled trench from R.8 to V.2 in neighbourhood of R.8., but to N.E. of it- this was hit twice. One shell set something alight in this trench- a smoky fire was burning for half an hour or so, and occasional small flames could be seen over parapet.

1(b) ACTION BY HOSTILE ARTILLERY.
10.10.p.m. 21.5.15. Heavy Howitzer and PIPSQUEAK shelled NEUVE CHAPELLE
22nd May 1915.
5.45.a.m. Germans bombarded our trenches opposite FESTUBERT heavily for an hour.
1.15.p.m. 10.5.c.m. Howitzer from direction of BOIS du BIEZ shelled our support trenches behind PORT ARTHUR-about 25% of the shell were blind.
1.30.p.m. 15 c.m. Howitzer shelled vicinity of M 26.
2.30.p.m. Some 10.5 shell fell over the 2nd Battery- bearing of scoop 121° true from M 32 a 0.10.
About 6.p.m. 10.5.c.m. Howitzer shelled GOOD LUCK Corner.
6.p.m. 15.c.m. Howitzer shelled RUE du BOIS.
6.15.p.m. 15.c.m. Howitzer fired one round in vicinity of M 27 a.
7.p.m. PIPSQUEAK shelled vicinity M 27 a and b.
10.c.m. gun shelled RUE du PUITS in afternoon.
RUE du BOIS shelled during late afternoon with Heavy shell-probably 8.27"- direction from behind BOIS du BIEZ.

2. INFORMATION.
TRENCHES:- From examining the ground round V.2. and FERME du BOIS, there are the following trenches:-
(a)A curly trench from R.8. to V.2., which does not go through R.7 but about 80 yards East of it, running mainly South.
(b)A very low command trench starting from East end of farm running North, but it could not be traced as far as V.2.
(c)A trench joining Q.10 and R.9.

O.M. Lynch-Staunton

Major R.A.

Brigade Major, Royal Artillery,
MEERUT DIVISION.

APPENDIX 223

S E C R E T .

TACTICAL PROGRESS REPORT
23rd May 1915.

1(a) ACTION BY OUR OWN ARTILLERY.
All batteries of the MEERUT Divisional Artillery carried out tasks allotted to them.
6.15.a.m. 2nd Battery fired to silence PIPSQUEAK at S 18 a 4'2-this was repeated at 1.40.p.m.
6.20.a.m. 66th Battery fired a few rounds at working party near 54.
12.30.p.m. 14th Battery fired on house 50 yards S.W. of 151- signalling seen going on there- 2 direct hits. This was repeated at 6.5.p.m.-3 more hits obtained.
1.2.p.m. 20th Battery registered their new zone from ORCHARD REDOUBT to V.6.
3.45.p.m. to 4.p.m. 7th and 66th Batteries shelled trenches on our front in reply to shelling of road near 7th Battery.
7.p.m. 19th Battery registered new zone.

1(b) ACTION BY HOSTILE ARTILLERY.
Some heavy shells fell near 44th Battery during the night.
10.p.m. 22nd May 1915. PIPSQUEAK dropped a few shell in vicinity of M 27 b.
10.p.m. 22nd May 1915. Heavy howitzer shelled 7th Battery O.P.
23rd May 1915.
6.15.a.m. and 1.40.p.m. PIPSQUEAK active from S 18 a 4'2.
10.a.m. to 11.a.m. LEICESTER LOUNGE(O.P. at S 9 d 5'6) shelled by 10.5.c.m. Howitzer- This is new O.P. of 8th Battery.
12.30.p.m. Howitzer shelled BREWERY- 2 blind shell fell near 7th Battery O.P.
3.45.p.m. to 4 p.m. Enemy shelled road near 7th Battery.

2. INFORMATION.
Our Infantry holding trench from ORCHARD Redoubt to opposite V.6. state they can stand up and look over parapet and that there are either no Germans in that trench or that they don't show or take any notice of our people.
The House 50 yards S.W. of 151 is two storied, with single chimney on left top corner and white gutter at foot of dark tiles.
Infantry patrols of "A" Sub-section report that there are a number of square holes parallel to trench in front of their firing trench at point 54 and to the right- in line with these are two old "dug-outs".
IDENTIFICATION:- 66th Battery report "Grey uniforms, blue caps with red bands".

[signature]

Major R.A.

Brigade Major, Royal Artillery,
MEERUT DIVISION.

APPENDIX 224

SECRET.

TACTICAL PROGRESS REPORT

24th May 1915.

1(a) ACTION BY OUR OWN ARTILLERY

12.30.a.m. to 1.a.m. 19th and 20th Batteries fired on points V.9e, V.6e and 59(KEEP) at request of BAREILLY Brigade.
Batteries of the 9th and 13th Brigades R.F.A. carried out registration on their new fronts.
10.a.m. 5th Siege Battery fired with aeroplane observation at Machine Gun near FERME du BOIS- registered this point, also point on this trench on either side. Airman reported fire very effective, trenches flattened and hit on Machine Gun was followed by many violent explosions.
11.10.a.m. 8th Battery registered German trench E. of FERME du BOIS.
11.35.a.m. 20th Battery registered FERME du BOIS, FERME d'AVOUE, FERME du TOULOTTES-R.10, V.4, V.7e, R 17a.
5.p.m. 5th Siege Battery fired on trench running N. from FERME du BOIS in conjunction with 8th Battery R.F.A.-5 out of 6 rounds were hits in the trench.
The 28th Battery registered the following points during the day:-
DISTILLERY, FERME COUR d'AVOUE, FERME du BOIS-trench V.3-V.2, trench Q.14-Q.16, trench R.10-R.13-FERME du TOULOTTES-V.4.

1(b) ACTION BY HOSTILE ARTILLERY.

3.a.m. to 4.a.m. Heavy Howitzer shelled vicinity of M 27 d and RUE du PUITS.

2. INFORMATION.

9th Brigade R.F.A. completed registration on their new front-GARHWAL Brigade, and 13th Brigade R.F.A. on DEHRA DUN Brigade front. Liasion established between batteries and battalions of these Brigades.
13th Brigade R.F.A. established Liasion with 1st Highland Brigade R.F.A.(T.F.) of the Highland Division on its right.
9th Brigade R.F.A. established Liasion with 11th Brigade R.F.A. of the LAHORE Division on its left.

4th Brigade R.F.A. was relieved last evening by LAHORE Divisional Artillery and withdrawn from action.
MEERUT Division now holds line from ORCHARD to R.3 both inclusive.
MEERUT Divisional Artillery Headquarters returned to FOSSE at 4.p.m.

Major, R.A.

Brigade Major, Royal Artillery
MEERUT DIVISION.

APPENDIX 224(a)

SECRET. No.G.768.

Headquarters, Meerut Division.

24th May 1915.

Copy of a memo from H.Q. Indian Corps to H.Q. Meerut Division, No.G.399 dated 23/5/15.

With reference to Operation Order No.69, para 6.

1. The Lahore Divisional Artillery will rejoin the Lahore Division.

2. The 4th Bde R.F.A. will continue to support the Lahore Division front until such time as the Lahore Division Artillery is ready to take over; details to be arranged by the Divisions concerned.

3. Headquarters of 6th Bde R.G.A. and 2nd Siege battery will be attached to Meerut Division.
5th Siege Battery will be attached to Lahore Division.

Lahore Divnl Arty.
Meerut Divil Arty

For information and necessary action.

Crowe
Colonel,
General Staff,
Meerut Division.

Copy for information to:-

A.A. & Q.M.G. Meerut Divn.

M 20

M 23

From 200 yds S. E. P 18

Q. 18

Q. 17

Q 10 & Q 9.

Trench Q 15 – Q 12

~~Q~~ Round Q 20 – Q 13

Trench N W of N 15

N 30

P 18. ~~N~~ . ~~N~~ 15

APPENDIX 225

SECRET.

TACTICAL. PROGRESS REPORT.
25th May 1915.

1(a) ACTION BY OUR OWN ARTILLERY.

24th May 1915.

11.p.m. 8th Battery fired on front of 6th Jats on report of Germans massing.

11.p.m. 44th Battery fired at V.2.- but stopped at request of 9th Gurkhas who had patrols out.

11.40.p.m. 2nd Battery fired a few rounds at PIPSQUEAK at S 18 a 4'2 which was active on our support trenches.

25th May 1915.

1.p.m. to 3.p.m. 28th Battery registered V.7e and RUE du MARAIS.

2.p.m. 2nd and 8th Batteries carried out registration of the following points;-

P.28, Q.18, Q.9, M 20, N.23, Farm 200 yds S.W. of P.18.

3.p.m. to 3.45.p.m. 20th Battery registered as follows:-

(i) German support trench from 59(KEEP) - V.6.

(ii)Barricade on LA BASSEE Road at point 60.

(iii)Probably Machine Gun emplacement between 60 and 57.

19th Battery re-registered a few points in their new area during the day.

5th Siege Battery registered trench running N. from Q.15- Airman reported 4 hits on the trench.

(b) ACTION BY HOSTILE ARTILLERY.

7.a.m. Farm at M 33 a 8'7(Headquarters 9th Brigade R.F.A.)shelled by 10.c.m. gun for half an hour hitting the farm several times.

10.a.m. to 11.a.m. PIPSQUEAK shelled RUE du BOIS intermittently.

2.30.p.m. 10.5.c.m. shell killed a Corporal and one gunner and wounded one gunner of the 44th Battery R.F.A.

6.15.p.m. PIPSQUEAK shelled road from PONT LOGY to about M 27 d.

2. INFORMATION.

AIRCRAFT:- 5.55.a.m. and 9.40.a.m. German biplanes seen to N.E. from 44th Battery gun position.

8.30.a.m. Hostile aeroplane seen travelling East over M 27 and M 28.

4.55.p.m. "Sausage" up true bearing $108\frac{1}{2}^{\circ}$ from S 10 b 1'7.

5.40.p.m. Two "Sausage" Balloons seen true bearings 115° and $150^{\circ}55'$ from S 31 b 8'7.

HOSTILE BATTERIES:- An Infantry patrol has reported a field battery in clump of trees near Q19, or the FERME de TOULOTTE's- this should be located and neutralized.

R.H. Lynch-Staunton

Major R.A.

Brigade Major, Royal Artillery,
MEERUT DIVISION.

APPENDIX 226

SECRET.

TACTICAL PROGRESS REPORT
26th May 1915.

1(a) ACTION BY OUR OWN ARTILLERY.

10.40.a.m. 2nd Battery fired on DISTILLERY in order to check zero line, corrector etc,.
10.45.a.m. 8th Battery registered trench midway between V.1. and V.2.
10.50.a.m. 2nd Battery fired a couple of rounds at screen or notice board seen being put up in German trench near V.2.- the screen came down when fired at.
12 noon. 20th Battery registered point V.6e and support trench from point V.6. to point 59(KEEP).
2.p.m. 8th Battery fired a few rounds at PIPSQUEAK Battery near Q.19.
3.20.p.m. 2nd Battery fired 40 rounds H.E. at V.2-R.7-R.8 and knocked the trench about.
4.45.p.m. 8th Battery engaged V.2 with H.E.
5.5.p.m. 20th Battery fired at PIPSQUEAK battery at S 18 a 4'2 and silenced it.
44th Battery carried out registration during the day.

(b) ACTION BY HOSTILE ARTILLERY.

9.45.a.m. to 10.15.a.m. 10.5.c.m. howitzer shelled vicinity LA BASSEE Road near PONT du HEM firing one round every 30 seconds from direction of LA RUSSIE.
2.15.p.m. LEICESTER LOUNGE(S 9 d 5'6) was shelled.
3.20.p.m. PIPSQUEAK shelled RUE du BOIS- one direct hit on RITZ.
5.p.m. PIPSQUEAK shelled RUE du BOIS S 9 c and front line trench opposite.
5.45.p.m. Heavy howitzer dropped occasional rounds into vicinity of M 34 a.

2. INFORMATION.

German biplane passed over 44th Battery position at about 6.45.p.m.

A.M. Lynch-Staunton

Major R.A.

Brigade Major, Royal Artillery,
MEERUT DIVISION.

APPENDIX 227.

SECRET.

TACTICAL PROGRESS REPORT
27th May 1915.

1(a) ACTION BY OUR OWN ARTILLERY.
9.30.p.m. 26th May 1915. 2nd Battery fired at PIPSQUEAK just N. of point Q.65.
27th May 1915:-
8.a.m. 20th Battery fired at working party who were visible sand-bagging second line trench just S. of LA BASSEE Road and dispersed them.
3.p.m. 8th Battery registered road Q.20-Q.12.
3.30.p.m. 8th Battery obtained 2 direct hits on fortified house 200 yards N.W. of R.28 with H.E.
3.30.p.m. 44th Battery searched for PIPSQUEAK about M.18.
4.p.m. 28th Battery registered N.29.
4.45.p.m. and 6.p.m. 2nd Battery fired at S 18 a 4'2 where PIPSQUEAK was reported active.
4.50.p.m. 20th Battery silenced PIPSQUEAK at S 18 a 4'2 which was active.
5.34.p.m. 20th Battery registered all 6 guns on battery at S 18 a 4'2.
6.p.m. 44th Battery fired on hostile working party about Q.15, Q.16.

(b) ACTION BY HOSTILE ARTILLERY.
7.10.a.m. 10.5.c.m. Howitzer shelled RUE du BOIS S 9 d and open ground N. of RUE du BOIS.
9.30.a.m. PIPSQUEAK shelled support trenches in S 9 d.
11.a.m. 44th Battery billet and Headquarters 13th Brigade R.F.A. was shelled by 15.c.m. Howitzer- no damage.
About 12 noon. Several 15.c.m. shell fell near DEHRS DUN Brigade Head-quarters.
3.p.m. to 4.p.m. Heavy howitzer shelled vicinity of WINDY CORNER (S 3 c 6'0)- 2 direct hits on REVOLVER HOUSE(S 3 c 5'4).
4.30.p.m. 15.c.m. howitzer had 2 direct hits on the RITZ(S 9 d).
4.50.p.m. PIPSQUEAK from S 18 a 4'2 was active.
Infantry reported being annoyed by enemy howitzer fire all day.

2. INFORMATION.
WIRE ENTANGLEMENTS:- New wire on iron posts about 3 feet high from R.8. to about 100 yards from V.2. Parapet of this trench has also been improved.
Wire in front of new trench W. of FERME du BOIS.
HOSTILE BATTERIES:- True bearing of flashes seen at 9.55.p.m. 26th May 1915 from M 33 a 5'4- 151°.

R.M. Lynch-Staunton

Major R.A.

Brigade Major, Royal Artillery,
MEERUT DIVISION.

APPENDIX 228

S E C R E T

TACTICAL PROGRESS REPORT
28th May 1915
\-

1(a) ACTION BY OUR OWN ARTILLERY.

10.a.m. 44th Battery fired on German front line in reply to shelling this was repeated at 5.30.p.m.
10.45.a.m. 2nd Battery fired 3 rounds battery fire on night lines in reply to enemy shelling our support trenches.
11.20.a.m. 20th Battery registered new wire near R.8.
11.30.a.m. 20th Battery obtained 4 direct hits on house at P.16.
11.30.a.m. 19th Battery registered "MOUND" S 17 a 8'0 and searched for PIPSQUEAK near DISTILLERY.
12 noon. 20th Battery obtained 4 direct hits on house at P.16.
12 noon. 2nd Battery fired on enemy's front trench near FERME du BOIS.
12.26.p.m. 2nd Battery fired two battery salvoes on night lines in reply to enemy shelling- this was repeated at 12.30.p.m.
12.30.p.m. 28th Battery fired 15 rounds at V.2. in conjunction with the 13th Brigade R.F.A.
1.45.p.m. 8th Battery fired 30 shrapnel and 20 H.E. on German trench by FERME du BOIS Orchard from R.8 to 200 yards to the West. This was repeated at 4.p.m.
2.20.p.m. 44th Battery registered R.8 and Q.16.
3.26.p.m. 2nd Battery fired three salvoes on night lines in reply to enemy shelling.
3.p.m. to 3.30.p.m. 28th Battery fired on trench at point V.2. with H.E. and shrapnel in conjunction with 2nd Battery firing on trench V.2. to R.8.-parapet a good deal knocked about, also some of the new loop-holes in parapet destroyed. The 2nd Battery bombarded this trench from 3.45.p.m. to 5.40.p.m. with good effect.
* 4.45.p.m. 20th Battery opened fire on German front trench 50-V.8.
* 4.50.p.m. 28th Battery opened fire on German front trench V.2. - V.3.
* 5.p.m. 19th Battery opened fire on German second line trench V.3. - V.3.
5.30.p.m. 28th Battery fired on German Observing Station- a tree with ladder at S 23 d 2'6. There appears to be either a "dug-out" or else a single gun emplacement close to this tree.

* This in retaliation to PIPSQUEAKS and 15 c.m. Howitzer shelling the RUE du BOIS, FACTORY and RITZ between 3.30 and 4.p.m.

(b) ACTION BY HOSTILE ARTILLERY

11.a.m. PIPSQUEAK dropped a few shell in support trenches near V.1.
12.30.p.m. PIPSQUEAK shelled neighbourhood of RITZ in reply to our shelling of their trenches.
3.26.p.m. Enemy shelled LEICESTER LOUNGE and neighbourhood.
3.30.p.m. PIPSQUEAK fired on RUE du BOIS for some time and 15 c.m. Howitzers also joined in at 3.50.p.m. firing on FACTORY and RITZ- this probably in retaliation of our shelling V.2. and trench V.2 to R.8.
5.p.m. 10.5 c.m. Howitzer shelled vicinity of M.27 d intermittently for about an hour.
8.15.p.m. RICHEBOURG was shelled and a large house set on fire.

2. INFORMATION.

AIRCRAFT:- 8.15.p.m. Hostile aeroplane passed over 14th Battery flying in direction of BETHUNE.
OBSTACLES:- A great deal of wire entanglement has been put down by enemy in last 48 hours opposite trench V.2 to R.8. Parapet has also been much improved. Latter has suffered to a certain extent from to-day's shelling by our 18 pounders, but requires heavier metal to demolish thoroughly.

Major R.A.
Brigade Major, Royal Artillery,
MEERUT DIVISION

APPENDIX 229

[S E C] R E T .

TACTICAL PROGRESS REPORT
29th May 1915

1(a) ACTION BY OUR OWN ARTILLERY.
6.30.a.m., 8.15.a.m. and 9.30.a.m. 44th Battery fired at German working parties.
8.45.a.m. 8th Battery fired on house (probably an O.P.) at S 23 d 8'7, on LA BASSEE Road.
9.25.a.m. 8th Battery shelled trench V.2 - R.8 as a retaliatory measure.
9.30.a.m. 2nd Battery fired 25 rounds at German trenches in retaliation to enemy shelling our support trenches- this was repeated at 10.50.a.m. 2.45.p.m. and 6.10.p.m.
10.30.a.m. 20th Battery registered a battery S 30 a 5'1 who's flashes were observed during the morning.
12.15.p.m. to 1.15.p.m. 8th Battery bombarded trench R.8 to Q.15-with 30 shrapnel and 20 H.E.- this was repeated from 5.p.m. to 5.45.p.m.
12.25.p.m. to 2.30.p.m. 2nd Battery engaged enemy's trench from V.2 (exclusive) towards R.8 with deliberate fire- this trench appeared to be well knocked about.
2.15.p.m. 28th Battery commenced firing on V.2. and on communicating trench connecting V.2-V.4 with V.2-V.3, deliberate observed fire employed to batter parapets. A good deal of damage was done, sandbags, timber and cooking pots were seen flying in the air.
3.30.p.m. 44th Battery searched vicinity of Q.18.
5.50.p.m. 2nd Battery engaged loopholes near V.2. in retaliation for fire on our trenches- 6 of the 12 were destroyed.

1(b) ACTION BY HOSTILE ARTILLERY.
7.a.m. Slow shelling by enemy of WINDY CORNER, LANSDOWNE POST and vicinity PONT LOGY and up LA BASSEE Road by howitzers and PIPSQUEAK commenced and continued for about 3 hours.
9.a.m. Heavy howitzer shelled RUE du BOIS (vicinity S 10 a) and PIPSQUEAK shelled vicinity of ROUGE CROIX.
11.a.m. to 1.p.m. PIPSQUEAK fired on our trenches with bursts of gun fire on RUE du BOIS in vicinity of S 9 d.
12 noon. 15.c.m. howitzer shelled our communication trenches in vicinity of S 15 a also vicinity of S 8 b.
2.45.p.m. PIPSQUEAK shelled from RITZ to LEICESTER LOUNGE S 9 d 9'8- probably in reply to 28th Battery shelling V.2.
3.15.p.m. FACTORY and RITZ shelled by 15.c.m. howitzer in reply to 28th Battery shelling V.2.
5.p.m. PIPSQUEAK shelled ROUGE CROIX with a few rounds.
5.45.p.m. PIPSQUEAK shelled Cross roads M 32 d 7'8.
6.p.m. PIPSQUEAK shelled vicinity of M 33 d.
6.15.p.m. 10.c.m. gun shelled from M 33 a to M 26 d for half an hour, searching and sweeping.

2. INFORMATION.
AIRCRAFT:- 5 balloons up at 3.30.a.m.- 3 in S.W. and 2 in the South. German biplanes were seen flying Southwards from 44th Battery position (M 31 d) at 4.p.m., 6.20.p.m., 6.30.p.m., and 6.45.p.m.
RETALIATION:- Our Infantry state that our retaliation on their trenches when our own trenches are shelled increases their HATE.
WORK:- More work reported done on FERME du BOIS last night.

30th May 1915.
6.a.m. PIPSQUEAK very active on front line trenches of DEHRA DUN Brigade.

[signature] Major R.A.

Brigade Major, Royal Artillery,
MEERUT DIVISION.

S E C R E T.

Copy No. 6

APPENDIX 229(a)

O P E R A T I O N   O R D E R   No. 37.

by

Lieutenant-General Sir Charles ANDERSON, K.C.B.,
Commanding Meerut Division.

Reference Maps:-
FRANCE 1:40,000 Sheets 36 & 36(a)
and Trench Map.

30th May 1915.

Information. 1. (a) The following temporary redistribution of 1st Army will come into force from 6.0 a.m., 31st May 1915.

(i) 8th, ×49th, Lahore & Meerut Divisions will form Indian Corps.

(ii) 7th, °51st and Canadian Divisions will form 4th Corps, and 1st, 2nd /th Divisions will form 1st Corps.

× W. Riding
° Highland
London

(b) Indian Corps will hold from present left of 4th Corps ‖(about TOUQUET) to the present right of Indian Corps (LA QUINQUE RUE exclusive) as a defensive front.

‖ 2 miles NE of ROUGES BANCS.

Intention. 2. The Meerut Division will hold the line from a point midway between V.1 and R.6 to the QUINQUE RUE, Exclusive.

The Dehra Dun Brigade will hold the Northern portion and the Bareilly Brigade the Southern portion. The point of junction will be the forward communication trench 100 yards south of Q.7, inclusive to Dehra Dun Brigade.

Reliefs. 3. (a) On the night 30th/31st May.- Garhwal Brigade will hand over the ORCHARD Redoubt S.10. a b, and the trench in front of it to the Jullundur Brigade.

Dehra Dun Brigade will take over from its present right to Q.7 from the 152nd Highland Brigade.

(b) On the night 31st May/1st June.- Garhwal Brigade will be relieved by Ferozepore Brigade.

Dehra Dun Brigade will give over from V.1 to halfway between V.1 and R.6 to Ferozepore Brigade.

(c) On night 1st/2nd June.- Bareilly Brigade will relieve the 154th Highland Brigade from 100 yards south of Q.7 to QUINQUE RUE Exclusive.

Dehra Dun Brigade will take over the portion of trench from Q.7 to the communication trench forward, 100 yards south of that point inclusive.

All details of reliefs will be carried out by Brigadiers concerned, in intercommunication, and the usual reports will be made to Divisional Headquarters as soon as the reliefs have been concluded.

Artillery. 4. The movements of artillery have been ordered separately. The 6th Brigade R.G.A. has been directed to join the 1st Corps temporarily. The group of French Artillery now in Meerut Divisional Area will remain in its position.

Billets. 5. (a) On relief, Garhwal Brigade will move into billets in VIEILLE CHAPELLE and LES LOBES WEST.

(b) That portion of Meerut Divnl Ammn Column now at CORNET MALO will move tomorrow to PARADIS, north of Church.

Reports. 6. Reports to FOSSE.

[signature]

General Staff,
Meerut Division.

Issued to Signal Company for distribution at 6.0 P.M.

Copy No. 1 & 2 Indian Corps
3 Dehra Dun Bde×
4 Garhwal Bde×
5 Bareilly Bde×
6 Meerut Divl Arty×
7 Meerut Divl Engrs×
8 4th Ind Cavalry
9 107th Pioneers
10 Lahore Divn
11 51st High.Divn
12 Meerut Sigs
13 A.D.M.S. Meerut
14 A.A. & Q.M.G.
15 D.A.A.G.
16 D.A.A.& Q.M.G.
17 Meerut Divnl Train
18 No.1 Group H.A.R
19 to 26 Diary & Files

× With map showing new billeting area.

APPENDIX 230

S E C R E T.

TACTICAL PROGRESS REPORT
30th May 1915.

1(a) ACTION BY OUR OWN ARTILLERY.

6.5.a.m., 6.30.a.m., 7.50 a.m., 8.35.a.m., 2.40.p.m. 2nd Battery fired salvoes on enemy's front trenches in retaliation.

6.30.a.m. 2nd Battery engaged loopholes near V.2. in retaliation- 2 of remaining 6 were knocked out(see Tactical Progress Report of 29th instant).

11.a.m. 44th Battery registered places where PIPSQUEAKS were suspected.

12.3.p.m. 2nd Battery registered a point in enemy's new earthwork M 16 a 6'5.

1.15.p.m. 2nd Battery registered point where tape runs into new earthwork M 16 b 3'7.

2.p.m. 44th Battery registered for night's shooting-trench from Q.15 along ridge towards Q.10.

2.25.p.m. to 3.15.p.m. 2nd Battery fired 100 rounds on V.2. towards R.8.- trench a good deal knocked about and 8 germans seen bolting.

4.p.m. 8th Battery fired 100 rounds at slow rate on trench R.8 to Q.16- some damage done.

During the afternoon the 28th Battery fired about 100 rounds on parapet in vicinity of V.2. and damaged it considerably.

(b) ACTION BY HOSTILE ARTILLERY.

6.a.m. PIPSQUEAK shelled RUE du BOIS, near LEICESTER LOUNGE S 9 d.

2.45.p.m. PIPSQUEAK shelled trenches in S 10 c.

3.45.p.m. 21.c.m. Howitzer shelled vicinity M 33 a. M 33 b. and very active all the afternoon.

4.p.m. 10.5.c.m. howitzer shelled vicinity M 26 intermittently for three hours.

4.p.m. to 6.30.p.m. 44th Battery position shelled considerably by 15 c.m. Howitzer - one aiming post damaged.

2. INFORMATION.

AIRCRAFT:- Two Sausage Balloons in view at 10.45.a.m. bearing from S 3 c 7'5- 150° and 162°.

12 noon. Sausage Balloon seen in direction of LORGIES.

4.30.p.m. Sausage Balloon seen true bearing from M 32 a 3'6-173°.

RETALIATION:- Retaliation on enemy's front line trenches was continued to-day. It is thought that there is some result as there seemed to be less shelling ~~xxx~~ of our trenches. The Infantry state that they approve of the system.

[signature]

Major R.A.

Brigade Major, Royal Artillery,
MEERUT DIVISION.

APPENDIX 230(a)

S E C R E T.

Copy No. 15

OPERATION ORDER No. 30.
by
Brigadier General R. St. C. LECKY R.A. C.R.A. MEERUT Division.

Reference:
Map FRANCE 1/40,000 Sheets 36 and 36 a 31st May 1915.
and Trench Map.

INFORMATION. 1. (a) The following temporary redistribution of the 1st Army came into force at 6 a.m. to-day:-
(i) 8th, 49th(WEST RIDING), LAHORE and MEERUT Divisions form INDIAN Corps.
(ii) 7th, 51st(HIGHLAND) and CANADIAN Divisions form 4th Corps, and the 1st, 2nd and 47th(LONDON) Divisions form 1st Corps.
(b) INDIAN Corps will hold from present left of 4th Corps (about TOUQUET-1 miles N.E. of ROUGES BANCS) to the present right of INDIAN Corps(LA QUINQUE RUE exclusive) as a defensive front.
(c)(i) The MEERUT Division will hold the line from a point mid-way between V.1. and R.6. to the QUINQUE RUE exclusive.
(ii) The DEHRA DUN Brigade will hold the Northern portion and the BAREILLY Brigade the Southern portion. The point of junction will be the forward communication trench 100 yards S. of Q.7 inclusive, the to DEHRA DUN Brigade.

RELIEFS. 2. (a) On night 30th/31st May: GARHWAL Brigade handed over the ORCHARD Redoubt S 10 a and b, and the trench in front of it to the JULLUNDUR Brigade.
DEHRA DUN Brigade took over from its right to Q.7 from the 152nd HIGHLAND Brigade.
(b) On the night 31st May/1st June: GARHWAL Brigade will be relieved by the FEROZEPORE Brigade.
DEHRA DUN Brigade will give over from V.1. to halfway between V.1. and R.6. to FEROZEPORE Brigade.
(c) On night 1st/2nd June: BAREILLY Brigade will relieve the 154th HIGHLAND Brigade from 100 yards South of Q.7. to QUINQUE RUE exclusive.
DEHRA DUN Brigade will take over the portion of trench from Q.7. to the communication trench forward, 100 yards South of that point inclusive.

ARTILLERY. 3. (a) One section of each 9th Brigade R.F.A. Battery was relieved during night 30th/31st May by 18th Brigade R.F.A. Remaining 2 sections per battery will be relieved during night 31st May/1st June after 12 midnight. Time of relief and hour of handing over command of Artillery support of line as far South as V.1. will be arranged mutually by Officers Commanding 9th and 18th Brigades R.F.A. and will be reported in due course.
(b) 5th Siege Battery R.G.A. was withdrawn to join 1st Corps last night.
(c) On relief 9th Brigade R.F.A. will take up new positions already indicated to [illegible] to support BAREILLY Brigade front. Until such time as this Brigade is ready to take up this duty, the G.O.C. R.A. HIGHLAND Division is arranging for Artillery support of this front.
(d) The Group of FRENCH Artillery now in the MEERUT Divisional Area will remain [illegible].

GROUPING. 4. (a) 13th Brigade R.F.A. will remain grouped with the DEHRA DUN Brigade.

APPENDIX 23

SECRET TACTICAL PROGRESS REPORT

31st May 1915.

1(a) ACTION BY OUR OWN ARTILLERY.

12.15.a.m. to 12.45 a.m. and 2.15.a.m. to 2.45.a.m. } 4 Batteries of the 4th and 9th Brigades R.F.A. bombarded parapets damaged during the day in hopes of catching working parties repairing same.

7.30.a.m. 44th Battery shelled DISTILLERY- a house behind it was on fire.

10.5.a.m., 2.17.p.m., 3.23.p.m., and 4.45.p.m. 2nd Battery fired in retaliation for enemy shelling.

11.a.m. Two PIPSQUEAK batteries which were spotted during the night were seen to be firing repeatedly- an attempt to engage them failed as range was too great.

11.30.a.m. 20th Battery checked registration on trench Q.16 to Q.13.

12 noon. 8th Battery registered FERME COUR d'AVOUE and farm at Q.12.

1.45.p.m. 2nd Battery registered enemy new earthwork and communication trench.

2.19.p.m. 8th Battery retaliated on enemy at R.8 to Q.15 and on new white sandbag parapet 50 yards N. of this.

5.5.p.m. 2nd Battery fired on germans seen in trenches. About this time same battery registered Redoubt N.E. of V.2. where german working parties were seen.

6.10.p.m. 28th Battery fired on Machine Gun emplacement 100 yards E. of V.2., obtaining two direct hits.

(b) ACTION BY HOSTILE ARTILLERY.

12.40.a.m. PIPSQUEAKS opened fire on our trenches in answer to our bombardment.

2.20.a.m. PIPSQUEAKS shelled our trenches hard, in reply to our second bombardment.

PIPSQUEAK shelled trenches in front of RUE du BOIS occasionally during the morning.

9.30.a.m. 15.c.m. Howitzer shelled St VAAST Corner and vicinity.

2.p.m. 15.c.m. howitzer shelled REVOLVER House(S 3 c 5'4) and road up to St VAAST for about 1½ hours, including first aid post:- Direction believed to be AUBERS Ridge.

3.p.m. to 5.p.m. German heavy guns shelled following vicinity continually for about 2 hours- M 26 b, M 32 d, S 2 b, S 3 d, M 27 d:- Direction believed to be VIOLAINES.

6.30.p.m. PIPSQUEAK shelled vicinity of M 33 b.

6.45.p.m. 15.c.m. howitzer shelled FORESTER's LANE and WINDY CORNER- direction believed to be LORGIES

2. INFORMATION.

HOSTILE BATTERIES:- 8.25.p.m. 30.5.15.- Flashes seen from S 9 d 7'7 3½° L. and 4° 45' L. of LA BASSEE Church- approximate range from S 9 d 7'7 3,000 and 3,300 yards.

11.30.a.m.31.5.15:- Flashes of PIPSQUEAK located near M 30.

1.45.p.m. Flashes and dust of two field batteries located from LEICESTER LOUNGE(S 9 d 7'7) true bearings 140° and 138°.

WORK:- A considerable amount of work has been done to parapet of trench V.2. to R.8., also vicinity R.9.; parapets of trenches have been heightened.

A busg screen has been put up in front of battery located at S 30 a 5'0

A new german trench appears to run from near R.13. to FERME du BOIS and 200 yards East of FERME du BOIS,- this trench appears to be very strong.

Work in FERME du BOIS considerably strengthened.

A new trench appears to be made behind FERME du BOIS. No wire visible in front of any of these trenches, which are linked up by communicating trenches.

FIRES:- Big fire in LA BASSEE 300 yards East of Church.

AIRCRAFT:- German aeroplane flew over 2nd Battery at 8.30.a.m. and then returned.

[signature]

Major R.A.
Brigade Major, Royal Artillery,
MEERUT DIVISION.

www.ingramcontent.com/pod-product-compliance
Lightning Source LLC
Chambersburg PA
CBHW081400160426
43193CB00013B/2074
* 9 7 8 1 4 7 4 5 3 5 0 6 9 *